PETER COLLINS

*All about
the boy!*

Ed McDonough

This book is published by:
Mercian Manuals Ltd
353 Kenilworth Road
Balsall Common
Coventry
CV7 7DL
+44(0)1676 533304
www.mercianmanuals.co.uk

Distribution worldwide by the same.

© Ed McDonough

ISBN 978-1-903088-43-2
ISBN 978-1-903088-45-6 (Klemantaski special edition)

All rights reserved. No part of this publication may be reproduced, stored in a retrieval system, or transmitted, in any form or by any means, electronic, mechanical, photocopying, recording, or otherwise, without the prior written permission of the publishers.

CONTENTS

Dedication & Acknowledgements — v

Foreword — vii

Introduction - Who was Peter Collins? — 1

Part One — The racing career -
The early years — 1947-1951 — 11
The Grand Prix driver — 1952-1955 — 45
The Ferrari years — 1956-1958 — 159

Part Two — What they said about him... — 265
What they wrote about him... — 309

Appendix A - List of races — 317
Appendix B - Louise's letters — 323

Bibliography — 327

DEDICATION

This book is dedicated to Richard 'Dickey' Green and the other behind-the-scenes team members from the 1950s. They were an integral part of the running of Aston Martin, Cooper, H.W.M., Vanwall and the other race teams, and they rarely received the credit they deserved.

ACKNOWLEDGEMENTS

There are many people to thank: Louise Collins King, Sir Stirling Moss, Michael Green, Richard Green, Neville Hay, Ted 'The Ferret' Walker, Graeme Simpson, John King, Guy Loveridge, 'Mick' Marriott, John Moody, Tony May, Peter Vale, Sue Palethorpe, John Francis, Mike MacDowel, Tim Parnell, John Pearson, Anthony Pritchard/T.C.March Collection, Peter Sachs & Klemantaski Collection, Don Truman, Denise McCluggage, LAT, my friend Peter Collins of the same name, Mike Jiggle, Anthony Carter, Michael Whittall.

I would like to apologise to those people who I would have liked to have included and did not manage to, and to anyone I have forgotten here.

Photos not credited are from the author's collection. Every attempt has been made to correctly identify photographers where possible.

FOREWORD

It has given me great pleasure to have been involved with this book which, fifty years after his death, is honouring Peter's wonderful life. A half a century can fly by and the memories of my life with Peter in 1957 and 1958 make me feel as though they happened yesterday.

Peter simply loved life, motor racing, his family and me. He was full of fun and joy but very serious about his racing and the cars he drove. We had a great marriage, even though it took a lot of people by surprise. We met on a Monday and were married the following Monday. It led to the happiest year and a half of my life. We were very, very close through every minute of it so we packed a lot of living into a short eighteen months.

That period of racing was very different from today. The atmosphere we experienced was enjoyable, although there were painful moments. The camaraderie between the other drivers, our friends, the press and all the people that made the racing possible made it a very special and satisfying way of life, even though we were constantly on the move.

It was a big change for me when it ended. I went back to work in the theatre and television in the United States, and later in England, so I didn't see our racing friends very often. In a way, that keeps that period suspended in time. It was a lovely time and I am so happy to have been a part of it.

Louise King

INTRODUCTION

Who was Peter Collins?

This is not a facetious question. Whenever the subject of Peter Collins comes up against the back-drop of motor racing history, the first words out of most peoples' mouths seem to have the names of Collins and Mike Hawthorn inextricably linked almost as if they were one entity, never apart and each without a separate existence. Though they were friends and eventually team mates, however, they were not inseparable. They linger so closely together in memory because they were two of the three great British racing lads…the golden boys…and because their stars fell as quickly as they had risen. Stirling Moss, of course, is the third 'boy' who fortunately is still around with us today to recount some of the tales.

Peter Collins sits in the Cooper at the Prescott International meeting. He was only 17 at the time. Photo - LAT

All about the boy!

Though what has been written about Peter Collins has very much reinforced this link with Hawthorn, Collins had his own life, his own friends, his own career and very much his own personality. When the opportunity to write this book came about, occasioned by the tribute to be paid to him in August, 2008 on the 50th anniversary of his death at the Nurburgring, it seemed clear that the task was to draw a vivid and living account of Collins in his own right. As you will see, a number of people came forth…or were ferreted out…who knew him and his family and had tales to tell. Many of these stories are as much about the period…the late 1940s and early 1950s as about Peter Collins. That was, for many, a very special time. The war was over and some semblance of normality returned. Many of the accounts here mention that that was 'an easier time', and that was especially true of motor racing. Peter Collins was one of those people who made his name in racing when it was a very different activity than it was even twenty years later, never mind now.

My friend, commentating colleague and supreme motor racing historian Neville Hay, it turned out, 'knew the boy' and had connections with many of the people who participated in this book. With Nev's help, I started making the rounds of these folk, and the stories poured forth. It seemed reasonable, then, that many of these accounts should be told as they were related, and thus was made the decision to present the Peter Collins story in two halves: the chronology of his racing history, and those tales which tell us 'all about the boy' from the perspective of some of the people who knew him. It is fashionable to say 'don't write a book that is a bunch of race reports.' Well, that is fair enough, so what I have tried to accomplish here is providing a 'live' account, as it were, of how many people saw Peter Collins, and a thorough description of his races and what they said about him. Some of the former is integrated into the latter, to cast light on some of the issues.

For readers who were and are real Peter Collins fans, you can imagine what it might have been like for the author to get first hand accounts of Collins' life and times. I sat with Neville Hay at his home in the Isle of Man…or Isle of Persons as he calls it... for some days listening to his tales. Nev went to school with Peter's sister, worked at the Collins' Kidderminster Motors, went to the races to see Peter, was driven home by him on occasion, and shared trips to the pub. That was riveting. Because these were first-hand accounts, you will see that some of them have not been edited to any great extent. Some of them are often contradictory, which is also inevitable. People saw Peter Collins through the glass of their own perception. Some people knew a fair amount about him, and not many knew him well. Hardly anyone could or would claim to have had a deeper insight into the inner person of Collins.

Neville also took me on a ride into the past, Peter's and his own, as we spent a day gathering some of the photos you see in this book. It started with a trip to the Black Boy Hotel in Bewdley, Peter Collins' local, where he spent many evenings, where he had a number of acquaintances, and where Neville Hay himself was his occasional escort. The journey then went to the bungalow at Mustow Green where the Collins' were living at the time of Peter's birth, next door to which was the location of the first family garage. Then the road took us to Shatterford Grange, the imposing later Collins family home which looks over classic countryside and rolling fields. Not far away was the house which Peter was negotiating to purchase for himself and Louise at the time

Introduction - Who was Peter Collins?

of his death. And finally to the rather poignant Stone Church and graveyard, where Peter is buried. This was particularly striking as no other close members of the Collins family are there and the grave has a distinctly lonely feel about it.

Above: The Black Boy Hotel at Bewdley, not far from Kidderminster, which was a central point in Peter Collins' social life. Mike Hawthorn brought Louise back here after Peter had been killed in Germany.

Below: The Collins' bungalow at Mustow Green where Pat and Elaine Collins were living when Peter was born in 1931.

All about the boy!

Louise Collins meets Elaine and Pat Collins for the first time at Shatterford Grange in 1957. Photo - Louise Collins King Collection

Introduction - Who was Peter Collins?

Honeybrook House, near Shatterford Grange which Peter was negotiating to purchase at the time of his death.

The site of Kidderminster Motors as it is today. Pat Collins owned the adjoining properties as well.

All about the boy!

This simple grave at the church at Stone is where Peter Collins is buried.

Equally fascinating was the development, for me, of a clearer picture of those early days of the 1950s when Britain emerged from the post-war doldrums and started to become a force to be reckoned with in motor racing. Peter Collins drove Coopers, J.B.S., H.W.M., BRM, Aston Martin, Allard and Vanwall long before he went near an Italian car at all! Some of the tales from those teams are every bit as intriguing as the revelations about Collins himself. While motor racing history records the often frenetic and sometimes bizarre antics of the Ferrari and Maserati teams, life at Aston Martin, for example, was no less marked by strokes of genius and complete disaster, and H.W.M. was a manufacturer that seemed to be able to play a part in the World Championship while having hardly any finance at all!

Collins, like Moss, 'put himself about' a bit…he

Introduction - Who was Peter Collins?

did sprints, hillclimbs and rallies too. He managed to get himself into a Sunbeam Alpine for the Alpine Rally in 1953 and 1954, and thereby hangs another fascinating tale. I was extremely fortunate to get a closer than expected feel of what that might have been like when I was able to compete in the Rally des Alpes Historique in 2007...in the very car used by Peter Collins. Coincidentally, that car, beautifully preserved, is in the ownership of Peter Shimmell, the publisher of this book!

A chance to drive one of the Healey 100s that ran so well at Le Mans in the historic 1953 race added to the excitement that constituted 1950s motor racing, a period of great adventure, when the first hints of modern technology would begin to appear in a time when many of the cars had been around since well before the war.

I hope this book casts some light into the corners of those early Fifties British racing efforts as well as onto Peter Collins himself, as his life was very much tied to the rise of British racing, especially in his early years. There may be many areas of interest and tales left out of this book, and I apologise for that. It is now getting clearer that fewer and fewer of the active participants in 1950s motor sport are still around.

Peter Collins caught against the back-drop of a typical 1950s motor race meeting. Photo - Courtesy Neville Hay

All about the boy!

Peter Collins - the bare facts

It was interesting that when Motor Racing magazine chose to declare Peter 'Driver of the Year' in 1956 and subsequently went on to trace the outline of his career, the story included hardly anything of a 'personal' nature about the then 25-year old. It was left to Chris Nixon's *'Mon Ami Mate'* to do the first real digging into the 'boy's' background, and I am indebted to the late Chris Nixon for his detailed work. I am not going to reproduce it all here, and Neville Hay draws a good portrait of what life was like around the younger Collins.

Peter was born on November 1, 1931 in a Kidderminster nursing home to Elaine and Pat Collins. They were living in Mustow Green, near Kidderminster, at the time and Collins Senior was running a prosperous transport business, which was based at the Talbot Garage next to the bungalow in Mustow Green. The income from the business was 'substantial', Collins was an astute businessman, and it wasn't long before he extended his efforts and investments into land and other business deals. There was a nanny to look after young Peter John Collins. When the first nanny left, young May Baker was taken on to look after him, and her recollections included comments that 'he always woke up in a bad temper' and that 'he was mad about his father's lorries from a very early age.' These were two characteristics that rather seemed to remain with him for most of his life, though the temper was very well managed, but it sometimes spread into other parts of the day! May Baker saw the temper as being directly inherited from his father!

Peter was afflicted with more than his share of illness, and had several visits to hospital for appendicitis, peritonitis, and a mastoid operation, all fairly serious affairs for an under-six-year old. He was at Bradley's Kindergarten at Chawton in 1938, and then moved to the kindergarten section of Kidderminster Girls High School for two years, then to King Charles Grammar School, where his own mother had been a teacher. The Collins' then sent him off to boarding school just before he was eleven and though it wasn't far from home, he was very unhappy there and soon converted to being a day pupil rather than a boarder. He was not academic, which was not a surprising occurrence amongst men who later turned out to be racing drivers! His father was a practical 'action' man, so wasn't unduly worried by Peter's lack of academic skill. His mother was, however, insistent so he then was again off to another boarding school, Bromsgrove, where he developed a liking for and skill in a number of sports, especially swimming. Swimming became his exercise and training, his competitive activity, and often his refuge from problems at home. Peter would often get a lift from one of his father's lorries passing the school and head off home. When he finally fell out with Bromsgrove he announced that he was off to become a racing driver.

That wasn't so much inspired by having much to do with racing, more to his increasing interest in things mechanical. He had spent most of his time hanging around the family garage business, learning to drive, doing a range of odd jobs, and his father seemed quite happy to set him up as an 'apprentice' when he was 16.

Pat and Elaine Collins did have an influence on Peter's interest in competition. Before the war, they did a number of rallies together and were doing trials in an MG when Peter was two. When he was eight, they did the Monte Carlo Rally in a Railton Straight 8. By this time Peter had outgrown his pedal car and when he

Introduction - Who was Peter Collins?

was nine, this got fitted with an old two-stroke engine. He spent many hours driving this around the garage and surrounding area, and so developed his driving abilities at a very early age. His father was quite pleased about this, and he could begin to see his own competitive ambitions being borne out by his son. Peter was allowed to go out on runs with the drivers and the business was thriving as the war approached. Pat Collins saw the inevitable about to happen and put his money and effort into building up the range of transport vehicles he owned. He made a very considerable amount of profit when he leased his vehicles to the Ministry of War Transport for the evacuation of British troops from Dunkirk.

Peter's sister Patricia was born in 1940, and they were very close, though being nine years older than 'Tricia', he didn't have a lot of time for her in those years. As he got older, he was more absorbed in the garage business, and became handy at stripping down gearboxes on lorries. His first attempt at competition, now that the war was over, was not very far away and his father played a big part in it, as he always would.

Shatterford Grange, the imposing later Collins family home.

All about the boy!

St. Mary's Church, Stone, Worcestershire.

The Peter Collins memorial window at St. Mary's Church, Stone, Worcestershire.

The inscription on the Peter Collins memorial window.

Plaque showing that the window was restored with help from the BRDC.

THE RACING CAREER
The early years 1947 - 1951

1947

June - Blackpool rally

Peter had been growing up in not only the mechanical environment of the family garage business, but his family were actively oriented towards motor sport competition. Having already seen his parents take part in rallies and trials, Peter set to work persuading his father to enter his 1938 Aston Martin in the Blackpool Rally. This was to be the first significant post-war rally and took place in the Peak District, which included most of the road sections, then ran to Blackpool for a number of tests. Peter's father was driving and Peter himself was navigating so it was his first motor sport event. The father and son team did not prove to be a great rallying success but they won the prize for the following day's concours event for the open car class. Thus Peter Collins could claim the dubious distinction of winning in his first competition.

What was interesting was that the rally was won by Ken Wharton, who would go on to distinguish himself as well. He had built an Austin Special with a Ford engine and this excited Peter enough to launch a furious period of designing a similar car. While considerable effort went into building what would become known as the 'Purple Peril', Peter became increasingly more occupied with his father's business. 1947 was also the year that the government nationalised transport and bought out Pat Collins' substantial and cleverly accumulated transport assets. With this money he purchased the site for the about-to-be-opened Kidderminster Motors in February 1948. Peter was very much involved in everything from bulldozing the new site to helping to set up the stores and offices in the new premises. Peter also got his first look at the French Grand Prix circuit at Reims when the family went on holiday in 1948.

The Collins family life became very busy as shortly after the holiday they purchased the rolling estate that contained Shatterford Grange, a large ten-year old house with considerable acreage. On November 6, 1948, Peter's 17th birthday, he applied for and got his driving license and was soon using the second 'Purple Peril' special to do trials with. There is little record of his results in these but whatever they were, they helped him to decide to do 'proper motor racing' and a decision was made with his father to obtain a new Cooper 500 c.c. F3 car.

1949

April 10 - Brough....almost

The first Collins Cooper, it seems, was purchased on March 10, 1949 and Peter and his father spent some time in getting used to driving and working on it. The first tests were done in company of Ron Lowe at Purton, an ex-RAF base near Wolverhampton. As an indication of the family attitude towards Peter's ambition of being a racing driver, not only did they buy the Cooper but Pat and Elaine Collins both drove it at those first tests.

All about the boy!

The new Cooper loaded onto the Collins trailer about to set off for home. Photo - Neville Hay

John Cooper, although he didn't seem to keep detailed records of the early Cooper transactions, remembered some of the first 'deals':

"...fortune seemed to smile on us. Among our first customers were Sir Francis Samuelson, followed by Stirling Moss (destined to reach the pinnacle of fame in motor racing) and Peter Collins, a natural born enthusiast whose father, Patrick had a large automotive dealership in Kidderminster, the carpet manufacturing centre on the River Stour. Moss had got wind of the fact that we were building a production 500 cc race car but he was at this time still at school." (Cooper, 1977, p.27).

Brough, in Yorkshire, was one of the early season events in 1949 and it was intended that Peter Collins would make his debut in the Cooper. He had been 'testing' locally as C.A.N. May has already described and this meeting would also see May have his first run in the ex-Moss Cooper. However, there was a near epidemic of flu and John Cooper and Stirling Moss were among those laid low by it, in addition to May himself. However, he managed to get the details of the Brough event for his book and of course for Iota which was the 500 Club's magazine. Among the happenings on that day, a young David Brown took over John Cooper's Cooper and left the airfield course and got "entangled with a tea-tent!" Various machines lost wheels and chains in practice and only five cars started the first heat and it was won by Eric Brandon. Bill Aston won the second heat.

Brandon also won the final, changing gear by pulling on the gear lever rod after the gearshift lever broke off. Don Parker won the handicap race and oddly there is no mention of Peter Collins. As it turned out, though the Cooper was entered by P.J. Collins, it never made it to

The racing career - The early years 1947-1951

the meeting as it was not ready to compete. In spite of this, at least one book records that Collins finished 8th though Sheldon and Rabagliati make it clear that the entry was a DNA! (Page, Rabagliati, Sheldon, 2007) Chris Nixon (1991) insists that the car was there, that Peter nearly made a mess of the start and finished 8th. However, as the family notes record that the first few weekends after buying the car were spent at Purton, there is something of a mystery about Peter Collins' first circuit race!

April 18 - Goodwood Easter Monday

C.A.N. May, having missed Brough, was determined to take part in the Goodwood race at Easter, which would be his first 500 event. He described the run-up to the meeting:

"My transport arrangements were that young Peter Collins would provide and drive a long-wheelbase Fordson truck, on the back of which it was found just possible to accommodate the two Coopers by placing them tail to tail and removing one rear wheel from each. Collins ran into a whirl of last minute fun-and-games with a broken engine-sprocket sliding member and clutch slip and when I delivered my car to his garage for loading he had rushed out for an eleventh hour test on the local airfield, so that I left for Bognor with (Fred) Fletcher, in my private car, without seeing young Peter.

"When by 8.00 pm on the Friday evening he had still not shown up at Bognor I began to wonder but shortly there came a reassuring phone call to say he had got as far as Farnham and was pressing on. It appeared that almost at the moment of setting out from home it had been discovered that the truck ear-marked for the journey was, unaccountably, not licensed, while *en route,* although displaying a notable turn of speed, it consumed petrol and oil in more or less equal quantities. Collins finally arrived at something after 10.00 pm" (May, 1951, p.85).

When the tired duo finally got themselves organised in the Goodwood paddock, next to Stirling Moss, they discovered that they were the only Cooper drivers still using leaf springs, all the others having converted to the latest solid mountings. John Cooper himself helped May sort out excess play in the rear hubs so he could pass scrutineering. After suffering a broken piston in practice, May replaced it with the spare engine he had bought from the Moss family. This was indeed the sprint engine mentioned later by May...set up to last for about a 60 second sprint run!

Peter Collins had not entirely repaired his clutch before leaving home and was getting some assistance from one of the Cooper mechanics to get it done in time for the race. There was a second practice session and both May and Collins managed to get in a few more laps before the two of them, with Fred Fletcher, worn out from very little sleep, climbed into the Kidderminster Motors Fordson truck and went off to find a bed for the night.

During the race, newcomer May started from row two and was soon forcing his way into the lead, which he held for about 100 yards before the engine blew to pieces...his sprint run well and truly over! Peter Collins never even made the start when his black Cooper just wouldn't start. This was eventually discovered to have been caused by an ignition short. The Collins racing career was not starting all that smoothly! Two races and nothing resembling a result for the very frustrated young Collins, anxious to show that he was indeed a racing driver.

All about the boy!

May 22 - Prescott Open Meeting

Collins had not entered any other events until the Prescott hillclimb, but on May 14, he had signed up as what C.A.N. May referred to as a 'stand-in' mechanic to join Fred Fletcher in assisting May for a race at Silverstone. The truck broke down near Birmingham on the way to the circuit. This gave Collins the first real chance to have a thorough look at the serious 500 c.c. opposition and to spend some time considering how the regulars dealt with the numerous problems suffered by the somewhat temperamental 500s. May stopped in the race when a cylinder head bolt sheared and Moss won the race.

However, a week later, Collins was back behind the wheel for the Prescott Open Hillclimb. Times were pretty close in the practice sessions for the 500s and when the timed runs began, Eric Brandon was fastest on 48.80 seconds, Clive Lones on 49.12, May 49.47, Don Truman's Bardon 8th in 50.17 and Peter Collins 9th with a time of 50.34 seconds. Considering the highly competitive nature of the class and the experience of his rivals, Collins' very first hillclimb was judged a good result.

June 12 - Prescott Members' Meeting

There were stories going round the next meeting at Shelsley Walsh that Peter Collins had already sold his new Cooper, which had been painted in a distinctive black with red wheels and a skull and crossbones on the petrol tank faring to Bill Cox, another new racer who had been doing trials and rallies. Collins had found another Cooper with a 1000 c.c. engine which was reputed to have been specially built for John Cooper's father Charles. This car had chrome plated suspension and all the latest Cooper mods. John Cooper later said he very much doubted that this story was true, as his father was very unlikely to have such a car! There are also arguments about exactly when the original Collins Mark II was replaced by the Mark III. Some reports have the Mark III entered at the very beginning of the season though this seems unlikely.

Collins was entered in the 'Up to 750 c.c.' class at the Prescott Members' meeting but with an earlier smaller engine. He finished 7th with Brandon winning and May in 3rd.

Sure enough Peter Cox showed up for the next Silverstone meeting on June 25 with the now ex-Collins car, which was immediately afflicted by a seriously leaking fuel tank, though repairs were made in a mobile workshop which travelled to all the events. This was Bob Gerard's workshop and it allowed many people to race who otherwise would have had to go home.

It was during this period that Pat Collins acquired one of the new and quick Norton 'double-knocker' engines and a great deal of testing went on at Purton before the Silverstone race. It would also seem that by now they obviously had a new chassis and again there are conflicting stories as to whether an earlier MK II had originally been bought and replaced by a MK III or, as the author agrees, a MK III had been bought in March and this had now been replaced by the stretch chassis T9...still a MK III but a version suitable for a larger engine. The earlier MK III was a Cooper T7.

July 9 - Silverstone 100 Miles

The 500 Club organised its most ambitious event to date at Silverstone by running a 100 mile race on the short circuit. This was preceded by several shorter races as well as one for 'non-production' 500s, that is, essentially home built cars. After an interval the main race took place at 4.30 pm and Peter Collins was present with a new Cooper but

The racing career - The early years 1947-1951

with the 1000 c.c. engine temporarily replaced with a Manx-Norton 500 c.c. unit which had been detuned and was running in the long race on a petrol/benzole combination to ensure reliability. This attention to detail seemed an indication of Collins' very serious approach to racing at this early stage.

Some of the cars broke down within the first few laps but the leading group of Bill Aston, George Saunders and Jack Moor pulled away from the pack at a rapid rate. Young Collins managed to pull himself up onto the back of this group in fifth, which became 4th when Moor dropped out in the Wasp. Saunders and Aston collided at Stowe and Don Parker took over the lead in the Parker Special, with Collins right on his tail, followed by Bill Grose. Then Parker and Collins exchanged the lead several times. After 23 laps Parker, who had not fitted a long-range fuel tank, went in for a top-up, leaving Collins out front and he stayed there until the 44 laps were complete.

C.A.N. (Austen) May described the finish:

"Collins passed under the finishing banner, received the chequered flag, pulled over to the left of the track and took the return road to the now-deserted paddock. The first people to greet him as he climbed a little wearily from his car, a bit dazed and very deaf, were Delingpole, Lowe (later of DEL-LOW) and myself. There was a lot of oil over the body but when we lifted the body I was actually able to lay my hand on the Norton engine's cylinder head. Then people came running and calling and Peter stiffly clambered back into the Cooper, Delingpole, Lowe and myself push-started the car and he drove back to the finishing area to join John Cooper and be applauded with suitable ceremony. So, in one gigantic stride, 'young Peter' came from comparative obscurity to the top of the class." (May, 1951, p.101-2).

This was certainly the moment when Peter Collins, in only his fourth event as a driver, had arrived, beating a class field, showing sound judgement in preparing his car and in calculating and driving the race.

July 17 - Summer Prescott

In spite of the title of this meeting, rain had made it seem anything but a summer event, though the hill had dried somewhat by the time the serious runs were to be made.

Peter Collins chases Don Parker in the Silverstone 100 mile race.
Photo - Motor Racing/BRSCC Archive

All about the boy!

Austen May mentions that Peter Collins was using his original JAP engine in the Cooper, the same car used at Silverstone the week before. The implication was that a Norton had been used at Silverstone, rather than the JAP as appeared in some reports and it does seem that this is the case. Nixon argues that it was indeed the Norton 'double-knocker' used at Silverstone. With 500 c.c. engines being so easy to change, it is remarkable that there is any record at all of which engine was used when! However, the engine type meant little when, on the damp surface, Collins arrived at Orchard Corner in a front-wheel slide, fell off the inside of the corner but fortunately landed down on some hay bales which had been knocked over earlier. According to May: " 'young Peter' stepped out unhurt, the photographers seized avidly on a heaven-sent opportunity, the car was retrieved between the first and second climbs but was not passed by the scrutineers for a further run." (May, op. cit. p.104).

IOTA, the monthly journal of the 500 Club reported Collins' excursion thus: "P.J.Collins, running the Silverstone winning Cooper, now using its sprint JAP motor, flashed through a gap in the hedge, created by Wilkes' Rover during practising the previous day, and dropped smartly into the gully which faces the unwary at this point. Fortunately the Rover had succeeded in depositing some bales in the gully and these nicely cushioned the Cooper's fall. Collins stepped out quite unhurt and a cursory glance revealed no damage to the car, though by the time this had been retrieved and got back to the paddock the scrutineers reckoned their examination would not be over in time for him to have another try that day." (IOTA, Aug.-Sept. 1949, p.11).

July 30 - Zandvoort - Dutch Grand Prix

The Dutch Grand Prix was taking place at Zandvoort on July 31, so the Dutch RAC decided to put a 500 c.c. race on the programme the previous day and this attracted Stirling Moss, John Cooper, Curly Dryden, Bill Aston, Don Parker, Eric Brandon, and others including Peter Collins, with his Cooper-Norton. Accommodation was organised for drivers and there was reasonable prize money available. Stirling Moss ran in the first practice session with the 1000 c.c. engine in his Cooper in hopes that he could convince the organisers to let him run it in the Grand Prix itself, but this was not permitted.

At the start, John Habin's car wouldn't fire and his mechanic rushed out to push him, then stepped back right in front of Moss who knocked him flying. Moss looked like he might stop at the end of the first lap but he was waved on and moved into the lead on the 3rd lap. Peter Collins, in his very first Continental race, was going well but had a plug lead come loose so he was forced to make a quick stop. This dropped him well back though he managed to finish 8th, with Moss winning from Bill Aston. Peter Collins, still not 18, was now an 'international racing driver!'

August 20 - Silverstone International Trophy Meeting

A fifty lap 500 race was to support the BRDC's International Trophy race and this was an invitational event, so a strong field was put together, which included Collins and his 'travelling companion' Austen May. May comments that the 500s were located behind the pits, not segregated from the 'real racers' as per the usual practice. There was indeed a great deal of snobbery in motor racing at the time and many people tended to look down on the 500 teams. A huge battle took place in the race between Moss and Brandon which went Brandon's way by two tenths of a

The start of the 500 race supporting the 1949 International Trophy race. Dryden, Reece, Moss and Bladd line up at the front. Collins was 8th. Photo - Ferret Fotographics

second. Curly Dryden was 3rd, and Austen May had his engine seize. Peter Collins didn't have a particularly sparkling race as he came in 8th, some 90 seconds behind the leading pair.

September 3 - Silverstone SUNBAC Meeting

Many of the 500 runners went to Blandford on August 27. May has Collins there but a non-starter, though it appears he did not appear! He did go to Silverstone for the short, 4 lap race a week later. May and Collins went to Silverstone together and in the early laps May led Collins who had the JAP engine back in his Cooper. Collins swept past his friend who didn't give up, caught him up again, and was able to sit there as Collins' engine seized and he was forced to retire. May should have finished 3rd but couldn't change gears and lost the place to Whitehouse while Ken Carter won.

September 11 - Prescott International

Some of the pioneer 500 drivers and cars showed up at Prescott and did very well, Colin Strang in his Strang finishing 2nd in the large 500 class with Jack Reece winning, Don Truman 4th, May 5th, Collins, with the JAP engine in the car, 7th and the Tiger Kitten of veteran Clive Lones 8th.

September 17 - BARC Goodwood

Though the Collins 'team' was optimistic about their chances at the Goodwood meeting, a cloud hung over them as

All about the boy!

*A young Stirling Moss in the late 1940s early 1950s.
Photo - Ferret Fotographic*

Charlie Smith, who had prepared Peter's engines, had been killed during practice for a motorcycle meeting at Blandford, just a week after the car race meeting had taken place there. Smith had been something of a preparation genius and was to be missed. Pat…or 'Percy'…Collins, Peter's father, had managed to secure what appears to be a second of the special 'double-knocker' twin overhead camshaft Norton engines and this was now in the Collins Cooper.

Peter Collins was not entirely satisfied with the performance of the Cooper with its new engine in the first practice session, so he asked Stirling Moss to give it a try. Moss managed to make the Cooper go some five seconds quicker than Peter had. In spite of all the effort going into

The racing career - The early years 1947-1951

the practice periods, the grid was based on ballots drawn from a hat! While Collins was closer to the front, Austen May had drawn last position. Collins, wearing, for some reason, a Southampton Speedway team helmet and inspired by Moss' handling of the car, pushed the 'double-knocker' right to the front with Curly Dryden behind him. The Dutch driver Lex Beels harried Dryden and he eventually got past, taking Stan Coldham along with him. But Collins had gotten the most out of the new engine and had learned something about technique after making the wise decision to get Moss to try the car...Stirling wasn't in this race so he obliged. Though not a major event, it was another good victory for 'the boy' who had now triumphed on the somewhat 'hallowed' ground of Goodwood.

The IOTA report for October-November 1949 added that the bookmakers had changed their odds when the news had got out that Collins had a new 'double-knocker' and he was favourite in the betting. The rumours at the time had this engine producing 48 bhp, which was interesting in the light of papers which Collins had indicating the power curve stopped at 43 bhp!

September 24 - Shelsley Walsh

For the Shelsley meeting the 500 c.c. cars would be running in the 750 c.c. class and thus Peter Collins made the decision to remove his recent Norton acquisition and replace it with an early V-twin JAP which had been enlarged to some 700 c.c. This first attempt to use the Cooper chassis with a variety of different size engines didn't quite work as intended and the unit blew up, so the Norton went back in. There was thus only one larger-engined car in the group and that was the single-seat Austin of George Symonds who won the class from Fry's Parsenn and Peter Collins, about a second slower than the larger car.

The Pat Collins team mechanics struggled with engines at the Shelsley Walsh meeting. Note Peter Collins shirt and tie under his overalls. Photo - Motor Racing/BRSCC Archive

All about the boy!

Monaco as a 500 race was supporting the Grand Prix for the first time. Moss won his heat, Schell his, with Austen May 3rd and Moss won the final with May in 5th.

Above: Peter Collins at the 1950 British Grand Prix. Photo - LAT

Left: The 500 drivers are presented to the Royal party at the 1950 British Grand Prix. Moss and Collins on the right, Prince Bira to the far left. Photo - BRDC Archives

The racing career - The early years 1947-1951

May 27 - Goodwood 500 Trophy

Goodwood hosted the BARC 500 International Race and had a very large entry, including a number of cars from Scandinavia. Again, the event was run in two heats of seven laps and fifteen laps for the final. Paul Emery made it look like he would disappear in Heat 1 with his Emeryson but the ignition failed and he retired. Eric Brandon took over the lead with Collins right behind and Denis Poore in a Parsenn was third. Curly Dryden dominated the second heat, beating Bill Whitehouse and Don Parker and that opened the door to a real clash between Collins and Dryden in the final over 36 miles. Peter Collins was noted for his ability to run wheel to wheel with very tough opposition even at this stage in his career and the pair put on a magnificent racing display, something that would happen quite often in this first full year of 500 c.c. racing.

The race was full of incidents, part of the appeal of this class of racing. Don Parker and Leonard crashed into each other and Denis Poore's Parsenn rushed into the pits alight; Aiken's Iota had a suspension breakage and Bill Whitehouse also dropped out while near the front. This all allowed John Cooper to move up to 3rd spot behind Dryden and Collins, who finished 0.6 seconds behind the winner. Collins had put the Norton engine back into the 'older' chassis as he was not happy about the handling of the new one.

Peter Collins (5) on the front row at Goodwood.
Photo - Ferret Fotographics

All about the boy!

May 29 - Blandford

Several British drivers headed to Aix-les-Bains in France the next day for a race there, won by Harry Schell. A number of those who had gone to Monaco had also remained on the Continent.

The rest of the Brits headed to Blandford on the Holiday Monday where the two heats and a final format was used for the 500s. Dryden's Cooper-Norton took the first heat fairly easily from Headland's Cooper-JAP and Alan Brown in a similar car. Heat 2 was a closer race altogether, which Collins led virtually all the way until Alf Bottoms sneaked past on the last lap with George Wicken back in 3rd. Bottoms asserted himself in the final and after Dryden went off, he headed Collins to the flag. Collins would run in some twenty competitions in the Cooper in 1950 and only seven of these would be races, many being sprints and hillclimbs. His ability to learn a new circuit, such as Blandford where he had never been before, was becoming obvious and one of his skills was being able to turn very quick laps in practice and run with the leaders at the beginning of a race. Though there was a large number of new drivers in 500 racing, very few of them became regular winners. Peter Collins was quickly one of the few.

June 10 - Shelsley Walsh

With some of the 500 competitors again overseas, Peter Collins was at Shelsley where there was fairly fierce competition in the 500 c.c. class. This finally went to Jeremy Fry's Parsenn in 42.89 seconds, Collins in the Cooper in 43.27 and Clive Lones with the Iota-Tiger Kitten in 43.82.

June 11 - Prescott Members' Meeting

Peter and Pat Collins had been working on a rather special twin-cylinder JAP engine of 750 c.c. capacity and after leaving Shelsley they immediately set to work installing this engine in the Cooper and then set off for Prescott to compete the very next day. The smallest class at Prescott was the 'Up to 750 c.c.' group and Collins was over a second faster than all the 500 c.c. cars, Clive Lones coming second. Collins broke the existing 750 record on both of his runs which had stood since 1939 so the Collins team was well pleased with their ability to find an extra advantage with their increasing knowledge of the formula. They had also earned their bonus fuel company payment as promised before the season had started.

June 24 - Bo'Ness Hillclimb

The 750 c.c. engine remained in the Cooper for the Bo'Ness event where Collins took another class victory in his third of five straight hillclimbs. The Bo'Ness climb is a half-mile long, located not far from Edinburgh. Peter had broken the record in the dry practice session and then it rained for the timed runs. He still won but didn't manage to break the old record here. Ken Wharton was after the outright record in his 998 c.c. Cooper and Collins would get used to competing with Wharton in many events over the years.

July 2 - Rest and Be Thankful

The Collins Cooper continued in good form, coming second a week after Bo'Ness, proving just how versatile the Cooper could be. This climb at Arrochar was part of a Collins family holiday to Scotland so they didn't seem to mind the trip to Loch Long, west of Glasgow. As the course had been shortened there was no chance of breaking old

The racing career - The early years 1947-1951

records and there was also no class for 750 c.c. cars so Peter was up against Wharton's bigger engine. Peter had had the Cooper get away from him on the second run, sliding, over-correcting and climbing a bank, but nevertheless setting a good time.

July 8 - Silverstone 500 Club meeting

The highlight of this 500 Club meeting was the 100 mile race for the Commander Yorke Trophy. Following last year's success the Collins team was disappointed with troubles throughout the weekend, resulting in a non-finish in a race won by Ken Watkins' Cooper-JAP. Peter was persisting with the older Cooper chassis as a lot of work was going into the new one, trying to solve the handling problems caused by the weight distribution. Thus a fair amount of time was spent at Purton, moving fuel tanks etc in order to get a better balance in the car.

August 3 - Bouley Bay

There was a welcome break of several weeks before the competitors had to make the trip to Jersey for Bouley Bay, Peter Collins taking another victory with the Cooper still in 750 c.c. trim. This meant he had had three firsts and two seconds in the last five consecutive hillclimb events and this again boosted his image to a wider audience. He broke the old course record and won his class by a full four seconds.

August 26 - Silverstone International

The Silverstone International Trophy meeting was remembered mainly for the dire showing by the V-16 BRM on its international debut in the hands of Raymond Sommer. Two BRMs had been entered, one for Raymond Mays which was not ready on time. Sommer was impressive in practice in the wet but when the flag went down for Heat 1, the car shuddered and died, the transmission broken. This was the start of the BRM's starring role in so many cartoons and jokes of the time. The works Alfa Romeos of Farina and Fangio won the heats and Farina won the final. The race was notable for a stirring performance by Moss in the HWM who finished 6th in the final.

After a stirring 500 c.c. race supporting the British Grand Prix, the International Trophy 500 event was relegated to an early morning start, with a grid of 36 cars. Moss had a new twin o.h.c. Norton engine in his Cooper and was very fast in practice, quicker than several of the cars in the Formula 1 race! Eric Brandon, Sommer, Ken Wharton and Alf Bottoms were among the front-runners. The early laps saw a ferocious battle between Curly Dryden, Sommer, Moss, Ken Carter and Alan Brown. A second group was headed by Don Parker in the Parker, Harry Schell in John Cooper's Cooper (soon to be disqualified for an unauthorized driver swap) and Peter Collins' Cooper holding off Eric Brandon's similar car. By halfway Moss was pulling away and there was a huge battle between the next five cars, with Collins now leading the second group. Moss won, eight seconds ahead of Sommer, Bottoms, Dryden, Carter, Wharton and then Collins. Sommer's presence in the race lifted the profile of 500 c.c. racing that bit higher, Collins now being seen as a leading member of those drivers in the international arena.

Collins was making another attempt to run the new lightweight version of the Mark III. It had the Norton 'double-knocker' engine but it was also new, said to have been taken from Geoff Duke's racing motorcycle by the Norton firm and sold to Collins. Unfortunately, this change had all happened rather suddenly and the new car had not been at all sorted so didn't perform up to expectations. When they got back home, it was discovered that the bracket which

25

supports the gearbox had broken and the gearbox was only being located by the chains, so Peter's seventh place wasn't perhaps as bad as he felt it was.

September 2 - Brighton Speed Trials

Peter Collins continued his pattern of participating in major international races and relatively minor speed events by running in two classes at the Brighton Speed Trials the following weekend, his first appearance at Brighton. Of course, Brighton in those days was seen as hosting the "world's most important short-distance straight sprint event" so it was another showcase for up and coming talent, attracting 206 entries and 100,000 spectators.

Raymond Mays clocked Best Time of the Day in his ERA, while Tony Rolt's Alfa and Ken McAlpine's Maserati were in the top ten with Betty Haig and Sydney Allard. One J.M. Hawthorn won the 'Up to 1100 c.c.' sports car class in a Riley. Peter Collins was running both of his Coopers in the 500 and 750 c.c. classes and he not only won the 500-750 c.c. class but set a new course record of 28.20 seconds. Don Parker's Cooper took the smaller class ahead of Dryden's Cooper-Norton with Peter 3rd in class tied with C.J. Tipper on 31.80 seconds. Collins' performance had also gotten him into the Top Ten, 10th fastest runner overall. He was timed at 95.2 mph in the 500 Cooper and at 104.8 mph in the 750 car.

If there had been doubts about how many Coopers the Collins family were running, it was made clear at Brighton when they were both seen together for the first time. The IOTA report for September-October in 1950 clearly states that : "Peter Collins arrived equipped with two Coopers, using the Norton-engined machine which had its first outing at Silverstone in the 500 c.c. class and his earlier car with specially built 750 c.c. JAP twin to win the 750 c.c. class in 28.20 secs." (IOTA, September-October 1950, p.4).

September 10 - Bugatti Owners' Club Prescott

There was only a week's break between Brighton and the next speed event, the Bugatti Owners' Club national hillclimb at Prescott, where Collins had scored his first win at that hill in June in the 750 c.c. class. This time, however he was after another class win and after taking third in the 500 c.c. class, behind Clive Lones in his Iota and Alan Rogers in a Cooper-JAP, Collins appeared in his second chassis with a JAP engine in the Cooper which had been enlarged to 1200 c.c. according to some reports and 1100 c.c. in others. With this powerful and difficult handful, Peter broke the 1500 c.c. record of A.F.P. Fane which had stood for some eleven years. It was clear in both the commentary on the day and in the reports afterwards that this achievement earned Collins the comment that he would soon be taking Best Time of the Day at the hill. His time was 47.29 seconds, more than two seconds quicker than his run with the smaller engine. This was only a half second slower than Raymond Mays in the ERA, who was 3rd fastest overall.

The atmosphere of the Prescott meeting was made somewhat gloomy when news filtered through that Raymond Sommer had been killed at Cadours in France in a Formula 2 race. He was the leading driver there and in front when his Cooper with an 1100 c.c. engine crashed. He was a much loved figure and in spite of the failure of the BRM at Silverstone only weeks earlier, he considered it the fastest road racing car in the world and predicted it would soon be winning.

The racing career - The early years 1947-1951

C.A.N. 'Austen' May in his Cooper at Prescott. The May and Collins families were close friends. Photo - Ferret Fotographics

September 23 - Shelsley Walsh

When the British hillclimb crowd moved to Shelsley Walsh two weeks after Prescott, new British Hillclimb Champion Denis Poore and his Alfa Romeo were there and took another fastest overall time in spite of wet conditions. Collins again brought both cars and held the lead of the 500 c.c. racing car class for much of the run with a time of 43.00 seconds until John Cooper himself reduced it to 42.29 and a new class record. In the second run, Clive Lones got the Iota Tiger Kitten down to a time just behind Cooper, leaving Collins third in the class.

Rain fell on Shelsley so it would then be hard work to beat any of the earlier times. In the 501 - 1100 c.c. class, Ken Wharton was the quickest in the 996 Cooper-JAP and as the next class, for 1101 - 1500 c.c. cars appeared, it looked like Denis Poore might do a double in the Cromard Special with a fast time of 42.53. Then Collins picked exactly the right moment to put in a stunning performance with the Cooper with the 1200 c.c. engine. He power-slid and tigered his way up the hill in 39.47 seconds, the first person to beat the 40 second mark that weekend, 1.3 seconds slower than Poore's overall winning time in the Grand Prix Alfa Romeo. Collins also got himself onto the list of the quickest drivers in wet conditions for his spirited run at Shelsley. He had very quickly moved into the elite of the hillclimb competitors and earned admiration for his handling of the rather fierce Cooper with the 'big' engine.

27

All about the boy!

September 30 - Goodwood

It was a sign of how desperately some people wanted to see the V-16 BRM win a race after the debacle at Silverstone. Not long before that Reg Parnell's two victories were greeted with such enthusiasm. In truth, though Parnell had done a good job in atrocious wet conditions, the BRM had won a 5 lap Woodcote Trophy race and a 12 lap Goodwood Trophy event, the opposition was limited and in fact Prince Bira came close to getting past the BRM in his Maserati. Nevertheless, it was something and again Peter Collins was present at an important race meeting where some degree of history was being made.

Collins himself had a mixed record at Goodwood with a DNF, a win and a non-start on previous visits. The 500 c.c. race was another short event, only five laps, putting pressure on all the drivers to get into the quick mode very rapidly, something that perhaps had been helped by Collins' recent outings at sprints and hillclimbs where all-out performance was mandatory for success. Regular antagonists Curly Dryden (Cooper-Norton) and Alf Bottoms (J.B.S.-Norton) were at the front but Bottoms stalled and Dryden was out in front. Stirling Moss surged through from the fifth row in his Cooper-Norton, getting past some 12 cars. Eric Brandon and Collins had their Cooper-Nortons behind Dryden and were virtually locked together in the wet, then Moss got between them and then past. Ken Wharton latched onto Collins but Peter held him off in a mature display of good wet weather driving. Dryden won from Moss, Brandon, Collins and Wharton. This race, however short, was typical of the 'training ground' aspect of 500 c.c. racing in the period, with the drivers having to learn to race in the worst possible conditions, sometimes with the best drivers there to aid the process.

October 7 - Castle Combe

The Bristol Motor Club-organised race meeting at Castle Combe had at least two clear outcomes: the circuit was recognised as one of quality, a real boon to the West country scene and second, Peter Collins achieved a new degree of prominence for his skill shown in the 500 c.c. race.

The 500s had two heats and a final and there was a serious entry for what amounted to the end of the season circuit event. Regulars Curly Dryden and Clive Lones again fought it out in Heat 1 with Ian Burgess in 3rd. While there was mayhem at the back of the grid for several starters in Heat 2, including Don Truman, at the front it was immediately a straight fight for the lead between Stirling Moss and Peter Collins. Collins out-drove Moss for the first few laps with Alan Rogers a way behind in 3rd. Collins, perhaps, had better gearing for the Wiltshire circuit but Moss flung his Cooper past Collins at Camp Corner on Lap 4 right in the middle of the corner. Collins tucked in behind and, head down, held the slip-stream and pulled out and into the lead again at Quarry bend. This pattern was repeated several times over the remaining laps, until back markers slowed Collins towards the end and Moss won.

With only one race in between, Collins was almost immediately getting ready to go in the race for 1100 - 1500 c.c. cars, his 1200 c.c. Cooper up against some impressive ERAs. In fact, it was Collins who was again making a big impact by taking the nimble Cooper off the line first and leading all the supercharged cars into Quarry. Bob Gerard and Brian Shawe-Taylor got past but Collins was holding off the other bigger machines. Collins continued to impress though finally Graham Whitehead got the ERA past. The crowd erupted when Collins pushed the Cooper back in front of Whitehead and took third overall at the finish.

Collins wins the 500 race at Castle Combe. Photo - LAT

All about the boy!

In the 500 final Moss had trouble getting off the line and was very near the back when the field came round. Curly Dryden was in front...again...but Collins was stuck on his tail with Ian Burgess, Rogers, Lones, J. Leary and Paul Emery, in the Emeryson-JAP, following. Peter Collins repeated his earlier battle with Moss, this time engaging Dryden every inch of the way. These two changed positions several times a lap, as Moss was working his way back through the field. Moss got up to 4th and was working on Ian Burgess when a piston ring seemed to fail and a cloud of smoke meant he was going no further forward. Collins re-passed Dryden and Dryden retook him on the grass as the cars went past the paddock. Collins was then in front at the crucial moment to lead Dryden over the line with Burgess just behind. It had been a fine performance, witnessed by many about to become Peter Collins fans!

October 16 - Altcar Sprint

The Waterloo and District Motor Club was organising the Altcar Sprint on part of the Altcar motorcycle circuit and had a good entry of 63 cars for their final event of 1950. This is a very short circuit and cars in the 1100 - 1500 c.c. 'largest' class were expected to set the quickest times. Peter Collins had the Cooper with the 1200 c.c. engine this time and was up against none other than Duncan Hamilton behind the wheel of Peter Bell's ERA which he had just purchased. Collins was quickest on the first run on 14.6 seconds with Hamilton nearly a second slower. Collins repeated this time on the second run, and it turned out to be quickest time of the day. Hamilton tied it on his second try but Collins was the overall winner on aggregate times, a spirited end to his 1950 season. He had now done two seasons of competition in nothing but Coopers, but that was about to change.

1951

The motoring press was full of reports on driver movements and new cars at the beginning of 1951. John Bolster reported on Alf Bottoms' plans to start a production run with a 'new' version of his J.B.S, a tubular chassis now replacing the previous section frame. Given Bottoms' marked success in 1950, it looked as though Cooper might have some more significant opposition in 1951 and Peter Collins was one of the people now looking closely at what would be competitive in the new year, though he certainly planned to start the year as he had finished 1950, Cooper-mounted.

Work had gone on during the winter months building yet another new engine, this one based on their 1098 c.c. JAP unit. There were many problems before this engine ran well but finally it seemed to be quite competitive, Peter testing on a bit of little-used hill near Chaddesley Corbett, outside of Kidderminster. Peter's numerous delivery errands for the garage gave him the chance to not only find new roads to test on, but also to practice as well!

The 'older' Cooper with the 500 c.c. engine was refurbished and suspension and wheels replaced. The new Cooper wheels were a big improvement on the originals. It was also early in the year that a decision had been made to do some sports car racing, so an Allard was purchased through contacts that had been made with Sydney Allard. While the Allard would be run under the Kidderminster Motors banner, with many Ford parts, it had a Cadillac engine in it. The chassis of this Allard later became the basis of the well-known Farellac-Allard now owned by Tony Bianchi and raced in historic events.

The racing career - The early years 1947-1951

March 3/4 - Burnham Rally

Whatever Collins and his father had in mind for circuit racing, they were 'lured' into another diversification, Peter entering his second rally. The North Staffs Motor Club ran a scaled-down Monte Carlo Rally with five starting points all ending up in Burnham-on-Sea.

The cars arrived from the various starts at Worcester and then headed to Prescott where the cars had to achieve set target times on the Prescott hill. The times proved to be challenging and a relatively small number of drivers managed to meet the targets, Collins in a new Ford Consul being one of those. A set average speed was next on the agenda as the cars had to cross Bristol to Burnham where a large crowd turned out to welcome them. After an overnight stay, the town mayor set the cars off on an elaborate sprint course on the closed seaside promenade. John Buncombe in his powerful Healey Silverstone was by far the quickest car and won the event outright.

He was followed by Cecil Heath's Jaguar XK-120. The 'Over 1500 c.c. closed car' class was won easily by Peter Collins, who drove smoothly in the very first competition appearance of the Ford Consul. It would be the first win in what would turn out to be Collins' most successful season in his career in terms of the number of events he won. Of course, he was then about to move on to mix it with much more stirring company. The Consul, like the Allard and the Coopers, was run very much under the Kidderminster Motors banner.

Peter Collins in an early rally. Photo - LAT

All about the boy!

March 26 - Goodwood Easter Monday

Easter Monday saw the expected good crowd in Sussex and Collins was again running in two classes as he did so often the previous year. In the 'Earl of March Trophy Race for 500 c.c. cars', with the now veterans Alan Brown, Alf Bottoms, Curly Dryden and Collins making the early running, Bottoms and Dryden were both in the new J.B.S. cars built by Alf Bottoms and they were very impressive. Dryden got past Collins on lap 2, with Eric Brandon and Ken Carter right behind him. Brandon also got past Collins and he was also threatened by D.A. Clarke but he posted the fastest lap at 1 min. 48.2 secs, a bit over 79 mph. The First Easter Handicap was one of four handicap races, where Collins was listed as driving a 1098 c.c. Cooper-JAP though it was in fact the newly developed engine of 1260 c.c. Collins drove competently to beat his handicap and win the event, making up somewhat for not winning his first race. He again set the fastest lap.

The performance of the J.B.S. so impressed the Collins' that Pat Collins discussed a deal with Alf Bottoms and made his firm order only a few days later.

March 31 - Castle Combe

500s were the featured cars at the Bristol Motor Club's meeting only a few days after Goodwood on the rather soaked Castle Combe circuit in Wiltshire. Regulars Don Parker, Ken Wharton and Bill Whitehouse dominated the first heat of the 500 race in that order. In the second, Ken Carter led from Collins and Clive Lones in his usual Tiger Kitten-JAP, followed by Les Leston in a J.B.S. and A. Loens in Alf Bottoms' 1950 J.B.S. Loens very nearly crashed into Collins at Camp Corner, his wild driving taking him up the field and then into a field, though he reappeared later in the race. Collins finished two seconds behind Carter. Peter Collins had a rare DNF in the final and that win went to Ken Wharton. Collins seemed to have got himself well off the circuit into the hay bales and marker barrels and was forced to stop.

May 5 - Silverstone International Trophy Meeting

Again, Peter Collins was present at one of those great motor races remembered for disaster rather than proper racing. Not for the first time in 1951 British weather...rain, snow and hail...changed the course of events. The 1951 International Trophy should have been a great race with two heats and a final. Juan Fangio's works Alfa Romeo won the first heat from Reg Parnell driving Tony Vandervell's Thin Wall Special Ferrari. In the second heat it was Farina's Alfa which beat Sanesi's Alfa and Bira's OSCA but the final had to be abandoned after six laps when no one, officials, drivers or scorers, could see anything, such was the power of the downpour. Parnell was credited with the win.

The conditions hadn't been quite so bad for the 500 c.c. race. Moss' new Kieft was not there and 55-year old Clive Lones shot his Iota-JAP into the lead from Headland Bill Aston, Eric Brandon and Alan Brown. This last pair moved to the front. Peter Collins was up into 5th trying to pass Headland, but then lost third gear. He was trying to keep the engine revs up apparently and went into Woodcote much too fast, sliding backwards and rolling over. His feet got momentarily caught in the steering wheel as he was being chucked out but he ended up unhurt. Brandon won from Brown. The car apparently got well up into the air and having deposited the driver on the ground, soon came crashing down next to him.

On the programme as well as the Formula 1

The racing career - The early years 1947-1951

Collins went flying over the bales and was thrown out of the car at Woodcote corner, but was uninjured in this crash. Photo - BRDC Archive

cars were races for production cars, under and over two litres. These were one hour races and the first featured a number of interesting and quick cars. There were BMWs and Astons and Roy Salvadori and Bob Gerard in Frazer-Nashes, Bert Hadley in a Jowett Jupiter and Dick Jacobs and Ted Lund in MGs. Amongst the 27 cars was a quartet of Dyna-Panhards, driven by Gordon Wilkins, R.M. Dryden, Peter Collins and one "Dave", an American with an extraordinary driving style! These were well out-classed but put up some of the best entertainment running for the hour nose to tail. Salvadori rolled his car and was sent to hospital, while Tony Crook won in his Frazer-Nash. The Dyna-Panhards almost finished line astern, with Collins 3rd in class and 21st overall. For Collins, this race was notable for being one of the longest of his career to date, if not the longest...and his days as an endurance driver were not that far into the future.

Peter was lucky to get into this race, as he had been taken into 'medical custody' after his crash and only just released in time. It was a good thing as three of the Panhards were entered by his father...at the behest of the Autocar's John Cooper...the other John Cooper!

May 12 - Altcar Sprint

The Waterloo and District Motor Club was in its traditional role of organiser of the Altcar Speed Trials at the motorcycle racing venue. The weather was a vast improvement over the horrors of Silverstone.

The Collins family and helpers had a fair bit of work during the days before the sprint repairing the car damaged at Silverstone and also getting the other Cooper and the Allard ready for its competition debut.

All about the boy!

In the class for 'Unlimited Sports Cars', Collins made a successful first appearance in the Allard which would become a regular mount for him during the year. Guy Warburton was there in his Allard and was quickest after two runs by an eighth of a second, the pair having recorded identical times in the first run. In the class for 'Racing Cars up to 750 c.c.', Collins had entered the Cooper in 750 form and just wiped out the opposition with two perfect runs. He repeated this with the other Cooper in 1260 c.c. trim, again fastest and tying with C. Heath for setting a new course record. Collins, according to the reports, 'flashed down the course in a wonderful demonstration of getaway and gear change'.

May 19 - Bugatti Owners' Club Prescott

Peter Collins already held the 1100 - 1500 c.c. racing car record at Prescott and brought the Cooper along and duly improved on his own time, with a new record as the result, also winning the class. Collins also brought the Allard to Prescott though heavy rain (now what was being referred to as 'Silverstoning!') made it impossible to achieve much. Best Time of the Day went to Michael Christie and also present were Colin Strang and Clive Lones who were the first drivers to appear in post-war 500 races. It was Pat Collins' intention that Peter use the Allard wherever possible to get more experience in it.

May 26 - West Essex Car Club Boreham

If the 500 crowd had ever felt they needed more wet weather racing practice, then this was the season for getting it!

A number of big names went to the West Essex Car Club event at the Boreham Airfield and the crowd was 'entertained' by more spinning than on an ice rink. Dennis Poore and the Alfa Romeo beat Tony Rolt's Delage and Reg Parnell's Maserati in the big Formula Libre race. Parnell had lapped the three-mile track at over 91 mph, raising hopes that Boreham might one day get used for Grand Prix racing!

By this point in 1951, it is to be noted that the motoring journals made fewer references to 500 c.c. racing and tended to use the term F3 for the 500 cars, which of course it had been for a little while. The F3 event was again in two heats and a final, with Eric Brandon in a Cooper-Norton holding off Les Leston's J.B.S.-JAP and George Wicken's Cooper-JAP Peter Collins appeared for the second heat in a new car. He had seen the rising fortunes of Alf Bottoms' J.B.S. concern and now had a new J.B.S.-Norton. He used this to good effect and when Alan Brown's leading Cooper-Norton faltered, Collins was past into the lead which he held. This was somewhat ironic in that Alf Bottoms had been killed in practice for the F3 race at Luxembourg and with one brother having been killed in a motorcycle accident and another injured at Brands Hatch, it was left to 'Pop' Bottoms to continue to run the car-producing business.

The final was over 15 laps of the quick but wet circuit and Collins lined up alongside Brandon, Jack Wescott, also in a J.B.S., Leston and Wicken on the wide front row. Westcott was the first to fall foul of the soaking airfield and spun, being passed by several cars while he was still at high speed...backwards. After two laps Brandon held the lead from Wicken, Paul Emery in his Emeryson and Peter Collins. With runners spinning on every lap, Brandon started to move away, now with only Collins on his tail. At least eight cars spun at Gilhooley Corner on lap five, proving the corner to indeed have the right name. Collins was actually pulling Brandon in when the wet flag came out at the end of 15 laps, satisfied with the new J.B.S., at least in the wet.

The racing career - The early years 1947-1951

Collins shown in the new J.B.S. 500 c.c. car. Photo - BRSCC Archive

June 2 - Ulster Trophy Dundrod

Though Peter Collins was amassing a significant amount of racing and general competition experience by mid-1951, virtually everything he had done was based in England. Indeed, he had had the chance to rub shoulders with some of the British and overseas stars but most of his racing was on home soil. So, in early June, the Collins 'equipe' ventured a bit further afield, to take two cars to the support races for the Ulster International Trophy meeting at the notorious and dangerous Dundrod road circuit.

A 'scratch' race for the 'Up to 1300 c.c.' cars was the first on the programme and Collins again had benefited from his ability to learn a new circuit quickly, putting the 1200 c.c. Cooper-JAP at the head of the grid and then blasting off into the lead for five laps of the 7 mile circuit. He came past the start line at the end of the first lap more than a dozen seconds ahead of Ron Flockhart in a J.P.-Vincent. But at the end of lap two Flockhart came past and there was no sign of Collins until he coasted slowly in. There was a rush to change plugs and he restarted but he had apparently holed a piston and soon posted another of his rare DNFs.

An apparent mix-up by the organisers meant that the 500 c.c. race would have only five starters. Drivers had found the expense getting to Northern Ireland too great but some ten entrants had their forms come in late and the organisers wouldn't accept them. Nevertheless, Collins again went off into the lead in his second outing in the J.B.S.-Norton.

He extended the lead, though Gallagher's aptly named Leprechaun (presumably up from the Irish Republic) was beginning to make up some ground and was touching 100 mph on the timing straight. Peter Collins decided not to push the car with a comfortable lead. Ninian Sanderson, later to go on to achieving some fame in D-Type Jaguars, retired his Cooper-JAP Collins thus came home a happy winner, eight seconds ahead of Gallagher after easing off the pace.

The main event was won by the Alfa Romeo of Giuseppe Farina from Reg Parnell in the Thin Wall Special Ferrari 4.1, in the presence of the Queen, wife of King George VI, and their daughter, Princess Margaret. Farina had set a new lap record at 94 mph for the Dundrod circuit. Pat Collins had met Mike Hawthorn at this meeting for the first time, Hawthorn driving in the sports car race. Peter had not yet met him.

All about the boy!

June 14 - British Empire Trophy Isle of Man

It was 'another trip abroad'...well, to the Isle of Man...twelve days later when the BRDC staged the British Empire Trophy meeting at Douglas. There were preliminary races for the Castletown Trophy, won by Reg Parnell in the Maserati and the Manx Trophy, which was taken by Dunham's Alvis.

There were 26 cars for the British Empire Trophy, a race which is a classic but has changed shape a number of times in its history and continues to do so today. In 1951 it was for what could be best called 'semi-production' sports cars...cars which had been built as production vehicles but which were permitted a number of modifications. There were no less than seven Frazer-Nashes in the 'Up to 3litre class', in the hands of people like Stirling Moss and Bob Gerard, while George Abecassis was in an Aston Martin DB2. The 5.4 Allards were on hand for Peter Collins and Sydney Allard himself. These had Cadillac engines and Curtis and Scott-Russell had 4litre Allards, while Reg Parnell was in a 3.8 Nash Healey.

Stirling Moss got beaten into the first corner on this challenging road course but there was some spinning and banging behind and at least one Delahaye was stuck against a stone wall. Moss managed to find a way past Gerard but there was still turmoil behind, and poor Peter Collins got caught up in it. Sydney Allard went too quickly into a corner, hit another car and they blocked the road, with three more cars bearing down on them. One went over another and into the air and all five were out, with no serious injuries. Collins didn't really get the chance to show what the Allard could do except that it was clearly up with the front runners. Moss went on to win a very long and hard race and set fastest lap.

June 23 - 50th Anniversary Shelsley Walsh

Following the Isle of Man event, Collins had four straight hillclimbs in the schedule, the first of which was the first visit of the season to Shelsley Walsh. This was the 50th Anniversary of the venerable Midland Automobile Club which continues to organise events on the equally venerable Shelsley hill, which was 46 years old then.

Collins was not particularly successful this time with the J.B.S. and finished out of the reckoning in the 'Up to 500 c.c.' class but was again untouchable with the larger Cooper, fastest in '1101 - 1500 c.c.' class on both of his runs. Ken Wharton managed Best Time of the Day and also took the big car class in the ERA. The drivers were grouped into teams for this event and the partnership of Collins, Wharton and Dennis Poore in the Alfa Romeo managed to scoop the team prize pretty easily, this trio scoring some of the top times of the day.

June 24 - Members' Meeting Prescott

There was no break at all as many of the competitors packed up at the end of the day at Shelsley Walsh and then were on their way to Prescott for the Bugatti Owners' Club Members' Meeting. Suitably Peter Stubberfield's 2.3 Bugatti set best time of the day, as Poore's Alfa lost its clutch, probably from the hard work the day before at Shelsley. Clive Lones, in a class for 'Up to 750 c.c.' racing cars, took his Tiger Kitten 500 up the hill a second quicker than Collins could manage in the Cooper. It is of historic note that C.A.N. May in a Cooper was 1/100th of a second behind Collins. May was the father of Tony May, currently a leading light, as was his father, in the Midland Automobile Club. However, when Peter ran in the '751 - 1500 c.c.' class with the 1260 engine, he continued his impressive winning streak beating C. Heath's Cooper.

The J.B.S. at Shelsley Walsh. Photo - LAT

All about the boy!

while Dryden looked liked winning the second until he got overtaken at the last minute and Peter Collins led the third heat from start to finish and set the quickest time of the day up to that point.

In the final it was the now veteran 500 c.c. drivers in command as Dryden, Les Leston and Peter Collins had the three J.B.S. cars at the front. Leston got a bit sideways and Dryden and Collins broke free but then Peter Collins was suddenly in the pits. Jack Moor got into the lead when Dryden spun near the end. Collins had rejoined and was the quickest car on the circuit. Parker, Moor and Collins won the heat money and Collins got an additional £10 for quickest lap!

Positions in the 500 F3 championship after this event still had Brandon in the lead, with Peter Collins now having moved into a clear 6th spot on 14 points to Brandon's secure looking 37.

August 4 - West Hants and Dorset Ibsley

The Ibsley airfield was the destination a week after Croft, more or less from one corner of the country to the other, as Ibsley is near Ringwood in Hampshire where the West Hants and Dorset Car Club was running an active day's racing. This pleasant venue admitted spectators at no charge and there was a very friendly atmosphere as well, so a large crowd showed up; the 500 and Formula Libre races being the main attractions.

While Sydney Allard won the 'Over 3000 c.c. sports car race' in his big Allard, Colin Chapman took the 750 Club Formula race in his Lotus. Peter Collins had decided to concentrate seriously on 500 c.c. events for most of the season, which meant he wasn't bringing the Cooper with the 1260 engine to races as he had done. Headland and Parker crashed into each other in the first 500 heat and Peter Braid thus

won while John Cooper was third. In the second heat there was a real battle from two of the drivers now recognised as stars of the formula, Eric Brandon and Collins. Peter Collins won the duel in the J.B.S. by only 0.2 secs with the Emeryson of Williams third.

The final was over 15 laps, with 20 cars surviving from the two heats. Andre Loens seemed to anticipate the starter's flag by a fair margin and charged in to the first corner ahead of Brandon and Collins. Though there was plenty of wild driving, Collins seized the lead on the second tour and looked to be moving away. However, on the 8th lap, Loens was past Brandon and catching Collins by dint of some spectacular cornering. Collins resisted the impulse when Loens went sliding past into the front and this was a good decision as Loens then slid wide and off the track, so Collins smoothly took over and held the lead until the end. Loens got back and looked to be trying to catch Collins again, relegating Brandon to third. The usually quick Curly Dryden was down in 4th having his own battle with John Cooper in 5th. Denis Poore's Alfa Romeo won the Libre race from Kenneth McAlpine in the Connaught. The concentration of 500 races during this period gave Peter the chance to develop his race-craft and he seemed to be a very mature driver, sometimes in the face of some very impetuous driving on the part of others.

August 6 - Gamston

As this was a Bank Holiday weekend, racing continued on Monday and the F3 crowd went northwards again to Gamston, another circuit new to Collins. As it was a Bank Holiday, so it rained, which added some interest as there were a number of big cars present. Collins had brought the Allard-Cadillac for the sports car race. This was meant to be run in heats and a final, but the organisers

The racing career - The early years 1947-1951

seemed to get overwhelmed by the weather and the cars as well and declared each as a separate race. Peter Collins thus took the Allard to its first victory, beating Frazer-Nashes and Jaguars, something of an achievement in the damp conditions.

Rain had ceased by the time the 500 c.c. runners were ready to race, though it was still very wet and slippery. The cars came around in a mass of blinding spray but it was Collins in front from Jack Reece's Cooper. C.A.N. May was 4th from Bob Gerard. Collins used the advantage of the spray to put some distance between himself and the field, while Gerard was attacking Reece. Collins' J.B.S. handled beautifully in the wet and he had a good distance on Gerard at the flag. Reg Parnell's ERA took the Libre race from Gerard's ERA and Poore's Alfa.

Peter Collins had gained 12 points in the F3 Championship with his two wins over the weekend and that had the result of moving him up to third in the overall positions. Brandon had 41, Alan Brown 28 and Collins 27. This included a bonus point for sharing fastest lap at Ibsley with Brandon.

August 11 - Boreham

It was back to Boreham within a few days of the Gamston meeting, and Britain was having a very wet August. Rain poured from after the first heats throughout the day. Peter Collins was at the front for the first five laps for 500 c.c. cars and tore off in front of the three Coopers of Leary, Lowe and Leapingwell. On lap two Bill Whitehouse had taken 4th in the works Cooper. There was a lot of battling behind Collins but he was pretty much in a league of his own and he took the win at 80.18 mph.

It rained for the second heat but there was nevertheless some good racing, with Alan Brown at the front with Curly Dryden and Bernard Ecclestone, who was going well but later had a spin. Then David Brake hit the bales and rolled three times in his Cooper. He had severe head injuries and died shortly after, thus becoming, unfortunately, Britain's first 500 c.c. fatality. Dryden eventually won from Don Parker.

Four varying races had done nothing to clear water from the track for the 500 final and it now rained even heavier...*Silverstoning*! Dryden and William's Emeryson led the cars of Brown, Moor and Collins after a blinding first lap. After just a few laps, it appeared that water had drowned Collins' engine as he pulled over, though it later turned out to be a spark plug wire which had become detached, possibly knocked off by the volume of water flowing over it...but that was the end of the race for him. Alan Brown's Cooper finally won from Dryden's J.B.S. and Moor's Wasp, with Parker 4th.

That left Brandon still in front in the F3 Championship (41 points), Brown second on 35, Collins still third with 27 and Moor on 24.

August 18 - Half-Litre Club Silverstone

It was now back to familiar ground for the closed race meeting run by the Half-Litre Club. There were short five and ten lap races for the 500s, an All-Comers race and a Production (500) race, both won by Charles Headland. The big draw of the day was a pair of 100 mile races. 31 cars lined up for the first one and Alan Brown was away into the lead, first of a five-car bunch, Collins being the fifth man in this train. John Coombes made a good showing in this race, moving into the lead but it was Collins who came up to dispute the position with him. After some 17 laps Charles Headland was now second behind Brown with Collins third.

All about the boy!

Headland retired leaving Brown and Collins as the undisputed leaders, though Collins was some 20 seconds behind. Then on lap 36 with only a few more to go, Collins sputtered past the pits with a severe misfire. The carburettor had come adrift and the car soon stopped for good. Brown dashed in for fuel, had a long stop and dropped three places. But 100 miles was proving a great distance for the 500s and the lead cars all broke down, putting Brown back into the first spot.

Les Leston won the second 100 mile race in a J.B.S from Ken Gregory in a Kieft, who was being 'managed' by Alfred Moss, Stirling's father and Eric Brandon was third.

September 1 - SUNBAC Silverstone

There was then an unusually long two week break and it was back to Silverstone again, this time for a more modest meeting run by the Sutton Coldfield and North Birmingham Automobile Club. Colin Chapman had a win in his Lotus in the race for 750 Formula cars, and the 500s had two heats, the result to be decided on the basis of the fastest time. Collins took an undisputed win in the J.B.S. from Les Leston, winning the first heat by twelve seconds. In spite of the fact that the battling was much more intense in the second heat, a brief shower had penalised this group. Alan Brown and Eric Brandon changed places several times a lap, and Brown spun at Stowe on the final lap giving the heat to Brandon. But Collins had set a quicker time so the final result was Collins, Brandon and Leston. Brandon and Brown had been running all season as team mates in the Ecurie Richmond team.

September 9 - Croft

The 500s were the featured cars yet again at Croft eight days after Silverstone, and the anticipated fight quickly became a reality as Curly Dryden led the field with Headland and Collins in hot pursuit. Dryden was then in trouble and Headland now led Collins while several cars had been ploughing up the adjacent field. Don Parker came from nowhere and took both Headland and Collins. The driving was less than smooth, especially from Headland. Collins then set a new lap record and promptly disappeared from the field and did not finish, leaving Headland to win from Parker.

Peter Collins then ran his Allard in the race for 'Unlimited Sports cars' and had no trouble winning from John Walton's Frazer-Nash and Dickson's Healey. He also raised the lap record average speed to 77.64 mph. The day's competition was ended with a novel knock-out sprint with a massed start and the fastest two in each heat working their way towards a final run-off. Peter Collins thus won his class, adding another victory for the Allard-Cadillac, beating Gillie Tyrer in his FN-BMW and F. Curtis in another Allard.

The Croft race had meant that Alan Brown had moved closer to Eric Brandon in the F3 Championship, Brandon now on 49 points from Brown's 45 and Collins on 33, six ahead of Jack Moor.

September 15 - Tourist Trophy Dundrod

The Allard was then shipped over to Northern Ireland as it was again Tourist Trophy time at Dundrod. Tom Cole was to join the official Allard team for this important race but was unable to come, so Ken Watkins was invited into the official squad in his Allard-Chrysler to join Peter Collins. This was Collins first big sports car race and it was interesting that he had been invited to join the official team, though quite what that meant was not clear as he entered his own car.

The start for this race, nearly four hours of

The racing career - The early years 1947-1951

hard endurance racing, was peculiar in that the Le Mans start was abandoned as the race was running in a limited handicap format. That meant that the drivers sat in their cars and started in groups according to the handicap they had been allotted. The race was notable for the presence of the Aston Martin team and the new DB3 and the C-Type Jaguars, and especially for Moss' great performance for the second year in succession. Moss broke his own record a number of times and the Jaguars were very quick.

Collins had been going well though steadily but after some twenty laps, the Allard broke the crown wheel negotiating the Hairpin and he was immediately out. Moss won from Peter Walker in another C-Type and Bob Gerard in a Frazer-Nash. Word filtered through that Eric Winterbottom's Frazer-Nash had crashed on the first lap and he had been killed. Lance Macklin retired the DB3 with a broken exhaust.

September 22 - Shelsley Walsh

As the 1951 season drew to a close, Peter Collins decided to bring all three of his regular machines to Shelsley Walsh for the Midland AC's popular event. Clive Lones immediately set a new 500 record in his Iota Tiger Kitten, and Collins put up the second fastest time until Ken Wharton went and beat them both in the Stirling Moss Kieft. Wharton would clinch the British Hillclimb Championship and set three new class records. Wharton took the class from Lones and Collins, who then jumped into the 1260 Cooper to easily win the 1101 - 1500 cc racing car class, a class that didn't get a great deal of support but which Collins always seemed able to win.

There were a number of important drivers at Shelsley...Salvadori, Parnell, Poore, Abecassis, Wharton...as well as all the hillclimb stalwarts. The class for production cars over three litres saw a battle between Allards and Jaguars and Collins set fastest time until Sydney Allard had his run and he managed to push Collins back to second.

However, Collins was a member of the Allard team which won the production team award and also a member of the winning racing car team with Allard and Poore. He also made it, once again, into the top ten runners during the course of the event.

Standings in the F3 Championship remained pretty much the same after Shelsley with Collins still in third behind Brandon and Brown.

September 23 - Westwood Park

This was a sprint meeting, virtually on the Collins door-step as Westwood Park is in Droitwich, a 700 yard run. The Allard and the J.B.S. were brought along, Collins setting the fastest time of the day in the Allard, which was something of a beast needing taming on this 'city' venue and Collins was spectacular. He then got into the J.B.S. and went out and set second fastest time of the day.

October 6 - Gamston

At Gamston for the penultimate meeting of the season, Collins had the Allard in the scratch race for the fastest sports cars, coming third to Howart's Jaguar XK-120 and Walton's Frazer-Nash. He then won the second sports car race and all this was fairly fortunate as he had missed practice. His parents had driven the Allard to the circuit and got caught out by local flooding and arrived very late. However, he was still

43

All about the boy!

allowed to compete and did very well out of it. In the race for 500c.c. cars Collins had the J.B.S. out in front the entire distance from Alan Brown and Jack Reece for a good win. This wasn't a major meeting but Collins seemed to have the measure of Alan Brown who was still just ahead of him in the F3 Championship.

October 7 - Blackburn W.M.C. Brough

A big crowd turned out the following day for the Blackburn W.M.C. meeting at Brough Aerodrome. As so often during the season, the 500s were having two heats and a final and points were at stake for the Championship. Reece, Brown and Alan Rogers held off Don Parker in the first heat, Brown particularly anxious to see if he could manage to catch Brandon for the title. In the second heat it was Collins facing Brandon and Brandon beat Collins to the line, with Charles Headland driving Stirling Moss' Kieft to third.

In the final it was Jack Reece's Cooper taking first at the start and in spite of assaults from Parker, Brandon and Headland, he emerged the victor, while Peter Collins disappeared early from the running, an unfortunate end to the season for him, in spite of a 3rd place in the Allard in the sports car race.

The results meant that the F3 Championship now had Brandon in front on 61 points, Brown on 47 and Collins with 36.

After the Brands Hatch race, the results were finalised and the first three stood, with Parker 4th, Headland 5th and Jack Moor 6th. Sadly, talented racer Curly Dryden had been killed in a crash at Castle Combe in October, on the same day Peter was at Gamston and would be missed by the 500 crowd. The loss of Dryden and Bottoms, both front runners in 500 c.c. racing, was something of an indication how dangerous the formula was. On the other hand, there were many accidents where the drivers escaped unharmed. Though it wasn't absolutely clear at the time, Collins would only do one more 500 race the following season before moving on to more serious formulae, though by no means more competitive racing than he had found in 500 c.c. competition.

44

THE RACING CAREER
The Grand Prix driver 1952 - 1955

1952

The motoring journals, in the early 1950s, were rather less packed with news and gossip of the 'off-season' and it would have been difficult to gauge the perceived significance of most drivers from the amount of press coverage they received...with the exception of Stirling Moss who seemed to appear fairly regularly. However, an early January *Autosport* reported that the Daily Telegraph had been entertaining Brands Hatch officials at a dinner and then all were taken to the Victoria Palace to see the Crazy Gang. Among the guests of honour...Stirling Moss. *Autosport* also had a note of a party given by new F3 Champion Eric Brandon and the guests there included, Moss, Alan Brown, Peter Collins and John Cooper. Apparently Brandon made a 'secret' recording of the conversations which made interesting listening...where is that now?

One of the more significant announcements was of the new H.W.M. for 1952. This had been a successful car in 1951 in F2 and now that the World Championship was going to be run to F2 regulations rather than F1, this was particularly important. The new car would have more power, better handling and lose some weight. The light alloy Alta engine would be retained but the head was modified and had been made considerably more efficient. Lance Macklin was down to be number one driver, with George Abecassis his regular team mate. Other drivers thought likely to drive for the team were Duncan Hamilton, Peter Collins and John Heath.

There have been various stories as to how Peter Collins landed his two important drives for 1952. Some say that he was harassing John Wyer at a party and Kay Petre told John Wyer about him. Other stories have Peter chasing hard for a good drive late in 1951 and that it was John Wyer's wife Tottie who had said to John: 'Oh, give the boy a try'. There may be truth in these tales but John Wyer would already have been well aware of Collins' exploits in 1950 and 1951. A test was arranged in January, before the Monte Carlo Rally, at the MIRA (Motor Industry Research Association) testing ground. This was followed by another test at Silverstone, where H.W.M. had been testing, and George Abecassis offered Collins a test in the H.W.M. It seems like a dream scenario, although H.W.M. had already announced that Collins was likely to be one of their drivers, so the reality must be that Collins had organised these tests and they were the point at which final decisions were made. Nevertheless, Collins had got himself into the position he wanted to be in...sought after by a professional race team.

January 22/29 - Monte Carlo Rally

Monte Carlo Rally time brought news that Scot David Murray would be entering a Ford 8 Anglia for himself in the event and would be starting from Lisbon, one of seven starting stages for the classic event. There was no mention in the early news of who his co-driver would be and it wasn't until the results came out that there was any awareness that Peter Collins had made another foray into rallying in David Murray's company.

All about the boy!

In fact, it was a great British win, as Sydney Allard took the overall victory in an Allard, the first time the event was won by a British driver in a British car. This was made even more newsworthy as Stirling Moss and Desmond Scannell were 2nd in a Sunbeam Talbot and only 18 cars made the finish without road penalties as the weather had been atrocious. Collins and Murray were 71st overall and third in the 1100 c.c. class with the 8 h.p. Ford Anglia.

Brief announcements, with no details, appeared in the motoring press in late February and early March indicating that Peter Collins would probably join Stirling Moss as an entrant at selected international F3 races. This was not meant to imply they were going as a team, though apparently some readers interpreted it this way. In fact, Moss was being declared an official member of the Jaguar team, while Autosport said that Peter Collins would drive an Aston Martin at Le Mans, probably sharing with Lance Macklin and that he had been confirmed as a member of the H.W.M. squad with Macklin as well. The same issue of Autosport also reported on the award ceremony for the 500 c.c. Championship which had taken place at the Park Lane Hotel in London, with Eric Brandon getting the main award and several drivers, including Collins, receiving large photos of themselves taken by Autosport's George Phillips in lieu of just another trophy. The February issue of IOTA now had Peter Collins down as a "one-man J.B.S. team" for the J.B.S. company. That would turn out to be something of an overstatement as he only did one more 500 race in 1952.

The 1952 H.W.M. had numerous improvements and a more effective looking body, but could not compete with Ferrari throughout the season. Photo - David Hodges

The racing career - The Grand Prix driver 1952-1955

Entries for the Luxembourg 500 c.c. Grand Prix were announced and there were early entries for Peter Collins in his usual J.B.S.-Norton and Moss in his Kieft and it was thought that this would be a major overseas F3 event. In mid-March, details of the H.W.M. plans were revealed to the public, with John Heath announcing that 1952 would see the company's most ambitious year, in fact he called it "the most ambitious programme ever attempted by a British manufacturer". The first-line team of drivers would consist of Lance Macklin and Peter Collins and for the moment they would make an assault on the French Formula 2 series and a third car would be entered for Frenchman Yves Giraud-Cabantous. Moss, it was thought, might drive a fourth car in some events up until late July when Moss was supposed to start driving an ERA for Leslie Johnson and then George Abecassis would be in the H.W.M. team. The first appearance of the new car was scheduled for Goodwood on Easter Monday where Abecassis would drive and on the same day Collins and Macklin would be at Pau for the first French race. Abecassis had been doing the testing on the new car and it handled better and had more power. Everyone who saw the new car was impressed by how well prepared it was.

*George Abecassis tests the new H.W.M. at Ibsley early in 1952.
Photo - Ferret Fotographics*

All about the boy!

In the same week the Automobile Club de l'Ouest revealed the official list of acceptances for the 24 Hours. Aston Martin had five entries accepted, though at this stage it wasn't entirely clear whether the works cars were all to be the 2.9litre cars (the new DB3) and it was thought that perhaps one would be. Further information then made it clear that the entry would consist of DB3s for Parnell/Abecassis, Macklin/Collins, and Thompson/Poore, while private entries would go to Mann/Goodall and Clark/Scott, both pairs in DB2s.

On April 14, the Goodwood Easter Monday meeting took place. This was a race for Formula 1 cars, in spite of the fact that clearly Formula 1 was going to be a non-event in 1952 and Grand Prix races would be run to F2 regulations, though this took some time to sink in for many teams. A mixed field showed up and the race was won by Froilan Gonzales in a Vandervell Ferrari 375 from Mike Hawthorn in a Cooper-Bristol, with Duncan Hamilton's Talbot-Lago 3rd from Abecassis in the works H.W.M. The Lavant Cup for F2 cars was run on the same programme. Abecassis crashed at the Chicane on the second lap and the race went to Mike Hawthorn's Cooper-Bristol. Ecurie Richmond had now bought Cooper-Bristols for their regular drivers Alan Brown and Eric Brandon and they were 2nd and 3rd behind Hawthorn. Hawthorn also took the Formula Libre race and this was a significant day for Mike, prompting his backers to put together a Continental programme for him. Hawthorn had not gone the F3 route of Moss and Collins but had chosen sports cars before he got seriously into single seater. However, their paths would now begin to cross.

April 14 - Pau Grand Prix

While Hawthorn was winning and Abecassis was crashing at Goodwood, the H.W.M. team was in the Pyrenees at Pau. It was only just becoming clear to the teams, who had set out to race in Formula 2, that they would in fact be competing for the World Championship as Formula 1 had just fallen apart.

Ferrari was not slow to realise the implications of the changes and had a full team at Pau, with 500s for Ascari, Villoresi and Scotti. There was a mixture of four Gordinis, privateer Ferraris and Maseratis and the three works H.W.M.s as had been promised. The Ferraris of Ascari and Villoresi were fastest in practice by a couple of seconds but Macklin did well to get the H.W.M. on the front row. De Graffenried's 4CLT Maserati and Fischer's Ferrari were next, then Manzon in the newest of the Gordinis and Peter Collins. This was the first round of the series known as "Les Grands Prix de France" of which there would be eight races in this French Championship.

Although this was essentially Peter Collins' 'bigtime' debut, it was clear that the H.W.M. would have to work hard to stay anywhere near the Ferraris. Ascari went straight into the lead, dogged at first by Macklin until Villoresi stormed past. Peter Collins had had a brake pipe fracture before the start so there was a rush to repair that. From 14th in the early laps, Collins progressed up to 9th and then 8th and then had a recurrence of the brake problem and axle failure and he retired on lap 43 out of 50. Macklin also had a broken brake pipe and lost many laps getting it fixed. He came back and got back up to 7th but was unclassified at the end. Collins had, by all accounts, driven very well in his first Grand Prix. Giraud-Cabantous spun on a patch of oil on only the fourth lap and was unable to get going again.

April 27 - Marseille Grand Prix

Two weeks after Pau, a very similar entry showed up at Parc Borely in Marseilles for round two of the Championship. This was a twisty little venue, only 1.6 miles

The racing career - The Grand Prix driver 1952-1955

around but would be very challenging over three hours racing. Robert Manzon became almost a French hero by getting the new Gordini onto the front row of the grid with Ascari in the Ferrari again quickest and Villoresi again also on the front rank. Macklin only managed row three some six seconds off the pace and Peter Collins was 11th quickest two rows further back with Giraud-Cabantous next to him but a second slower. Giuseppi Farina was in the Ferrari team with Ascari and Villoresi so it was a strong field.

Farina made an aggressive start from the second row and held onto Ascari for many laps, eventually forcing his way past until Ascari took the lead again a few laps later. Farina, as always pushing hard with what appeared to be little thought for the consequences, took over when Ascari went in for new tyres. Farina had a good lead but didn't slow and paid the price by sliding off and damaging the car. Manzon was now second behind Ascari but he had swapped cars when his transmission broke while leading Macklin. Manzon took over Bira's car and Macklin looked like he was going to get a good result until his fuel tank split.

Manzon climbed back through the field and of course the French spectators loved it. This slightly overshadowed the fine job being done by Collins who got up to fifth when he had a repeat of the Pau axle problem. Though Collins was running in 7th at the finish, he was listed as unclassified, having lost too many laps in the pits. His French team mate Giraud-Cabantous again retired fairly early in the race.

The team had been lucky to have cars to race at all as the team's transporter driver ran off the road while attempting to swat mosquitoes and the cars had to be loaded onto vans to get to the circuit.

May 10 - Silverstone International Trophy

A lot had been happening in the two weeks between the French race and the big International Trophy meeting at Silverstone. The H.W.M.s had undergone a thorough examination and a great deal of work had gone into getting them more reliable. On the driver front, there was considerable annoyance when Ferrari announced that Farina and Villoresi wouldn't be coming to Silverstone, presumably because they had injuries during and after Marseilles. Villoresi had a serious road accident but then the cars turned up the next day at Naples for the race there with Taruffi also in attendance, though Villoresi didn't drive. Even without the works Ferraris, there were five H.W.M.s, the Aston-Butterworths, three Altas, four Connaughts and three Gordinis. There were also the three Cooper-Bristols for Mike Hawthorn, Reg Parnell and Alan Brown. The local betting was clearly on the rising Mike Hawthorn. The H.W.M.s were in the hands of Collins, Macklin, Abecassis, Tony Rolt and Duncan Hamilton.

For the very first time, Mike Hawthorn and Peter Collins were lined up next to each other for the start of Heat 1, Collins really pushing the car hard in practice to get onto row one. He was joined by Behra's Gordini and team mate Macklin, with the other three H.W.M.s in the second heat. The heat turned into a serious thrash between Hawthorn and Behra, running very quick laps, while Collins and Macklin also had an active race between themselves but appeared to be doing something to save the machinery for the final which would be over 35 laps. In Heat 2 Manzon took an early lead from pole and Duncan Hamilton kept the H.W.M. flag flying by running in second, well flying until the differential gave out on lap six and put him out. Abecassis had his diff go as well

49

Peter Collins about to practice in the H.W.M. at the 1952 International Trophy race at Silverstone.

The racing career - The Grand Prix driver 1952-1955

and that worried John Heath, though Tony Rolt did a good job to finish third behind Manzon and Fischer's private Ferrari 500.

For the final the front row lined up with Manzon, Fischer, Hawthorn and Behra and it was Hawthorn who got it all right and beat everyone off the line but Manzon's Gordini gearbox was fragile and he dropped right to the back. Before people had a chance to realise Manzon was gone, Hawthorn was also in gearbox trouble, having trouble finding gears, thus letting Behra fly into the lead. But almost immediately, on lap four, Behra had the same problem as Manzon and it was Rolt and Macklin leading, ahead of Fischer. Macklin overtook Rolt and the two British H.W.M.s moved away from the pack. After all the fuss of the last few years about BRM as the great British motor racing challenger, it took this small team to produce some results. Lance Macklin took the flag after thirty-five laps and De Graffenried's Maserati was third from Fischer.

Hawthorn had stopped to have the gear lever which had snapped off repaired and Peter Collins came in after five laps with dirt in the fuel system and from then on was driving very quickly for the rest of the race, finally making up enough ground to finish 9th. He had been all the way down in 23rd on lap 6 so it was a pretty dramatic drive for most of the race. If he had not stopped...a big if...he would have been well in contention for the lead.

May 18 - Swiss Grand Prix

The Swiss Grand Prix and racing at the Bremgarten Forest circuit had had a serious number of accidents associated with them and this meeting sadly was no exception. The Italian motorcyclist Frigerio had been killed in the morning bike races and Rudi Caracciola had been seriously hurt when his Mercedes crashed in the sports car race. Again a large entry had been put together for the Swiss Grand Prix, though Ascari was away trying his hand at the Indianapolis 500 and Villoresi was still on the mend from his road accident. The two works Maserati A6GCMs had been entered for Fangio and Gonzales but apparently were not quite ready and failed to show up. The Ferraris of Farina and Taruffi were at the front of the grid with the plucky Manzon in the Gordini 16 next to them. Collins, for the first time, was the quickest of the H.W.M.s on row three. Collins had managed a time faster than Behra's Gordini, de Graffenried's Maserati 4CLT and the next H.W.M. of Stirling Moss. George Abecassis was a half second slower than Stirling and on row five sat Lance Macklin almost four seconds slower than Collins.

Not too surprisingly Farina shot off into the lead of the 62 lap race round the tough and dangerous 4.5 mile circuit. Taruffi stuck to his tail with Andre Simon initially third in the other works Ferrari but it was soon Stirling Moss who drove superbly to grab 3rd before he needed to rush into the pits for new plugs. Farina had the magneto break on his Ferrari and stopped and Simon was called in to hand over to Farina. This moved Behra up the field but he also had to make a stop for his exhaust to be repaired. Privateer Ferrari driver Fischer moved up to second after Farina had managed to break another car, so Taruffi won from Fischer and Behra. Sadly all the H.W.M.s were out: Abecassis had a stub axle break and he ran over the bales and overturned, with only a slight concussion as a result. Then Collins had his stub axle fail and he spun to a standstill, causing John Heath to withdraw the Moss and Macklin cars in case the same should happen to them. The wheels had come off on both the Collins and Abecassis cars. Moss was up into third again on lap 24 when he was called in. The wheel of the Collins car

51

All about the boy!

bounced over the bales and was headed for a crowded spectator area but fortunately it hit a tree and bounced clear. Collins was pretty lucky to get the car stopped as he had been accelerating very hard out of the Forsthaus corner at the time the axle broke.

The opening lap of the Swiss Grand Prix in the Bremgarten Forest. Photo - LAT

The racing career - The Grand Prix driver 1952-1955

May 22 - Luxembourg Grand Prix

The well publicised Luxembourg Grand Prix on the Findel circuit had been high on the list of must-do events for many British drivers. It was of course essentially for 500 c.c. cars...and bikes! There were two 500 c.c. heats and a final for cars and three motorcycle races as well. British drivers and riders won every single event.

F3 regulars Don Parker, Alan Brown, Charles Headland, Ken Wharton and Ninian Sanderson were in the first heat. Brown crashed out while in the lead on lap three and Wharton pressed Parker very hard. Parker managed to be in front at the end of the twelve laps. The second heat had Andre Loens leading Stirling Moss' Kieft. Moss was doing a number of 500 races in addition to all the other events he was now doing as Britain's busiest professional racing driver. Eric Brandon, Ken Carter and Les Leston chased this pair. Leston suffered a broken gear lever and an impressive Loens then had his chain fracture. Brandon sneaked past Moss and Carter but then his driveshaft broke so he was out. Peter Collins, with his J.B.S. was in the second bunch and managed to finish fourth behind Moss, Carter and Arthur Gill's Mackson-Norton, with Leston 5th by dint of holding the remains of the gear lever in place and driving with one hand.

On the basis of the best results in the heats, the 25 lap final consisted of all British drivers. Peter Collins was on the fifth row in 11th spot and wasn't looking particularly likely to get a good finish. It was Leston in his repaired car which made the best start from back in the 4th row and at the end of lap one Moss' Kieft led Parker, Leston, Coombs and Carter. Wharton was quickly out with a broken exhaust. The lead was changing every lap and so were the next five or six places. By 10 laps, Collins had worked his way up to third behind Carter and Leston and Stirling Moss had a plug lead off and had dropped to ninth. Les Leston was driving superbly and was in front on lap 15 and, with a number of cars struggling on this tough circuit, Collins was secure in third, so Leston won from Carter and Peter Collins with John Coombs 4th. Moss finished in sixth and he would do several more 500 races, while this turned out to be the swansong for Collins' J.B.S. with which he had done so many events since May of 1951. The J.B.S., which had been towed to Luxembourg by Pat Collins who was on holiday near the French coast, was then sold to John French who took it to the USA. That was the last of Peter's races in 500s.

May 25 - Montlhery Grand Prix

By late May the serious racing season was well under way with an event every weekend and in some cases two per weekend. The Eifelrennen was being held on the same date as the race at Montlhery and, as there were races for F3, it was of interest to drivers such as Moss and Wharton. John Heath sent two H.W.M.s to the Nurburgring for Moss and Duncan Hamilton where they were up against mainly German drivers. Rudolf Fischer's Ecurie Espadon Ferrari 500 won the seven lap Eifelrennen from Moss, in spite of the fact that the H.W.M.'s fire extinguisher went off in the cockpit. Ken Wharton's Frazer-Nash was third ahead of Hamilton. Also in the race was Paul Pietsch who was described at the time as going very well in spite of his age. At the time this book is being written he is still going, as is the other competitor Hans Klenk, just about the very last of the pre-war and immediate post-war drivers of significance. Paul Pietsch is the oldest survivng Grand Prix driver.

Meanwhile, the Grand Prix de Paris was taking place at Montlhery, the third round

All about the boy!

of the French series. Ascari was again not present though Villoresi was back and Peter Whitehead was there with a new Alta. The race looked very much like it was going to be between the Ferraris and the Gordinis but it was Manzon who got onto pole in the Gordini from Taruffi and Villoresi, with Farina, Behra, Rosier, Prince Bira and Peter Collins next. So Collins managed to be the quickest of the non-Ferrari/Gordini set, with Whitehead next. Macklin was 2 seconds slower than Collins and Giraud-Cabantous another 4 full seconds behind that.

The two Gordinis charged into the lead but Taruffi soon went past them and for a short time, Harry Schell's Maserati had come through amazingly from the back row to the front until it retired just as dramatically. Peter Collins lasted an even shorter time, having another magneto failure on lap 2. The lead changed regularly for the first dozen laps. Behra retired and when Farina's car started to go off-song, he stopped and took over Villoresi's car while Simon took his. Villoresi had not completely recovered from his road accident. When Taruffi went past Farina, Farina in his usual aggressive style, overdid it and went off. Manzon was going well until he too was forced out near the end. Taruffi won, with Simon in second and Rosier third. Peter Collins had taken over Lance Macklin's H.W.M. and though he was running in 4th, they were eight laps behind Taruffi at the finish. Giraud-Cabantous also had the magneto curse but was in 6th spot at the end.

Peter Collins had taken over from Macklin when he came in to refuel. He reported that both front dampers were not working and that there was a fuel leak from the tank, so it was an example of Collins pushing on for many laps with a very difficult car, in great discomfort, just to get to the finish.

June 1 - Monaco Grand Prix

Most of the motor racing world was focussed on Monaco this weekend but the Formula 2 cars had gone to Chimay for the Grand Prix des Frontieres. John Heath entered an H.W.M. for himself and a second car for Belgian racing journalist Paul Frere, with a third for Charles de Tornaco. When the lead Gordini of Claes and the Ferrari of Laurent took themselves off on lap one, the race eventually provided a rare H.W.M. victory for Frere, while Heath crashed out. Somehow, Heath had agreed to Collins going to Monaco with Astons for the sports car race there. The Frere car which won was the car Collins would have driven himself.

Monaco 1952 was remembered as the year that the Grand Prix was run for sports cars and for the accident to Luigi Fagioli.

Most people seemed to think that Stirling Moss would dominate the main race at Monaco, after he had been forced to retire in the race for cars up to 2 litres. His C-Type Jaguar was however beaten to pole by Pierre Levegh in the streamlined Le Mans Talbot, with Stagnoli's Ferrari on the outside of the front row. Reg Parnell was next with the Aston Martin, then Manzon's Gordini and Macklin, also in the Aston. Back in the middle of the fifth row, next to Marzotto's Ferrari was Peter Collins, making his debut appearance in the Aston Martin DB3, and this was also his first time round the Monaco circuit.

Moss did indeed get away quickest at the start with the Ferraris of Stagnoli and Pagnibon, Manzon, Carini's Ferrari and then Levegh and Parnell. Levegh was then straight into the pits with a misfire from which he later retired. Moss eased away and when Stagnoli hit the wall Manzon went into 2nd. Within the first ten laps, Reg Parnell had gone into the pits with

54

The racing career - The Grand Prix driver 1952-1955

overheating and then Collins was forced to do the same but they both resumed. Meanwhile Manzon was catching Moss and on lap 24 the Gordini went past the Jaguar.

At this point, after Mascarenhas' Allard had leaked considerable fuel, especially at St. Devote corner, making it very slippery, Parnell's Aston gave up and he was trying to push it out of the way with very little assistance. The officials had said they needed a crane to lift the Aston and in response Reg lifted the back end himself, attempting to move it. Stagnoli spun on the slippery surface and hit the Aston and then Manzon was bearing down on them in the lead. He got round the Ferrari but hit the Aston and Moss, right behind, did the same. Tony Hume's lapped Allard then joined the pile-up with five cars strewn about the road. Parnell had been caught between the Aston and a hay bale and had injured his leg. Stagnoli managed to drive away and spectators helped Moss extract the Jaguar, bend the wings back and get moving again.

All this put Bruno Castellotti's 2.7 Ferrari into the lead. Eventually Moss got going again but after 20 laps he was black-flagged for receiving outside assistance and retired. The Astons of Collins and Macklin had both been into the pits and were not having a very good day. Marzotto moved up on Castellotti and went into the lead on lap 46. Castellotti was second and Stagnoli soldiered on to take 3rd. Macklin retired on lap 73 but Collins kept the only remaining Aston Martin going into seventh place, being fortunate to get the ailing car to the finish.

Sadly, the injuries to Fagioli, suffered in practice for the support race, were more serious than had been thought at first and the great Italian driver died three weeks later.

A fascinating aside to the Monaco story was the discovery of an ex-Aston Martin team mechanic, Richard 'Dickey' Green, living in California through the website of his equally enthusiastic son Michael. 'Dickey' Green was on the competition side at Astons during Peter Collins' spell with the team. Michael has kindly allowed me to extract from some of his father's notes and comments himself:

"My family began their long association with the marque in 1949 when my mother, then Doreen Sherwood, joined Astons as a secretary and would go on to work in the Racing Department under John Wyer. My father, Richard Green, joined in 1952 and it was here that he and Doreen met. It should be noted that my mother's two brothers also worked in the Feltham works, one in the drawing office, the other a panel beater. For many years our family revolved around Aston Martin, even when Richard and Doreen emigrated to California in 1956 they would continue a close association with Astons, Richard taking care of Joe Lubin's cars to name one. Richard would again join AM in the late 1950s, this time as Resident Engineer for Aston Martin, based in San Lorenzo, California. I too knew only Astons, having come home from the hospital in a Mk III 'notchback'"

His father recalled his early days with the company, which pretty much had coincided with the arrival of Peter Collins:

"The Tourist Trophy Race of 1951, run on the Dundrod circuit, (*where Collins was driving his Allard and did not finish* - EM) saw the introduction of the Aston Martin DB3. Driven by Lance Macklin, the car led for most of the race, only to retire finally with a broken exhaust system and low oil pressure. Powered by a 2.6 litre engine, the DB3 was in great need of more power and Aston Martin was considering supercharging as the most viable alternative. Discussions with Professor Eberan von Eberhorst and John Wyer determined that this

All about the boy!

was to be no bolt-on, belt-driven installation; rather, it was to be a chain-driven system and this called for a special timing case and certain modifications being made to the cylinder block. As Technical Representative (*for Wades Engineering manufacturer of superchargers- EM*) it was my responsibility to insure the installation was correct and that the end result was to the customer's complete satisfaction. Since, in this case, the customer was Aston Martin-Lagonda Ltd., I naturally spent many, many hours with team mechanic, the late Jack Sopp, to perfect the installation. During this period, Wade's overall policy was directed toward the industrial applications such as the drying of Technicolor film and the blasting of ships' bottoms by a system known as 'Vacublast' - not really too interesting when compared with working on Parnell's Maserati. One late evening, John Wyer suggested that since I spent so much time with the Aston Martin works, we should make the relationship permanent – a suggestion I accepted with alacrity!

"I joined the Experimental Department of Aston Martin (there was no Racing Department at this time) in the midst of their preparations of the lightweight DB2s, XMC76 and XMC77, for the 1952 running of the Mille Miglia. When this programme was completed all efforts were aimed at preparing the new DB3s for the May 10th Silverstone meeting (*where Collins was in the HWM - EM*). The weekend following the Silverstone meeting saw the introduction to the team of World Champion motorcyclist Geoff Duke. He and Reg Parnell raced the two Mille Miglia DB2s against the Mercedes Benz 300 SLs at Bern, and gave an excellent account of themselves when one considers that the cars were built up from production models.

"The next two events resulted in the splitting of our forces; three DB3s (now fitted with the new 2.9litre engine) were driven from Feltham to Monaco for the race around the famous streets, while Percy Kamish and I took DB3/1 to the Isle of Man for the British Empire Trophy Race. The result of the Monaco race was highly unsatisfactory. The modification from 2.6 to 2.9litres had been accomplished by off-setting the bores and the connecting rods at the wristpin end and all engines failed during the race. Parnell's was the first to go; he slid on his own oil and caused a spectacular crash that ultimately involved a Gordini, an Allard, and Moss' C-type Jaguar. At the Isle of Man, however, Duke made the fastest lap with the 2.6litre-engined prototype car that had already covered considerable test mileage at Montlhery during the early part of the year. Geoff led for most of the race but eventually retired with a broken crankshaft."

June 15/16 - Le Mans 24 Hours

The previews in the press regarding the Le Mans 24 Hour race were bubbling in their enthusiasm about this race with the new Alfa Romeo 'Disco Volante' promising to be very interesting and strong cars from Mercedes and Jaguar. It probably would not have taken much research to find out that the Alfas in their current form were far from being competitive, indeed they could hardly stay on the ground at speed, so it was clear to many that they were not going to be at Le Mans. The Aston Martin team was announced as Parnell/Thompson, Macklin/Collins, Abecassis/Poore all in DB3s and the privately entered DB2s for Mann/Morris Goodall and Clark/Scott. The press announced that the works Aston Martin team orders were that the drivers would be 'flat-out to the finish'. Knowing John Wyer, that seems highly unlikely and highly unlikely to have divulged real tactics anyway. The speculation was also that the Monaco overheating was due to the nature of the course and low gearing. 'Dickey'

The racing career - The Grand Prix driver 1952-1955

Green's comments would indicate that this was not the case.

Again, 'Dickey' Green provides the background to Aston Martin's trip to Le Mans:

"Our resources were stretched almost to their breaking point; we had three destroyed engines at Monaco, (Parnell's car had to be shipped to Paris for repairs) one car at Feltham with a broken crankshaft and Le Mans just twelve days away! We got to work. The Company's De Havilland Dove delivered two standard engines to Monaco and these enabled the cars to be driven to Le Mans where they were fitted with 2.6litre race engines for the twenty-four hours. Jack Sopp and I spent the next week rebuilding DB3/1 and completed our task at 5.10 pm on the Saturday afternoon. Our departure date was set for Monday - destination, France!

"By Monday morning, Charlie Burchett and his team had converted the car to a very attractive coupe which we hoped would have a lower drag coefficient than the open cars, thereby offsetting our relative lack of power. Jack and I set sail for France and completed our journey by ripping off the rear undertray as we passed through the gates of our final destination, La Domaine de Beauchamps. More work!

"Each year had its own minor adventures and 1952 was no exception. At La Domaine, the mechanics' quarters were converted stables that still retained the usual split stable doors. We had no showers other than a car-wash brush on the end of a garden hose that was slung over the stable door. Somewhere in the archives is a photograph showing Fred Lown in the act of showering, the cameraman being none other than David Brown himself. John King and I shared a room in 1952 and one day he left a bright yellow shirt lying on the bed. As it happened, the shirt was eaten by a cow that had wandered through when no one was about. John's only comment was 'She probably thought it was a bloody buttercup!' Every morning we were attacked by a vicious cockerel. Early one day, however, Eric Hind made a surprise attack on this monster, grabbed it by one leg, swung it through a large arc and about 40 rpm, and, on the fifth circuit, sailed it over a ten foot hedge. For the remainder of our stay, our chicken friend viewed anybody in green coveralls with well-deserved suspicion!

"Late Wednesday afternoon I departed from Beauchamps for Paris in David Brown's Land Rover with the engine to be installed in DB3/3 tucked securely in the rear compartment. With the new engine installed, the car was driven back to Le Mans by our French distributor Marcel Blondeau and took the place of the DB3 Pat Griffith had wrecked in the night practice.

"The Aston Martins made a sensible start to the 24 hour race and let the Ferraris, Jaguars and Cunninghams set very fast lap times in the early laps. Poore's Aston, however, came into the pits on only the fourth lap to report gear change problems and then carried on but even Ascari's Ferrari was having trouble in the early stages. Then Reg Parnell retired the DB3 after only some dozen laps when the rear axle failed, and things were not looking good for Astons. The C-Type Jaguars, had overheating problems in practice due to the newer streamlined front bodywork and the problems had not been overcome. Before the two hour mark Poore had the water pump break and both Moss and Ascari were out and with all the Jaguars out the three Mercedes were beginning to move towards the front. All the excitement however was being provided by Manzon, whose Gordini was flying in 2nd place."

All about the boy!

*The Aston Martin mechanics refuel the Collins-Macklin DB3 early in the 1952 Le Mans race.
Photo - Michael Green Collection*

The Collins/Macklin DB3 had moved into the top ten and was running a consistent pace. By five hours into the race 17 cars were out and, as the event progressed, the Manzon/Gordini was leading with Levegh (doing his famed solo drive) second. Sadly, just before halfway, the Manzon/Behra Gordini had a broken brake-shoe anchor pin and Amadee Gordini insisted the car be retired over the pleas of the two drivers. This left Levegh four laps in front of the two Mercedes, while Collins and Macklin had moved the Aston up to 4th, with Allard's Allard 5th. A few hours later the DB3 also succumbed to axle failure and that left the private Clark DB2 as the only surviving Aston Martin after Collins had begun to look secure in 4th. Levegh was leading when a con-rod broke at 23 hours, the popular view being that fatigue had meant he selected the wrong gear. The Mercedes of Land/Reiss and Helfrich/Niedermayer were first and second and Clark/Keens in the DB2 were 7th.

Richard Green summed up the Aston Martin situation after the Le Mans race from the point of view of a team 'insider':

"In the event itself, two cars went out with final drive problems. The Collins/Macklin car lasted the longest but retired shortly after the twentieth hour while lying third behind two 300 SL Mercedes. There was talk at the time about receiving a bad batch of hypoid gears from Salisbury but those of us in the shop could never understand the reason behind Salisbury's assembly specification that called for a tremendous pre-load on the taper roller races. We always felt that this, coupled with the excessive heat transference to the differential by our use of inboard brakes, was the key to the problem."

The racing career - The Grand Prix driver 1952-1955

June 22 - Belgian Grand Prix

John Heath had sent two H.W.M.s to Monza on June 8 for Duncan Hamilton and Johnny Claes and had not reaped much of a reward as Hamilton retired and Claes had finished 14th. Heath himself and Lance Macklin were at the Circuit du Lac at Aix-les-Bains on the same day where Macklin finished a good second on aggregate after two heats and Heath had retired in the second heat. Then it was time for the second World Championship race, the Belgian Grand Prix at Spa. News came through that Fagioli had died after his Monaco crash in the Lancia Aurelia and that cast something of a cloud over the meeting, as he had been held in high esteem. With the new Maseratis still not ready, Ferraris were unsurprisingly fastest from the Gordinis with Ascari leading Farina, Taruffi, Manzon and Behra. But one surprise was sprung by Mike Hawthorn whose Cooper-Bristol was the only other car to get under five minutes around Spa. Stirling Moss was on row five, making his ERA debut after much publicity over the previous months. The ERA with a Bristol engine was a strange looking device.

Paul Frere was the quickest of the H.W.M. team, Frere having a guest ride as he knew Spa well, with Collins just behind Moss and Macklin and Laurent further down the grid. The Ferraris blasted off into the distance after a wet start with Ascari and Farina in front. Moss took six cars by the exit of Eau Rouge but only made it halfway round the first lap before the engine went. Poor Collins' run of bad luck continued as the driveshaft broke on the third lap. Mike Hawthorn ran in 4th and even after a fuel leak, he managed to hold the position. Frere finished 5th and Macklin and Laurent were in 11th and 12th. Frere's 5th had earned two manufacturer's points, though there was no constructor's championship until 1958.

June 29 - Grand Prix De La Marne

The teams were at Reims immediately after the Belgian race for a round of the French Championship and the circuit had undergone major changes from the previous season, as the race no longer went through the tight and narrow Gueux village but La Hovette corner, the long right sweeper at the end of the pit straight had been built, so the course ran east of Gueux. However, the original road remains unchanged and visitors to Gueux can still see where the earlier route went...and in the Bar du Lac just before the road turns right there are photos of the old circuit.

Stirling Moss was back with H.W.M. for this race after his interlude with the ERA, joining Collins, Macklin and Giraud-Cabantous, Moss being the quickest by nearly two seconds from, not Collins or Macklin but Giraud-Cabantous. Mike Hawthorn, however, was a shade faster than Moss, though again it looked like this race would be between Ferrari and Gordini. Alan Brown managed to get the nose of his Cooper-Bristol alongside Ascari just after the start but it was Behra in the Gordini who led the first lap. Behra drove a sensational race and beat the Ferraris and this was probably the greatest win ever by the Gordini team. Collins had his engine expire on the 13th lap and Macklin had ignition failure on the 23rd. Moss finished 10th with oil leaking everywhere so it was left to Giraud-Cabantous to bring an H.W.M. to the line, with Hawthorn just ahead of him in 7th.

Collins had pulled himself behind the battle for 7th and 8th places between Moss and Hawthorn and certainly was no slower than that pair. Stirling Moss had done a good job for Jaguar to win the earlier sports car race in the C-Type from Guy Mairesse's Talbot.

59

All about the boy!

July 6 - French Grand Prix

This race was the 4th major race on consecutive weekends, though travelling was less of a problem for most of the teams at Reims as it was a relatively short trip to the fairly new road circuit at Rouen. The works Ferraris were all quicker than the opposition which was still the Gordinis. The Ferraris arrived at Rouen with engines with new front-mounted magnetos and a lot more power, so Ascari was on pole by a second and a half from team mate Farina.

The next four cars were all Gordinis...Behra, Manzon, Trintignant and Prince Bira and then Peter Collins, the only other driver managing a time close to the two quick works teams. Giraud-Cabantous was six seconds slower and Macklin a full nine seconds behind Collins. Mike Hawthorn's Cooper-Bristol was a second behind Macklin. The Ferraris held station through the entire race, with Farina and Taruffi behind the elegant and drifting Ascari. Behra stopped for repairs after a trip into a ditch. Manzon was not as quick as usual, though he held 4th for the entire race. At one stage Collins and Trintignant were fighting it out for 5th but it was clear that the H.W.M.s were not capable of mixing it seriously with the Ferraris or the Gordinis. Mike Hawthorn managed to pull himself up into this fight for 5th but he had a split header tank and had to pit and then retired. So Collins finished a quite reasonable sixth, with Macklin in ninth and Giraud-Cabantous in tenth. Collins had managed quickest time for any of the British drivers and that was seen as something of an accomplishment as the H.W.M.'s Alta engine was at least 30 bhp down on the Ferrari. Ascari was heard to be reminding everyone after the race that he had counted no less than four black cats hanging around the garage being used to house the Ferrari team. Ascari was particularly well known for his wide range of superstitions!

July 13 - Grand Prix de Sables D'Olonne

Again, all the teams packed up and headed for the tight 1.46 mile Sables D'Olonne circuit for the third straight race in the French Championship. This turned

Piero Taruffi in Ferrari number 12 is followed by Peter Collins at the French Grand Prix at Rouen. Photo - G.N.Boot

Collins in the hairpin at the French GP. Photo - LAT

out to be a surprising race for many of the drivers! Jean Behra crashed in early practice and was out of racing for at least a few weeks. It appeared that this would be another Ferrari-dominated round as Ascari and Farina led the grid from Manzon and Villoresi. Macklin was now a bit quicker than Collins and they sat on the third row with their French team mate two rows further back.

At the start it was the predictable Ascari/Farina duo leading with Manzon desperately hanging on, Villoresi next and then for a brief spell Macklin had the H.W.M. well up with the leaders but was soon in the pits. Peter Collins cruised competently in 7th. After several laps, Harry Schell had a big spin in his seized Maserati, just as the leaders were closing on him. Ascari, Farina, Trintignant and backmarker Cantoni all crashed into him and they were all out of the race. Manzon found himself in the lead but only briefly as his car was not running properly, so he stopped and handed over to Trintignant and took over Prince Bira's Gordini. Villoresi was thus in front from the

two H.W.M.s of Macklin and Giraud-Cabantous. Then Macklin retired and the Frenchman made a stop, putting the surprised but determined Peter Collins in second place. Belgian Johnny Claes had his Gordini two laps back in third and that is how they finished. Collins was rather bemused but equally had been rewarded for keeping the car going, as he himself had had a long pit stop.

July 19 - British Grand Prix

The motoring journals were predicting that Mike Hawthorn would give the Ferrari and Gordinis a good run for their money in the up-coming British Grand Prix at Silverstone, held the week after the French race. This seemed somewhat optimistic but in reality he was very competitive. Peter Collins was being declared the most dependable of the H.W.M. drivers who would have him, Macklin, Duncan Hamilton and Tony Gaze at Silverstone.

While, again, the Ferraris had the quickest

All about the boy!

practice times and dominated the front row, with Manzon squeezing onto the outside place, Hawthorn and Parnell were on the second row, with Hamilton the fastest H.W.M. on the next row while Collins led the next with Gaze and Macklin at the back of the very full grid. When the flag dropped and the cars came around at the end of a very busy first lap, Ascari and Farina led but there was reserve driver Dennis Poore in the Connaught in third, with Ken Downing in another Connaught in fourth, Parnell in his Cooper-Bristol and Eric Thompson in a Connaught, Manzon and Hawthorn. Ascari was going away, Manzon retired early and Dennis Poore held third. Stirling Moss, who had started on the fifth row in the G-Type ERA was trying to work his way through the field but not having much luck in doing so, finding the ERA without much power. Taruffi got up to 4th by 10 laps. Tony Gaze became the first H.W.M. casualty with a blown head gasket at 20 laps. Moss went out on lap 36 with engine problems, as did Hamilton eight laps later in the H.W.M.

Collins refuelled and took on some water

The start of the British Grand Prix with Alan Brown closest to the camera, Stirling Moss' E.R.A. and Peter Collins in the H.W.M. Photo - LAT

around the same time as Farina pitted for a plug change. Collins was then in for a long stop and quit after 73 laps with a severe misfire and Macklin was the only H.W.M. to finish in 15th, not a good showing after the International Trophy result. Ascari went on to win with Taruffi second and Hawthorn got ahead of Poore when the latter made a stop and suddenly the Connaught was looking like a threat, though they were very selective about which races they did. Collins'

The racing career - The Grand Prix driver 1952-1955

problem was diagnosed as magneto failure but, as they did strip the engine down between events, it was discovered the next time it ran that the crank had broken.

Stirling Moss won the 500 c.c. race and Taruffi took the Thin Wall Special Ferrari to victory in the Formula Libre event.

August 3 - German Grand Prix

H.W.M. had sent two cars to the Caen Grand Prix on July 27 for Andre Simon and regular Giraud-Cabantous but they both retired from a minor race won by Trintignant's Gordini.

After the British Grand Prix, all the major players had sorted themselves out after many hectic weeks and got ready for the German Grand Prix at the Nurburgring. The result was pretty much a foregone conclusion and Ascari and Farina were first and second in the works cars, with Taruffi fourth, Fischer's private Ferrari getting amongst them. There were the three works H.W.M.s for Collins in his Nurburgring debut, Claes and Frere, with Tony Gaze in his own car. Peter Collins had serious engine problems in practice with the crankshaft breaking on his first lap and although the car was repaired in time for the race, the organisers would not listen to the team's plea to be able to start on the grounds that he had not done sufficient practice. All the team cars suffered some malady or other and it was a pretty dismal meeting for H.W.M. They had arrived late and thus missed the first session. Had they been on time, they would have been able to do the repairs in order to race. It is an interesting thought, that though Collins was seeing himself as a professional driver at this stage, he didn't have or didn't exercise enough influence on the team to avoid such disastrous possibilities. In addition, routine maintenance, especially racing every weekend, was minimal and parts just wore out and broke.

August 10 - Grand Prix De Comminges

All three H.W.M.s had their by now standard problems with magnetos during practice and Collins was quickest of the trio on row four with Macklin and Giraud-Cabantous behind him. Macklin was into the pits after only three laps as he was a cylinder down and even the great Ascari had problems, stopping to take over Simon's car. A number of pit visits allowed Collins to move up and he was running very quickly but his timing chain and magneto went on lap 61, Macklin then dropped out eight laps later with the same magneto problem. Giraud-Cabantous finished 6th well down, while Ascari won again sharing with Andre Simon.

August 16 - Goodwood Nine Hours

Dickey Green described the run-up to the Goodwood race:

"The next meeting (after Le Mans) was the International Road Race in Jersey in the Channel Islands. After revising the pre-load figures on the final drive, we managed a third and fourth place with Parnell and Abecassis as drivers. This was followed by a minor event at Boreham which was won by Parnell and during which Abecassis retired with fuel filter problems - the first and last time we used fuel filters.

"In preparation for the Nine-Hour Race at Goodwood, we carried out a test program aimed at solving our continuing problem of excessive lubricant temperatures at the differential. Thermocouples and thermometers were installed in the differential of the two cars and Abecassis and Parnell completed some thirty laps of the Silverstone circuit as fast as

63

All about the boy!

The Aston mechanics take the Collins/Griffith car to the assembly area at Goodwood for practice for the Nine Hours. Photo - Michael Green Collection

possible without using the brakes. Bill James and I were the passengers and we took the temperature readings as we accelerated out of Woodcote Corner; this was difficult to do, since only the driver had any protection. After lunch, we repeated the program; this time, however, it was done faster - in anger - and involved heavy use of the brakes. After four laps, I left my lunch on Hangar Straight but the increase in the temperature caused by the heat transference certainly proved John Wyer's contention that we should move the brakes to outboard. Thus, the sacrifice was worth it!"

Peter Collins would later make a point of arguing with the team and John Wyer about this very issue.

With the H.W.M. team having gone to Zandvoort for the Dutch Grand Prix, Peter Collins was honouring his contract with

The racing career - The Grand Prix driver 1952-1955

Aston Martin and was about to have his third drive for the team in the DB3. The BARC was organising and the News of the World sponsoring the Nine Hours and it looked very likely to be one of the best races in the UK during the year. The weather turned out to be pretty awful but the crowd was huge. The C-Type Jaguars were favourites to win, and they led the grid with Moss and Peter Walker, Rolt/Hamilton and Whitehead/Stewart. The race was to start at 3.00 pm and run well into the hours of darkness and just before the start, the rain poured down on the Sussex circuit.

At the Le Mans start Moss led away from Rolt and Whitehead, followed by Allards, Reg Parnell's 2.9 Aston DB3, Levegh's Talbot, Abecassis in the 2.6 DB3 and the others. Before the lap was completed, Peter Collins had brought his DB3 up into 6th place and was in 5th on the next tour round. In fact the Astons were putting on a fantastic performance in the early laps in dreadful conditions. By only the fifth lap Collins was closing on both Moss and Whitehead. The leaders had done 30 laps in the first hour and the roadholding of the Astons was giving them an upper hand over the more powerful C-Types. Parnell had gone by Tony Rolt so one DB3 led, Rolt was next, then Abecassis in a second DB3. As the track started to dry out, the Jaguars asserted themselves and soon all three C-Types were in front from Parnell and Collins, driving very consistently.

On ninety minutes, Peter Collins pulled into the pits for fuel and Pat Griffiths took over. It was just after this that the first sign of Jaguar vulnerability appeared when Whitehead went off the road at Madgewick and hit the barrier hard enough to damage the bodywork and the gearbox. He got it back to the pits but it was withdrawn. Jack Fairman's Allard had stopped out on the circuit and Maurice Falkner's private DB2 ground to a halt with a big end gone. At two and a half hours Hamilton and Rolt still were in the lead, with Peter Walker and Stirling Moss second, Parnell/Thompson 3rd and Salvadori/Baird (Ferrari) 4th. Poore and Abecassis held fifth and the third DB3 in the trio, Collins and Griffith, was sixth.

Then one of the dramatic moments in Goodwood history took place. The Parnell/Thompson DB3 went past with smoke trailing from the rear, probably from the axle. Just before the three hour mark, Eric Thompson pulled in to refuel and hand over to Reg Parnell. According to the reports at the time, too much fuel was readied and a lot of it slopped over the car, on either the hot back axle or the exhaust pipe and this caused the Aston pit to erupt in flames. The two drivers got out of the way but the team personnel attacked the flames and team manager John Wyer and mechanics Jack Sopp and Fred Lown suffered burns. They were working desperately to keep the flames from getting to the fuel store which was not that far away. The fire was too big for them and eventually a fire crew got it under control, by which time the men were being taken to the hospital, John Wyer having serious burns to the arms and face.

Reg Parnell took over Wyer's job and it was only a matter of minutes before Poore came in to report that he only had top gear. They refuelled and Abecassis tried to get away but the starter jammed and had to be released. It then took several minutes to find top gear so Abecassis could struggle out of the pits back into the race, the Aston challenge now looking considerably weaker. At four and a half hours the two Jaguars were in front but Peter Collins had eased the DB3 up into third, ahead of the Tom Cole/Graham Whitehead Ferrari which was fast but

65

All about the boy!

beginning to lose its brakes. The two leading Jaguars were being driven smoothly to a prearranged plan and as the Poore/Abecassis Aston dropped back, the Cole and Salvadori Ferraris were trying to catch Peter Collins. As darkness approached, the weather had improved considerably and the atmosphere around the circuit was extremely pleasant. Abecassis had come in to hand back to Poore and he juddered out with only top gear but he was back before long to retire as there was no clutch and no way of getting the remaining gear. After six hours, Roy Salvadori had gotten his Ferrari past the Aston, so Collins/Griffith were now 4th, with the other Ferrari still threatening, so their position looked quite precarious. At 9.30, the Hamilton/Rolt C-Type suddenly stopped coming round, a half-shaft having broken and the wheel come off. But Moss still had a big lead and then just as suddenly he was in the pits with the axle gone. The Jaguar team set to work to replace it but this now meant that the Salvadori/Baird Ferrari led Collins/Griffith by one lap with the other Ferrari three laps back. When Baird went to take over from Roy, the starter wouldn't do anything, the battery was dead and four laps were lost in replacing it. Peter Collins now led the Goodwood Nine Hours.

The Aston team was not without worries as the DB3 did not sound well, though that turned out to be just a faulty exhaust gasket. Salvadori replaced Baird after only one lap and steamed out to try to make up the lost ground. Poor Roy was going so hard out of the pits that he spun when he got to Madgewick and the car wouldn't restart as the replacement battery wasn't much better than the one taken out. He got help and thus lost a further lap as a penalty. Stirling Moss then jumped back into the Jaguar, 16 laps behind Collins who was getting very clear signals and directions from Reg Parnell who was doing everything to keep Collins in front.

Reg's son Tim Parnell, himself an accomplished driver before he became BRM team manager, went to the races with his father as a young boy. He recalled how much Reg liked and respected Peter Collins and how seriously he took his job as John Wyer was being treated in hospital. Tim said:

"Oh yes, that is one race no one can forget. There was the fire of course but it was a very rare night race, and that didn't happen very often in England so the atmosphere was different. I remember my Dad hanging out a signal for Collins every lap, keeping him aware of his times, where the other cars were and how much longer he had to go. He really wanted Astons to win that race because it had been such a disaster and of course the crowd was cheering young Collins on...they wanted to see him win."

With thirty minutes to go, Collins held a good lead over Cole/Whitehead, a distance of three laps and Salvadori was a further three back. Collins then slid quietly into the pit lane as the flag came out and as he was joined by co-driver Griffith, a huge throng pressed in on them and fireworks were set off from behind the grandstand. This was Peter Collins' first major race win and ironically the only victory of the 1952 season, so it was significant in that it made him a key part of the Aston Martin team. His sensible but quick driving kept the Aston in the running for the entire event and the Collins/Griffith partnership had rescued what was about to be a disastrous day for Aston Martin. John Wyer was very grateful for what they had achieved and was willing to overlook some of young Peter's actions, like turning up late, because he knew how valuable he was. Pat Griffith and Peter got

Peter Collins in the Aston Martin on his way to victory at Goodwood. Photo - LAT

on very well and became good friends as well as a good team. Peter Collins' earnings from Astons for the entire year amounted to a not overwhelming £227, while Griffith earned £142 and a bit! This was one reason why Macklin left Astons, in fact it was the only reason and he came to regret it. Peter, however, was signed to a five-year contract by Aston Martin boss David Brown.

The inside view of the Goodwood race was, again, provided by mechanic 'Dickey' Green:

"And so to the Nine Hour Race at Goodwood, organized by the *News of the World* and documented many times by better pens than mine. Here, we experienced our first major fire; it consumed DB3/3 and resulted in John Wyer, Jack Sopp and Fred Lown all receiving fairly serious burns. I'm still not certain in my own mind that the cause of the spilt fuel has ever been accurately described; however, we all knew that the ignition was generated by the failure of an oil seal in the differential, just by the inboard brakes! For this race, DB3/3 had been fitted with the new 3litre engine - the connecting rods now offset at the big end rather than the wrist-pin end, which obviously should have been done in the first place.

"After the retirement of DB3/3, the Collins/Griffith car (DB3/5) went on to win. Even this did not occur without trauma, for in the last hour number two exhaust valve broke

67

and this resulted in a drop of 600 rpm. Furthermore, the fabricated exhaust manifold cracked and we could see the flames coming from the hood on the over-run at the end of Lavant Straight. On the last pit stop, John King poured water into the cockpit and over Peter Collins...remember this is at 11:00 pm...simply telling him to press on - which he did! At the conclusion of the race, the celebrations, prize-giving and so forth, John and I went to return the car to the hotel's garage. We couldn't have moved more than twenty yards when the engine died completely. Investigating, we found the coil laying in the undertray - the coil bracket had fractured!"

August 24 - Grand Prix De La Baule

Peter Collins had missed the Dutch Grand Prix which was on at the same time as Goodwood and H.W.M. had sent three cars for Macklin, Duncan Hamilton and Dutchman Dries van der Lof. Hamilton managed to travel back and forth to do both events and he finished 7th, ahead of Macklin in 8th, while the Dutch driver was down in 12th. The three Ferraris of Ascari, Farina and Villoresi had the top spots while Mike Hawthorn was 4th. Stirling Moss was another to be channel hopping but he was in 11th with engine problems in the ERA.

The following weekend Tony Gaze was the sole H.W.M. driver at the National Trophy race at Turnberry in Scotland, more famous for its golf course than motor racing. The main race was a Libre event which saw another appearance of the V-16 BRM. In the F2 race, Mike Hawthorn had been loaned a Connaught and he disappeared from a small field and won, while Gaze was 4th.

Meanwhile, the Grand Prix contenders, at least those in the French Championship, were at another seaside resort but this one was at La Baule near St. Nazaire at the mouth of the Loire. This was the final round of the French series. Ascari was well in the lead and had clinched the title. Peter Collins had seven and a half points so far but a good result could pull him up a place or two in the championship. H.W.M. had the usual three cars for Collins, Macklin and Giraud-Cabantous.

Ascari was just ahead of Manzon with Macklin on row six and Collins way down on the ninth row. Farina eliminated Manzon on the second lap. Just before halfway Behra had pitted and rejoined behind Rosier and Collins who had driven superbly to slice through the field. This was an important battle as Behra and Rosier were each after the championship for French drivers. Macklin had retired at 33 laps but by lap 49, Behra, Collins and Rosier were racing wheel to wheel. Collins came in for considerable praise in the French newspapers both for being able to keep up with the two French heroes and for not impeding their fight for the championship. Behra was in front and then retired, so when Rosier finished third overall behind Ascari and Villoresi, he took the French drivers' crown while Ascari won the major prize. Peter Collins thus came fourth and his three points pulled him ahead of Manzon in the final tally. The top ten were: Ascari, Farina, Villoresi, Behra, Rosier, Taruffi, Collins, Manzon, Bira and Claes and Simon tied on tenth. Giraud-Cabantous was 14th and Macklin 18th. While Collins' results were far from dramatic, he was clearly a force amongst the best drivers of the time, at least as far as this Championship was concerned.

September 7 - Italian Grand Prix

The Italian Grand Prix was the final round of the 1952 World Championship and thus attracted a large and impressive entry with nine Ferraris, eight Maseratis,

The racing career - The Grand Prix driver 1952-1955

three Gordinis and no less than eleven British manufactured cars, including the three H.W.M.s for Collins, Macklin and Gaze's own car for himself. Moss was driving a works Connaught and he and Hawthorn managed to get in on the third row of the grid by some clever slipstreaming. Wharton, Poore, Brandon, Brown and McAlpine also got onto the grid but the H.W.M.s didn't. They were just too slow. Ascari won from Gonzales in a Maserati and Ken Wharton's Cooper was ninth and Moss and Hawthorn retired. Thus the Championship went to Ascari, Paul Frere had scored H.W.M.'s only Championship points and Peter Collins didn't appear in the table at all in 1952. Collins was offered the chance to drive a Maserati in the race but the angry John Heath of H.W.M. refused to allow Collins to do so and Peter seemed to have accepted this.

September 14 - Circuit Du Cadours

Two H.W.M.s were sent to the Modena Grand Prix on September 14 for Macklin and Carini, neither did well with Carini 8th and Macklin retiring with transmission failure.

On the same day three works H.W.M.s went to Cadours for a race on the tough little street circuit. The inclusion of Collins and Giraud-Cabantous was expected but Tony Gaze was entered in a team car for this event. Louis Rosier had his quick Ferrari 500 on pole for the first heat but Peter Collins had done well to put the H.W.M. next to him at the front, though some five seconds slower. In the race Collins managed to remain fairly close to Rosier over the 15 laps and finished only eleven seconds behind. Collins also set the fastest lap, matching his practice time. Unfortunately, the engine was damaged in the process and Collins would not make the final. It seems somewhat strange that one of the other cars was not handed over to him for the final, or at least the engine.

Giraud-Cabantous had also managed to get onto the front row of his heat but only finished fourth. Tony Gaze was amongst those who were allowed into the *repechage* race...a sort of consolation race...and the best from this would also get into the final. Gaze managed to win this 10 lap race so was in the final. Collins' place was empty on the front row of the 30 lap final which was won reasonably easily by Rosier from Harry Schell, De Graffenried third, Giraud-Cabantous 4th and Gaze 5th.

That was pretty much the end of the season and certainly was the finish for Peter Collins. There was a race at Charterhall on October 11 and private H.W.M.s went for Gaze, Albert Wake, and Ian Stewart. Dennis Poore managed to win this in a Connaught, while Moss was 4th and Gaze retired after setting fastest lap.

Shortly after the Cadours race, the motoring press announced that drivers Harry Schell, Louis Chiron, Jean Behra, Maurice Trintignant, Lance Macklin and Peter Collins had gone to Paris to act as judges in the 'Miss Automobile' contest being held at the Moulin Rouge...at least Collins was getting a share of the 'glamour' of early '50s motor racing! In October, Peter was spending a good amount of time on the Aston Martin stand at the Motor Show.

By mid-November, quite strong rumours were circulating that Mike Hawthorn was being sought as a driver by Enzo Ferrari and this presumably was one of the topics of conversation at the party given by Peter Collins' parents on the occasion of his 21st birthday at Shatterford Grange near Kidderminster. Motor racing was very well

69

All about the boy!

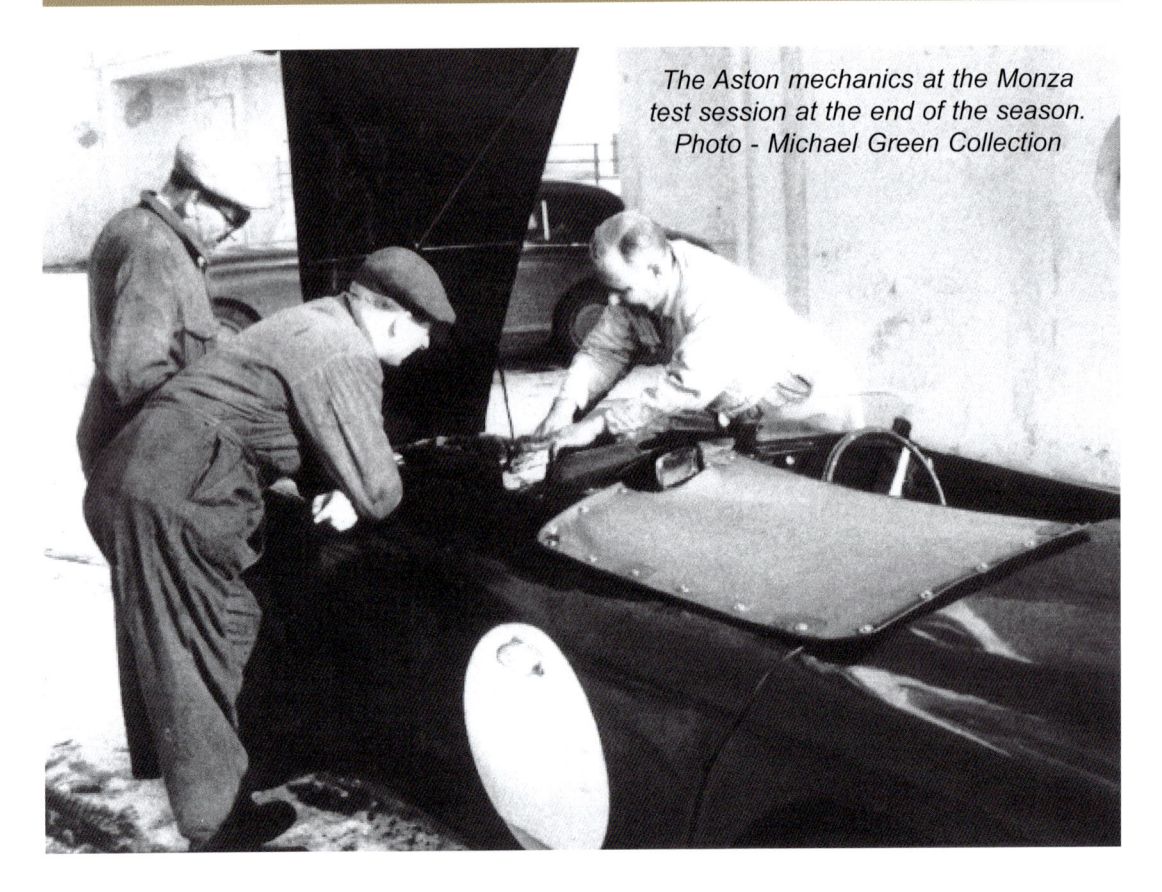

The Aston mechanics at the Monza test session at the end of the season. Photo - Michael Green Collection

represented by Stirling Moss, Reg Parnell, Ken Wharton, Bob Gerard, Duncan Hamilton, John Heath and George Abecassis, Lance Macklin, John Wyer, David Brown of Aston Martin, Alan Brown, Ken Gregory, Dennis Poore and many others. Speeches were provided by Moss, David Brown and John Heath, all very complimentary about Collins as both a person and a racing driver and he gave a speech himself before cutting an appropriately shaped birthday cake. It was a party on the grand scale, indicative of Collins' stature even at that relatively early point in his career. In some ways, it appears in retrospect that this very generous treatment of a young driver showed the respect in which he was held but it may have also served to pacify him in two teams whose cars were not adequately competitive. It is easy to say this now of course but eventually Peter would tire of the lack of performance. H.W.M. would more or less wind up but he really walked out on Aston Martin. That was all to come.

Meanwhile, Aston Martin's 'Dickey' Green had kept his notes up to date on developments going on towards the end of 1952:

"Our racing manager was hospitalised (after Goodwood) but not idle; his plans included a prolonged test to next year's cars with revised 3litre engines, modified hypoids, etc, etc. Bill James, Fred Lown, John King and I were charged with building these cars. (*The Green notebook dated November 3, 1952 gives the detailed specifications of DB3/4 ND DB3/5EM.*) December saw us off to Monza for testing, with Bill James and I in the transporter and Jack Sopp and John King in the Lagonda prototype - this was known as the 'Red Monster' - as escort. Our departure date coincided with what Londoners, in 1952, called the Five Day Fog, and some 2500 people died during this period. Our

The racing career - The Grand Prix driver 1952-1955

normal five-hour journey from Feltham to Dover took almost twelve hours on this occasion; in fact, the fog also blanketed part of France and we did not escape this miserable condition until we were approaching Chateau Thierry. John Wyer, and his assistant Brian Clayton, with drivers Abecassis, Collins, and Griffith, attempted the journey to Monza in the De Havilland Dove but because of the adverse weather, they completed it by train! At last, however, they arrived. The first two days' tests were conducted in fairly good weather but then the fog came and this was followed by snow! We cleared the track by lapping in the Lagonda and found that the lap times by the DB3 were not much slower than they would have been under ordinary wet conditions. Homeward bound for Christmas, we felt enough had been accomplished to set out 1953 specifications with some confidence - and so we had ended out 1952 season."

1953

Reports circulated in the journals towards the end of January about Aston Martin testing at Monza where they had gone to try out the changes made since the testing before Christmas. Peter Collins had put in many laps with the DB3 and had done an official lap, with outside observers, of 2 mins 17.4 secs at an average of 102.72 mph which had improved on the existing sports car record for Monza set by Mercedes by nearly a second and a half. The Aston Martin team for Sebring was also announced as consisting of Geoff Duke, Collins, Parnell and Abecassis, with David Brown deciding to accompany the team to Florida. At that stage the official Le Mans team was nominated as Duke, Collins, Dennis Poore, Eric Thompson, Parnell and Abecassis. Other early season news included the revelation that H.W.M. had built an all-new engine which bore only 'superficial' resemblance to the original Alta and that it had been constructed at H.W.M.

Above: An early season shot of the 1953 H.W.M. that had an engine which had been seriously revised.

In the early months of 1953, Peter had been speaking to David Brown at Aston Martin and had gotten his support to find a base in Paris. David Brown helped to convince Pat Collins that this was a good idea, though he didn't really need much convincing. For Peter it would achieve two things: escape from home and the occasional wrangles with his father and the opportunity to avoid National Service. Peter Collins managed to escape notoriety about this, partly through securing a 'job' with Majestic Automobiles who were the distributors for Aston Martin in France. Peter did actually show up at the company on Avenue de Versailles, doing some sales, promotion and general chores. Some stories say he never talked about the 'real reason' for being there...avoiding National Service, but in fact he was fairly open about this with George Abecassis and Pat Griffith. Peter very much enjoying being in Paris, where he was hugely popular. He had a flat in Rue Bayen near L'Etoile and was a regular at Harry Schell's

71

All about the boy!

L'Action Automobile bar. He and Schell were good friends and there is no question that Peter made the most of the social opportunities in Paris.

In the run up to Sebring there was even national publicity about Aston Martin's American adventure, as it was the first time a British works team would be going to the USA for an international race.

March 8 - Sebring 12 Hours

Aston Martin was by far the most professional team at the Sebring race, which was to be the inaugural event of the FIA's new World Sports Car Championship. The works Gordinis should have been the main opposition but at the last minute the team decided not to go. Sebring was still a new venue, an airfield in the middle of nowhere with limited amenities and very little atmosphere. John Wyer immediately announced his unhappiness about the fact that the circuit could not even be recognised by the drivers due to the wide-open expanses. This led to an increasing number of oil drums being brought in to mark the track. These increased in number over the days before the race and this was thought to be an improvement, though in fact there would be a sting in the tail for Aston Martin.

The Astons qualified well, though the field had been reduced by several cars during practice as the rough surface took a toll on some of the cars. At the Le Mans start the C-Type Jaguar of Dave Hirsch led from a pair of American-powered Allards with Peter Collins putting in a brilliant drive in the Aston, followed by the John Fitch/Phil Walters Cunningham. Reg Parnell had trouble getting his car started when the flag went down but by some superb driving he had managed to get into 4th by the end of the first hour.

Peter Collins, who was now a full-time Aston driver, putting his sports car commitments ahead of those with H.W.M., soon took the DB3 past all the Americans except John Fitch. He had had a fight for many laps with the Cunningham and this was something the crowd of 12,000 appreciated for the two cars were very close. Collins took the lead for a few laps and then lost it again and came in for fuel. He went out and regained the lead, eventually pulling out a 30 second cushion until he was back in at 3.00 pm to hand over to Geoff Duke. Duke of course had a great reputation as a motorcycle racer but was only out for a few laps before he came across the Jaguar XK-120 coupe of Norm Christianson. The drivers got their signals mixed while trying to avoid another car and collided and in an instant, both cars were out of the race. Not long after this, the other Aston struck one of the notorious oil drums, smashing the front and this required a stop for a new headlight assembly, which dropped them back. The Fitch/Walters Cunningham took the lead and went on to win, the Aston a lap behind at the finish...they had lost more than a lap making repairs so they would have been the victors!

John Wyer commented on the incident:

"In the race Collins made a very good start and for the first two hours had a battle with Walters, in which the honours at first were even but then Peter pulled away and when he came in to refuel had a lead of more than half a minute. But soon after Duke took over he crashed, hitting a marker barrel and another car. The De Dion tube was fractured and the car was withdrawn. Peter Collins was understandably furious and complained bitterly at having been partnered with an inexperienced driver. I was sorry for Duke but a good deal more sorry for Peter, for the team and for myself." (Wyer, 1981, p.41).

The racing career - The Grand Prix driver 1952-1955

Peter Collins had one of his fairly rare moments of very bad temper, and made it clear that he thought the team should not have paired him with someone he considered an amateur. While Duke did not have a great deal of experience racing cars, he had had some and had proved he could be quite quick. Peter's attack on him was pretty personal and Duke was prompted to decide he really didn't want to be involved if this was what it was going to be like.

After Sebring, 'Dickey' Green reported on Aston Martin preparations for the next race, the daunting and demanding Mille Miglia:

"Back at Feltham, Willie Watson, who worked for W.O. Bentley, conceived the idea of making the DB3 lighter by reducing the overall size of the car. The general lack of accessibility with the DB3 was also a problem that wanted solving, for it was almost impossible to carry out any operation without removing the entire body - a time consuming task at best. John King, Bill James and I worked steadily on the prototype DB3S while the remainder of the shop prepared DB3/3, 4 and 5, plus one of the lightened DB2s (XMC77) for the Mille Miglia. Eighty-hour work weeks were not unusual during this period.

"DB3S/1 was complete in late March and made its first run at Charlgrove, a disused airfield we used for testing purposes. The chassis was completely new, with the original Salisbury hypoid now replaced by a new aluminum 7 1/4 inch spiral bevel unit that was produced by David Brown. With this system, we used a central slide location rather than the Panhard rod to locate the De Dion tube. There was, however, a great deal of carryover from the previous car - the suspension and braking systems for instance, were virtually the same. I recall the time when John King and I fabricated the fuel tank brackets from scratch. They were such an odd shape that when we completed the job, the drawing office came into the shop to make the detailed drawings! We were looking for a 4% increase in overall performance at this early stage; this was achieved without problem and we departed from Charlgrove well satisfied with our initial run.

Testing of the new DB3S at Charlgrove. Photo - Michael Green Collection

All about the boy!

"Early April saw us en route to Italy where we made headquarters at the Casa Maggi in Calino, just outside of Brescia. This was the home of Count Maggi, patron of the Mille Miglia and driver of Alfa Romeos in the Twenties. During this voyage we made a short detour while Fred Lown, driving a DB2 chassis that was fitted out with plywood fenders and Plexiglass windscreen, delivered this rolling chassis to Bertone in Turin. It was on then to Monza to start our preliminary shakedown tests, where for two weeks, the drivers practiced in DB3/1, now in supercharged form. These sessions took place just after dawn, with the cars returning just after lunch. This gave us time to carry out normal maintenance and to make any modifications that were necessary. One such modification was to install a plain old brass door-bolt into the door section itself; we had discovered that body flex under certain conditions unlatched the door! Apart from the DB2 splitting its oil cooler and fuel tank and DB3/1 suffering a broken sub-frame on the chassis and a slipping clutch, all went well!"

After Sebring, Collins was back in the UK and spent some time at H.W.M. where considerable work had been undertaken to try and make the cars more competitive for 1953. An all-new de Dion rear end had been constructed and the new arrangement allowed lower seating for the driver and better access to the rear axle to change ratios. The suspension had been stiffened and endless minor changes had been made as well. The overall frame length had been reduced and the pre-selector gearbox had finally been replaced by a synchromesh box, at least in some of the cars. The Alta block had been retained but almost everything else about the engine was new, with a newly designed cylinder head coming from the pen of Harry Weslake. The intention was to get cars for Collins, Macklin and Duncan Hamilton ready in time for the Easter meeting at Pau, though this did not happen. That race on April 6 was won by Ascari from Mike Hawthorn, both in Ferraris.

Instead, Peter turned his attention to the Mille Miglia which he was about to undertake for the first time, a race that would become something he saw as rather 'special'.

April 25/26 - Mille Miglia

The 1953 Mille Miglia was remembered for essentially one reason... Juan Fangio. Fangio had been entered in one of three Alfa Romeo 6C 3000CM sports cars. Over the previous two years, there had been constant announcements about Alfa Romeo's 'Disco Volante'...a great new sports car. The lovely shaped first cars turned out to be totally unsuitable for competition and a second version, the 6C 3000CM, was designed and built. These were of a different type and designation than the original cars but the name 'Disco Volante' stuck. Cars were entered for Sanesi/Gagno, Kling/Klenk and Fangio/Sala. Kling led at Rome and then crashed and Fangio led briefly and his steering control arm fractured on one side after half distance and he thus started his epic drive to the finish with steering on one wheel only. He finished second, behind the Ferrari 340MM of Giannino Marzotto.

Bonetto was third in a Lancia D20, Tom Cole 4th in another Ferrari 340MM and then came the Aston Martin DB3 of Reg Parnell who was accompanied by the photographer Louis Klemantaski. The rest of the top twenty was entirely Italian except for the 16th place Aston Martin of Peter Collins and Mike Keens.

Much had been expected of Stirling Moss and the Jaguars and from John Fitch in a Nash-Healey. Less was perhaps expected from the Astons, though they had made

The racing career - The Grand Prix driver 1952-1955

thorough preparations, and had spent a great deal of time ensuring the cars would be reliable.

'Dickey' Green explained the drill for refuelling and servicing the Astons:

"Fred Lown and I, accompanied by Bob Walsham and a tyre fitter from Avon's, made tracks for L'Aquila, some 453 miles from the start, in the transporter. Ours was the job of establishing a third refuelling depot. We were next to Ferrari and their chief mechanic, Meazza, had reserved a section of the main street for us. Just adjacent was a side street where we were able to park the transporter. Refuelling in this 1000 mile event bore no resemblance to normal pit work, since the enthusiastic public were always packed tightly around you. L'Aquila was also a control point where all the cars had to stop to have their route card punched. The usual driver's drill was to stop with all four wheels locked up and the car sliding in a great cloud of dust and then accelerate away at maximum rpm. You could always tell the 'triers' by their race number, which was, in fact, their starting time. I still recall seeing both Marzotto, the eventual winner, and Fangio driving an Alfa 6C 3000 coupe accelerating away from the control to the wild applause of the crowds!"

The DB2 of Tommy Wisdom was an early retirement once the event had got underway, the transmission failing just after Mike Hawthorn had dropped out in his Ferrari 250 MM. The Alfas led the early stages, Sanesi going spectacularly quickly until he was out and they were pursued by Farina, who also had some time in the lead in a Ferrari, Kling, Marzotto, Fangio and Bonetto. Parnell had been in the scenery before Rome and showed up there with a number of dents. Nevertheless, he kept up a good pace and held 5th for most of the second half of the race. Peter Collins, with Mike Keen as his co-driver, had also been going well but was having suspension problems and had a long stop to secure the steering rack. This also slowed his pace after the stop.

'Dickey' Green reported that all the team DB3s arrived and refuelled at his depot without incident but that the DB2 (XMC77) driven by Tommy Wisdom had retired at Ancona. That meant that he and Fred Lown had to backtrack in order to pick up the DB2. On the way some Italians told them that a green British car was stranded south of Presaro but that turned out to be Moss' C-Type Jaguar. By the time they got back to Calino, the rest of the team was nicely tucked up in bed!

The Mille Miglia had been the last major race for the DB3 and Parnell's fifth place was the highest place achieved by a British car. Reg Parnell had driven the car from Florence to Brescia with a broken Panhard rod mounting so that the DeDion tube had no lateral location and on the Futa Pass the throttle cable had broken so Parnell had to make up a system that had the throttle full on, so he finished the race on the Lucas ignition switch. Perhaps not as dramatic as Fangio's broken steering but pretty brave as well. Equally determined, Green reported back that Collins' 16th place had been managed with the steering rack secured to the chassis with baling wire and Abecassis had retired near Florence, also with a broken steering rack mount. Peter had been forced to drive slowly into the control for repairs after he had hit a bridge when their steering rack mount had broken.

Collins had gotten target times from John Wyer before the start and was focussed on achieving these times. In fact, he was making marked progress through the field and without the mechanical failure would probably have managed third overall. John Wyer realised that

All about the boy!

that would have been a great achievement as the cars were just not fast enough to beat the Ferraris.

After the Mille Miglia Wyer prevailed upon Collins to remain at Monza for serious testing of the DB3S and that got him into some difficulty with H.W.M. However, Wyer was very impressed with Peter's testing ability. They did over 500 miles, setting quick times, before the engine went. This was then replaced with the 3litre unit from the Abecassis/Griffith Mille Miglia car, the same engine Collins had in the previous Monza tests with the DB3. He went some four seconds faster and overall the team were very pleased with the results. A total of some 828 miles had been covered in the testing at Monza.

'Dickey' Green recalled the testing session that took place after the Mille Miglia which was meant to be a preparation for Le Mans some six weeks later and the run-up to the Silverstone race:

"We left Brescia for Monza to meet Eric Hind who, accompanied by Peter Collins' father, had brought DB3S/1 from England in their Ford transporter. The test proceeded well with Peter doing most of the driving and we had our improvement in performance with little increase in bhp. As always, a number of flaws were quickly discovered. Professor Eberhorst had retained the inboard rear brake system and we soon discovered, when attempting to check the condition of the rear shoes, that it was impossible to remove the drums with the spiral bevel unit in situ. A modification to the chassis was made to overcome the problem but this was never satisfactorily resolved until the brakes were moved outboard, this solution finally being insisted upon by John Wyer."

Green recounted that the team's Le Mans experience had indicated to them that it was only necessary to change the left-hand wheels during the 24 hour race and therefore they designed a jacking system which allowed only one side of the car to be lifted clear of the ground at any given time. This was done by welding a 2 1/2" diameter tube at right angles to the chassis rail, matching a hole of 3" diameter in the body side. This allowed a jacking bar to be inserted some ten inches into the chassis tube. A long jacking lever working on a cam arrangement, depressing the handle parallel to the body, raised the car clear of the ground. The team tried the new system during a check of the front brake linings.

Green recalls: " I was removing the front brake drum with both my legs under the car, when I must have jiggled the drum too hard, the jack cam went over centre and the car came down with a crash! The rear wheel was still on but my legs were trapped under the car. Fortunately, there was no damage to the car or to me. Poor Eric was not so lucky, however. While standing by the cockpit he was hit in the middle of the back by the jack handle and this resulted in a trip to the local hospital. Needless to say, John Wyer had us revert to the more conventional jacking system, at the same time, we thus lightened the car by at least ten pounds by removal of the jacking tubes!

"The Monza test car was fitted with a light alloy, twin plug head. Whilst Peter was driving, his lap times slowed because of the loss of some 600 rpm. The Professor, of course, had a theory regarding this loss of power and the theory involved the structure of the plugs. He believed that the front plug of any cylinder should be of a different heat range than those in the rear; the actual cause of the power loss was a broken rotor arm in the distributor! The car failed to appear on one lap and we found Peter sitting on the fender at the Lesmo and pointing to a very large hole in the block; a rod had broken!

The racing career - The Grand Prix driver 1952-1955

John Wyer was anxious to carry on with the test program, so with some modifications we installed the standard six-plug iron-head engine from one of the Mille Miglia cars and thus completed the thousand miles. We loaded the engineless DB3 into Collins' transporter and I drove DB3S/1 back to Feltham, arriving in early May after one of the best rides I've ever had! I returned home just in time for Silverstone, where the DB3s made their final works appearance, with Parnell and Collins finishing 1st and 2nd in the 3litre class, a great ending."

May 9 - Silverstone International Trophy

While the sports car teams were returning from Italy, the Formula 2 season had of course already begun. The World Championship was being run again to Formula 2 rules. H.W.M. sent three cars to Bordeaux on May 3 for Macklin, Prince Bira and Giraud-Cabantous.

Collins did not appear of course as he was at Monza, and the race was won by Ascari who was again stamping his authority on the category. The work on the H.W.M.s had done some good as they handled better but they were still three seconds off the pace. Bira managed 8th, while the other two cars didn't finish.

There was a large 46 driver entry for the International Trophy race at Silverstone and no less than five H.W.M.s were entered for Collins, Macklin, Hamilton, Jack Fairman and Frank Curtis. Fairman's car did not appear but the rest would be there to contest the two heats and a final. Hamilton was the quickest of the H.W.M.s in heat one, having qualified ahead of Moss in a Cooper-Alta. However it was Moss who moved up to finish second to de Graffenried in the heat with Hamilton 7th and Curtis 14th.

Heat 2 saw Macklin just quicker than Collins on row three and five seconds slower than pole man Ken Wharton in a Cooper-Bristol.

Peter Collins in the H.W.M. tries hard to hold off the faster Connaught of Kenneth McAlpine at the International Trophy. Photo - Anthony Pritchard/T.C.March Collection

All about the boy!

Hawthorn had the lone works Ferrari next to Wharton at the front. Hawthorn won fairly easily while Collins had a long fight with Harry Schell's Gordini 16 and they were catching Bobby Baird's Ferrari towards the end. Collins was 8th and Macklin 10th. Hawthorn drove a competent race in the final and led most of the way. Collins was a lacklustre 11th ahead of Hamilton and Curtis and Macklin retired after only eight laps.

A 'production' sports car race had preceded the International Trophy final and 33 cars were ready for the Le Mans start. Hawthorn (Ferrari) and Moss (Jaguar) were the first away. Hawthorn immediately pulled out a lead on Moss but Parnell's DB3 and Rolt's Jaguar soon got past Moss. Geoff Duke was still driving an Aston amidst rumours he would return to motorcycles only but he retired when the Aston's clutch went. Peter Walker's Jaguar came under pressure from Collins in another team DB3 while American Tom Cole had forced his 4.1 Ferrari past Parnell into second. The two 2.9litre Astons finished 3rd and 4th winning the 3litre class, ahead of the Jaguars, with Hawthorn and Cole in larger-engined Ferraris ahead of them, so that was a good result for the Aston Martin team. The day as a whole, of course, had added greatly to Mike Hawthorn's reputation, especially at home in England.

Peter Collins hung on to the back of Reg Parnell to finish 4th at Silverstone in the Aston Martin DB3. Photo - Anthony Pritchard/T.C.March Collection

The racing career - The Grand Prix driver 1952-1955

May 16 - Dundrod Ulster Trophy

Dundrod witnessed virtually the entire International Trophy field transporting itself across the sea to the Ulster Trophy meeting, a matter of days after Silverstone. In fact, for some, it was straight to the ferry at the end of the day at Silverstone.

The Dundrod circuit, just a few miles from Belfast, was notoriously bumpy and would suit some cars far more than others. It was again to be a two heats and a final affair. Moss gave up on the Alta Special he had at Silverstone and was in a Rob Walker A-Type Connaught, in the fairly early days of the Walker/Moss partnership. Stirling put this on pole by no less than 18 seconds from the little known John Lyons in a similar car with Duncan Hamilton a further two seconds back. Moss romped away to win the first heat from Hamilton. Hawthorn, again with the lone works Ferrari, was even quicker in his heat, eight seconds ahead of Wharton, with Collins three seconds faster than Macklin in H.W.M.s on the third row. Hawthorn won, though not by as much as Moss had and ignominiously Collins and Macklin both went out on lap 2. Hawthorn won the final, Moss retired and Hamilton was 6th. Apparently Macklin's car in heat 2 was Hamilton's car from heat 1. This ruse was discovered and that is why Macklin was given the signal to retire! Collins had had a severe misfire which couldn't be cured.

May 25 - Crystal Palace

On May 24, there was an F2 race at the wonderful and dangerous Chimay road circuit in Belgium, won by Maurice Trintignant, while the following day the Coronation Trophy race would take place at Crystal Palace in London, as part of the celebrations for the coronation of Queen Elizabeth II the following week.

Crystal Palace, a great little circuit in south London, had been brought back into use. It was a great venue, where the spectators were safely placed only fifteen feet away from the track. Again this race would consist of the usual two heats and a final, all of ten laps each.

Moss was trying the Alta Special again, entered by Coopers but Rolt headed the grid for the first heat in the Rob Walker Connaught. Rolt won the heat from Wharton's Cooper-Bristol, an on-form Macklin and Moss. Peter and Graham Whitehead surrounded Peter Collins' H.W.M. in their Cooper-Alta and Cooper-Bristol respectively and Peter Whitehead squeezed past Collins into the lead. They stayed in those positions for the ten laps, ahead of Jack Fairman in the other H.W.M. Collins could not get past the Whitehead brothers in the final, which was taken by Rolt from Wharton, with Macklin fourth, Collins seventh and Fairman ninth.

Gregor Grant wrote an appraisal of British racing drivers in Autosport the same week the Crystal Palace report appeared. He had Stirling Moss at the top of his list by far, with Hawthorn next, mentioning Hawthorn's ascent in only the space of a year. Peter Collins was tenth on the list and he was seen as one of the young rising stars. Indeed, of all those on Grant's list, it was only Moss, Hawthorn and Collins who continued to go on to bigger and better things.

May 31 - Nurburgring Eifelrennen

This was again a period when there were races almost every weekend. There was another Coronation Trophy race at Snetterton on May 30, again won by Tony Rolt but that was a fairly minor event. Amazingly, most of the rest of the teams were split between three other venues for F2 races. Can you imagine four (!) F2 races on two days? The main contenders went to the Nurburgring for

79

All about the boy!

the Eifelrennen, while a mixed nationality group went to Albi and the amateurs went to Montlhery.

At the 'Ring, where all the H.W.M.s had gone, Collins and Macklin were again joined by Belgian Paul Frere. Peter Collins' car dropped a valve in practice and lacking a suitable workshop, repairs were done with a few hand tools. This seemed to have the right result because this car was then the quickest of the trio in a straight line. Baron de Graffenried took his Maserati A6GCM into the lead, followed by the little known Kurt Adolff in the Ecurie Espadon Ferrari F500 which Rudolf Fischer had been racing. This was, of course, the only Ferrari there and neither Ascari nor Hawthorn were entered in any of the F2 races that weekend. Adolff managed to block Moss in the Alta Special and the H.W.M.s for the better part of a complete lap and that allowed Toulo de Graffenried to build up a useful lead.

While Stirling Moss was struggling to get the Alta to handle, both Peter Collins and Paul Frere got past him and the sometimes team mates then had an exuberant battle for much of the race. Frere seemed to hold the advantage on the tighter parts of the challenging Nurburgring while Collins could get past him on the straight sections. This pair were the highlight of the race and they were pulling themselves closer and closer to the Maserati on every lap. It looked very likely that Collins would manage to get past on the final lap and hold off Frere to the line. But suddenly Collins fell back. His fire extinguisher had come loose in the cockpit and wedged itself under the pedals, and Collins went off the road briefly, side-swiped a tree but managed to regain control and carry on. The significance of Collins getting into the trees at the Nurburgring was of course unknown to all present, as they watched him desperately try to catch Frere. Frere pulled up behind de Graffenried and finished only two seconds adrift. Collins came in 15 seconds further back in a very good third spot but the delay behind Adolff at the beginning had really had a cost to the H.W.M. team. Moss was down in 6th and Macklin had retired with another magneto failure. The H.W.M. performance was noteworthy in that the de Graffenried car was the latest Maserati works machine and the Swiss already had two victories to his credit in 1953. Stirling Moss won the 500 c.c. F3 race by four minutes from Eric Brandon.

At Albi, Roberto Mieres, the very talented South American driver, had finished 4th in the heat to Rosier's win but in the final Rosier decided to drive his Formula 1 car. This was a race for both F1 and F2 so Mieres came through to win. Roberto Mieres now lives in Uruguay and still takes part in historic events. He reminisced with the author at a recent Monaco Historic meeting, saying that those were the great days of his career. His early years in Europe had been characterised by his desperate attempts to convince teams to let him race and he freely admitted he could never quite get used to the fact that "it worked!"

Meanwhile, at the Coupe de Printemps at Montlhery, Marcel Balsa took his BMW Special to victory over a small field.

June 7 - Dutch Grand Prix

The first round of the World Championship had taken place back in January and it had been won by Ascari from Villoresi, with Gonzales' Maserati 3rd and Hawthorn's Ferrari 4th. The Grote Prijs van Nederland at Zandvoort was the first European round of the Championship after several non-championship events in the intervening months.

H.W.M. had not made the trip to Argentina

The racing career - The Grand Prix driver 1952-1955

but were back with, sensibly, two cars for Collins and Macklin. They were up against the full might of the works teams from Ferrari, Maserati, Gordini and Connaught, which brought three cars for Salvadori, boss Kenneth McAlpine, and Stirling Moss. There was no Monaco race at all this year after the Grand Prix had been replaced by the crash-filled sports car event the previous year.

The H.W.M. team really didn't have a chance at Zandvoort and the most they might hope for was reliability and a reasonable place at the end. Ascari, Fangio and Farina dominated the front row and this looked like being a close contest, although it would be only for Italian cars! The circuit had just been resurfaced and was very slippery. Ascari took off at the drop of the flag and was seen no more. It was Farina who took up the chase with Fangio having transmission trouble from which he eventually retired. Hawthorn was much slower than Ascari and it was Gonzales, who had stopped and taken over Bonetto's car, who was the centre of attention as he worked through the field, past Hawthorn into third.

After making a good start and moving into seventh, Moss then started to drop back and was running much of the race in eleventh spot. Lance Macklin had his throttle control break on only the seventh lap after starting from row six and Peter Collins, starting a row further back, just put his head down and drove as hard as he could until he found himself in eighth place at the end, one up on Moss whose injection system was not working very well.

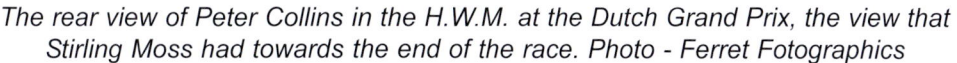

The rear view of Peter Collins in the H.W.M. at the Dutch Grand Prix, the view that Stirling Moss had towards the end of the race. Photo - Ferret Fotographics

All about the boy!

June 13/14 - Le Mans 24 Hours

Another week, another race...but this time it was Le Mans, rather more than just another race.

As far as Aston Martin was concerned, it was a good year for Jaguar! Astons had entered three cars, the new DB3S, for Abecassis/Salvadori, Parnell/Collins and Thompson/Poore. The back-up drivers included Pat Griffith and Geoff Duke who didn't appear. For Astons, the race was essentially a disaster. After the first hour, Parnell and Collins were in 14th position and Thompson/Poore 18th. The Salvadori/Abecassis car had already had a five minute pit stop so was well behind. Moss and Peter Walker were leading in their C-Type with Ascari/Villoresi next and Rolt/Hamilton 3rd, also in a C-Type. The famous story is that Rolt and Hamilton thought they were going to be unable to start so went on the razzle the night before the race, only to discover they were in. They made the start still 'under the influence!' With the Alfa Romeo 6C 3000CMs, the Ferraris and Gordinis all in the picture, it looked like it would be a great race.

Reg Parnell ran off the road in the second hour, causing considerable damage to the car, so one Aston was out and Collins never got a drive. Fangio's Alfa had a piston go. Rolt/Hamilton led at the end of the 4th hour. The Salvadori/Abecassis DB3S pulled back to 17th but went out with no clutch after 74 laps. Ascari and Villoresi vacated 2nd place to the Sanesi/Carini Alfa. After 182 laps the final DB3S quit with ignition problems and that was it for Aston Martin. Rolt and Hamilton droned on until the finish, four laps ahead of Moss and Walker, with the Walters/Fitch Cunningham third. None of Alfas or Lancias finished and only a few of the Ferraris. The Healey 100s did a fine job finishing 12th and 14th, the least expensive of all the cars in the race.

The DB3S driven by Peter Collins and Reg Parnell. Parnell went off the road and Collins didn't get a race. Photo - Ferret Fotographics

This prototype Healey 100 finished very well up the order; the author did a track test with this car some 55 years later. Photo - Archive Gasnerie

Again, we have a 'behind the scenes' account of what was going on around Le Mans time from 'Dickey' Green:

"Back at Feltham, DB3S/2, 3 and 4 had been under construction for Le Mans which had still been six weeks away. John Wyer made a point in his book that the DB3S failed through inadequate and hurried preparation; certainly we were all getting very weary on our 90 hour per week diet! Poor Reg Parnell was very upset at crashing his car at Tertre Rouge on the 16th lap, while the other two cars retired, one with a slipping clutch and the other with broken tappets. As a spare we had with us DB3S/1, now fitted with a new engine. Reg, always looking at the next race, wanted to drive this car in the Empire Trophy Race which was taking place on the Isle of Man just four days later.

"He drove alone across France and back to Feltham, picked up Eric Hind (still with a back problem) and continued on to his farm in Derby. Here he collected his own car, and the two of them completed the journey with Eric driving the remaining distance in the DB3S. They arrived in time for the first practice, where Reg made fastest time - a feat he repeated on the following day in the presence of John Wyer. He lost pole position to Stirling Moss in a C-Type Jaguar but retained his former position by breaking the lap record twice in the final practice. Then, disaster struck! Eric was returning the car to the garage when a rear driveshaft universal broke. We had returned from Le Mans with the transporter that Wednesday afternoon. At about 10.00 pm one of the factory police knocked on the door of my apartment and advised me that Mrs. Wyer had called the guard house and would I please return the call. She soon put me in the picture and asked if I could do something. I contacted Fred Shattuck (he, at least, had a phone) and around midnight we unloaded a transporter and removed a pair of driveshafts from the Le Mans cars. I then advised Jack Stirling, our Managing Director, of the plan, took XMC77 and drove through the night to Liverpool to catch the first flight, a DC3 that arrived on the Isle of Man at 8.00 am. Eric and I installed the new driveshafts and Reg, after a wonderful drive, demoralized the opposition by winning the British Empire Trophy Race at a record speed. What followed was a fair night out!"

All about the boy!

Le Mans marked Roy Salvadori's first drive for Aston Martin, a team he became a key member of and enjoyed the benefits of being there even though Astons didn't pay as well as some of the other manufacturers. He commented, about Le Mans:

"My first race for Aston Martin was Le Mans in 1953 and the story of this race sums up how well Aston Martin looked after their drivers and the sheer pleasure of racing for the team. Much of this pleasure was derived from travelling to the races and for me an overseas race with Aston Martin was a holiday in itself. At this time motor racing was my relaxation and I did not take holidays. I know that Peter Collins felt the same way and even went to the extent of taking along his bucket and spade!" (Salvadori and Pritchard, 1985, p.42).

June 21 - Belgian Grand Prix

Peter Collins remained in France and then travelled the brief distance to Spa for the second round of the World Championship, only two weeks after the first race at Zandvoort. Again, H.W.M. did not have high expectations and it wasn't too surprising that Paul Frere was quickest of all the non-Italian cars at Spa. He managed to be two rows and eleven seconds ahead of Collins who himself was another eleven seconds faster than Macklin who was next to him on the grid. While Fangio and Gonzales led initially, it was Ascari who outlasted and outran the others to win yet again from Villoresi and Marimon. Peter Collins lasted only four laps and had the clutch break, while Macklin had his engine give up on the 19th tour. Frere made it to the finish in 11th but was not officially classified.

Just after Spa, the BRDC announced the present standings for their annual Gold Star competition for British drivers. Hawthorn headed the table from Peter Whitehead, Moss, Rolt, Wharton, Hamilton, Parnell, Walker, Collins, Ian Stewart, Abecassis, Nuckey, Salvadori and Baird. It was clear that with the exception of Hawthorn, it was sports car drivers who were getting the points well ahead of the British Grand Prix drivers.

July 5 - French Grand Prix

No H.W.M.s had gone to the F2 race at Rouen the week before Reims and even with a small field at Rouen, Stirling Moss was unable to get the Alta Special higher than fourth in the F2 class in this combined race for F1 and F2 cars. Farina was the outright winner and Harry Schell's Gordini took the F2 section.

The more important event was the Grand Prix at Reims the following week, the next round in the World Championship in which Alberto Ascari already had a big lead. All of the H.W.M. cars were on the seventh row, with Collins in a sandwich comprised of Macklin and Giraud-Cabantous. Macklin was five seconds quicker than Collins so there was some guessing about which car had the quicker engine. A review of the three chassis used in 1953 does not reveal any pattern indicating that any one was consistently quick or slow and the driver's performances are varied and rather inconsistent. The cars made no impression in the race, with Macklin going out after nine laps with another clutch failure. Collins and his French team mate soldiered on to 13th and 14th, though not classified as they were eight and 10 laps behind. A look at the lap times during the race has the three H.W.M.s at the bottom of the list in the order Macklin, Collins and Giraud-Cabantous, a full 20 kph slower than Fangio's quickest time.

The racing career - The Grand Prix driver 1952-1955

This race was Mike Hawthorn's finest in his relatively short career as he fought for lap after lap with the great Fangio. Hawthorn's Ferrari led at the final flag by one second over Fangio's Maserati, with Gonzales four tenths of a second further back, Ascari 2.8 seconds behind, another three seconds to Farina and a further eight to Villoresi. This race has been acclaimed by many pundits over the decades as the finest Grand Prix ever...anyone there on the day had no doubt that it was.

What was very clear at this time was, that although Mike Hawthorn had not gone the single-seater route of Moss and Collins in the early years of the decade, his move into the Ferrari team had propelled him to prominence on the Grand Prix scene which even over-shadowed Moss and well eclipsed the accomplishments of Collins at the time, though there were many who said he was not the better driver.

July 10/16 - The Alpine Rally

The Rootes involvement in the 1953 Alpine Rally, or more properly the Rallye International des Alpes, came about largely as a result of competition manager Norman Garrad's travels in America where he had seen a market for a two-seater sports Sunbeam. The Sunbeam Talbot had a long history of rally success and had done particularly well in the 1951 and 1952 Monte Carlo and Alpine rallies and to take

Peter Collins and Ronnie Adams in MKV 23 before the start at the team's base in Bandol. They didn't look too friendly here and they certainly weren't by the end! Photo - Rootes Archive

All about the boy!

advantage of a likely market, the company set to work to produce a new car. Thus the new Sunbeam Alpine, aptly named, was constructed based on the Talbot engine and chassis. Engine performance was improved and there were stiffer coil springs, larger anti-roll bar and harder settings for the shock absorbers. Weight remained fairly high as side plates had been welded to the frame and a cross member fitted below the engine to provide strengthening, now that the roof was gone.

Stirling Moss and Sheila van Damm did some well publicised high speed runs at Jabbeke in Belgium and Leslie Johnson and Moss did high speed laps at Montlhery, all aimed at giving the new car a positive launch. The name Talbot was also dropped at this time, though coupe versions continued both as road and competition cars. It is interesting that some of the press insisted on referring to the new open cars as Sunbeam-Talbots or Sunbeam-Talbot 'Alpine'!

*Peter was often referred to as the 'tousle-haired youth'...this is why.
This is at Marseilles before the start. Photo - Rootes Archive*

The racing career - The Grand Prix driver 1952-1955

Rootes had a tradition of using racing drivers in major rallies and Stirling Moss had proved himself a real asset to the company. For 1953, the team would include Moss and John Cutts, George Murray-Frame and John Pearman, Peter Collins and Ronnie Adams, Leslie Johnson and David Humphrey, Sheila van Damm and Anne Hall and John Fitch and Peter Miller. Peter Collins and John Fitch drove down to the team base at Bandol directly from the race at Reims. There was considerable wining, dining and partying in the run up to the July 10 start.

Peter Miller, Fitch's co-driver, gave a detailed account of the antics that went on before and during the event, of which there were many. The teams drove the cars to the *parc ferme* on the old port at Marseilles where they were to remain until the start at 10.00 pm:

"Stirling, Peter and I looked around the shops and I bought a French seaman's blue-and-white-striped-cotton sweater, which turned out to be most useful later. We went into a waterfront restaurant about 7.30 pm and ordered a large meal, finished off by an orange souffle. We had eaten half of the tasty dish when a rally official came bursting in to find us. He said that if convenient to us our cars were due to start in fifteen minutes! We ran down the quayside stuffing the remaining morsels of souffle into our mouths and all had violent indigestion as a result." (Miller, 1962, p.30).

The Alpines then started in the order: Moss (504), Murray-Frame (508), Collins (509), Fitch (510), Van Damm (511) and Johnson (512) at one minute intervals. Peter Miller reported that all his stop watches failed to work as they left the start line and he was forced to

Peter and Ronnie Adams, looking happier here, just before the start at Marseilles on the first evening. Photo - Rootes Archive

87

All about the boy!

rely on his wrist watch!

When Fitch and Miller were arriving in the control at Cortina the next day, Collins and Adams had arrived a minute before. Peter Collins put his hand into Miller's window and said "Put these in your pocket Pete. You might need them in the morning!" They were all five wheel nuts from the left rear wheel of the Fitch/Miller car! All the Sunbeams had this problem and they were very lucky to have the wheel remain on the studs.

The 1953 event had a 2000 mile route and included 31 of the highest European mountain passes. The record entry set off on the first stage from Marseilles to Cortina d'Ampezzo. A number of cars fell by the wayside early in the event as the route went over the French cols and into Italy. After a stretch of autostrada, the field faced standing kilometer tests at Monza.

Conditions across Italy were less severe than expected and of the 91 teams making it into Cortina, a full 61 still had no penalties. Two female crews were in the lead and the 2600 c.c. class in which the Alpines ran was being led by Vegler's Ferrari. Gatta's Lancia took over this class by the end of stage two, which was a circuit of the Dolomite mountains, where Paolo Marzotto set overall fastest time. By the end of the third stage at St. Moritz, Stirling Moss was leading the Sunbeam Alpine pack and all the team cars seemed to be going very well.

Leslie Johnson was the first casualty from the team on stage four from St. Moritz to Val d'Isere when he lost top gear and the car could no longer manage the strain of being driven at 65 mph in 3rd gear. The British teams looked set to achieve a record number of Coupes des Alpes, the reward for going unpenalised. But

There were a series of speed tests at Monza soon after the rally got into Italy. The Collins car leads the team, all with hoods up to reduce drag. Photo - Rootes Archive

Collins swings the car through a tight corner in the Dolomites.
Photo - Rootes Archive

As the team started one minute apart, they remained fairly close together, so could have this group drink stop in Italy. Photo - Rootes Archive

this took a knock when the thus far quicker driven Alpine of Peter Collins retired with gearbox problems at Briancon. This was made worse when Hartwell's Sunbeam-Talbot coupe also stopped after hitting a marker stone and damaging the suspension.

The Stirling Moss/John Cutts car was the fastest of the Alpines and that car and those of Murray-Frame/Pearman, John Fitch/ Miller and Sheila van Damm/Hall all won Coupes, though there was a feeling that this year's event had been 'too easy'. Sheila van Damm and Anne Hall won the Coupes de Dames as well. The Gatta/Cottino Lancia won the 'Up to 2600 c.c. class', Porsche took the team award and a Porsche was the outright winner as well.

Peter Miller takes up the story of the Collins/ Adams retirement which was rather more complicated than it seems at first glance, as it wasn't Adams in the car when it finally stopped:

"We were having breakfast at 5 am on the last day, when, rather surprisingly, Ronnie Adams walked in, dressed in sports clothes and not in his usual rally kit. He announced that unless he drove certain sections that day he was pulling out and Collins could go on without him! Throughout the rally Adams had been rather upset that Peter had driven most of the tougher stages, while he had done the navigating. But Collins seemed the obvious choice for No. 1 driver and if Ronnie had any doubts about getting his share of the wheel, surely these should have been raised with the team manager before the 'off' - not on the final day, when the car was unpenalised (as were four others in the team) and in the running for a Coupe des Alpes!

"His withdrawal guaranteed the car's disqualification as two crew members were obligatory and driver changes were forbidden during the event.......Garrad had driven from St. Moritz to Cannes to await our arrival and so Cutts, as senior factory representative

Although the Sunbeam was not over-powered, Collins enjoyed getting the most out of it. Photo - Rootes Archive

The famous Stelvio Pass in Italy...one of the many dramatic rally stages used over many, many years. Photo - Rootes Archive

All about the boy!

Collins has just passed a group of spectators near the top of the Stelvio Pass.
Photo - Rootes Archive

present at Val d'Isere, tried to persuade Adams to continue and put his personal feelings after his duty to the team. But Adams was adamant! Rather than let Collins drive on by himself, David Humphrey (the retired Leslie Johnson's co-driver-EM) raced upstairs to change into overalls and continued the rally with him. They eventually retired the car dramatically at the Briancon control, where they arrived on time, but backwards - having lost all the forward gears. Pat Mennem got the newspaper scoop of the rally by his presence at the team row at Val d'Isere and then driving Adams back to the finish to face the music. Apparently Ronnie told him that he just couldn't stand driving with Collins for another day and had to have a showdown." (Miller, op. cit. p.38-9).

Four of the six factory Sunbeams entered had won Coupe des Alpes and were 4th to 7th behind the Lancias in the 2600 c.c. class.

Ronnie Adams would later tell Chris Nixon that he had been promised a '50-50' share of the driving and that Peter was out chasing girls just before the event. He also said Peter had almost fallen asleep while driving and he was generally critical of his driving (Nixon, 1991, p.75). Norman Garrad himself came in for severe criticism from Adams for not sorting out the problem, though this is at odds with some versions of the story.

July 18 - British Grand Prix

Collins and Moss were straight back to Silverstone, for practice for the Grand Prix started almost as the Alpine Rally was ending. Lance Macklin and Duncan

92

The racing career - The Grand Prix driver 1952-1955

Hamilton had earned reasonable places at Crystal Palace the previous weekend and this seemed to give the team something of a boost. Macklin managed to get his H.W.M. on row four with a good practice performance, though Hamilton was a full five seconds slower, Collins another four seconds behind that and Jack Fairman right at the back, way off the pace.

Ascari, Gonzales, Hawthorn, Fangio and Farina had the first five places on the grid and indeed they had the first five places in the results. Tony Rolt's Connaught was the quickest of the British cars, six seconds slower than Ascari. At the start Macklin made an incredible start and into the first corner he had gone from 12th to 3rd behind Ascari and Villoresi, though order was soon restored and he was quickly down to 11th. Hawthorn hit the Woodcote barrier and managed to get back to the pits for repairs. After several laps, the field settled down and Macklin and Collins, who had moved up a number of places, were having a good race with Behra's Gordini. Hamilton posted the first H.W.M. retirement when his clutch fell apart. This H.W.M. problem soon hit Macklin and he too was out and then the same happened to Jack Fairman. Finally Collins joined them, this time with no compression in the engine and he pulled to a stop at Chapel Curve...all the John Heath cars out. Collins had done 13 races in 1953 and was yet to have a really good result.

However, the sports car race supporting the Grand Prix then proved to be somewhat better. An interesting field, including Ferraris, Cunninghams, Jaguars and Astons had a Le Mans start with Reg Parnell's DB3S into the lead and Collins, who started 8th in the new DB3S, held 5th in the early laps. Tony Rolt in the C-Type sneaked past Parnell. On the 8th lap Rolt got sideways and Parnell went back in front. Rolt eventually had a piston break and Roy Salvadori took his DB3S past Collins

Collins gets the Aston DB3S well wound up in the sports car race supporting the British Grand Prix. Photo - Anthony Pritchard/T.C.March Collection

into second. Collins and Salvadori had a hard fight for the remainder of the 102 mile race and John Wyer was very pleased as they came in with Parnell, Salvadori and Collins getting the three top places.

Roy Salvadori said that his passing of Peter Collins had some consequences:

"I passed Peter going into Stowe and Rolt retired the Jaguar with a broken piston, so I finished second in an Aston Martin 1-2-3 with Spear's 4.1 litre Ferrari fourth. There were no team orders in this race, so I was free to pass Collins and we were still chasing after Rolt. Nevertheless I did notice a slight atmosphere in the Aston pits after the race!" (Salvadori and Pritchard, 1985, p.45).

July 26 - Aix-les-Bains Circuit du Lac

A week after Silverstone, a small field of F2 cars went to Aix-les-Bains. There were no works Ferraris though Marimon was there in the official Maserati entry. Harry Schell rather surprised Marimon by taking pole position but Marimon led at the start of the first of two heats. Schell was bumped by the Maserati and made a pit stop. Trintignant then pushed his Gordini in front and when he retired a surprised Jean Behra took the win with second going to Elie Bayol in his own OSCA. Macklin managed 4th, Collins 5th and Giraud-Cabantous 6th in the H.W.M.s. In the second heat neither Marimon nor Trintignant could start and Bayol held on longest to win the heat from Rosier and Macklin. Peter Collins had clutch failure on only the third lap. On aggregate, the results were Bayol, Rosier, Macklin...a full four laps down...and John Fitch, while Giraud-Cabantous was 5th but not classified as he was 12 laps off the pace.

The German Grand Prix at the Nurburgring took place on August 2 but there were no H.W.M.s present. The reason given by John Heath was that the organisers had not offered enough start money. This seems somewhat unlikely as the cars were already in France and as the cars had gone so well at the Eifelrennen in May it seems that they would have been made a good offer. However, Nixon says that the H.W.M. team was refused an entry. There were also other rumours circulating that things were not financially well at H.W.M. but that was probably no surprise to the team members. The Ferraris and Maseratis of Farina, Fangio, Hawthorn and Bonetto dominated the German race.

August 9 - Sables d'Olonne Grand Prix

The F2 privateers took themselves to the French circuit for another two-heat race to be decided on aggregate result of both heats. Stirling Moss brought the new Cooper-Alta and was absorbed getting used to the pre-selector gearbox which was giving problems. Behra won the first heat while Moss was 4th after losing some gears. Macklin retired in the first heat with engine bothers and Collins was 8th but not classified, having numerous problems in keeping the car running.

In the second heat, Collins managed sixth, Macklin crashed, so the overall results saw a win for Louis Rosier's private Ferrari, Chiron was second, Moss third, Giraud-Cabantous got 4th just for pressing on, Behra was 5th, Collins 6th and Macklin 7th.

This turned out to be Peter Collins' last race for the H.W.M. team. The Swiss Grand Prix was to take place on August 23 but that was the same weekend as Collins was committed to Aston Martin for the Goodwood Nine Hours. H.W.M. sent three cars to Bremgarten for Macklin, Paul Frere and local driver Albert Scherrer. They were well down the grid and

The racing career - The Grand Prix driver 1952-1955

oddly only the little known Scherrer finished, though he was too far behind to be officially classified.

August 22 - Goodwood Nine Hours

Just before Goodwood, the motoring press announced that Peter Collins would share a C-Type Jaguar with Stirling Moss at the Nurburgring 1000 Kilometers race a week after Goodwood. That must have got some interesting discussion going in the Aston camp!

Whatever might have been intended for the German race, Jaguar intentions at Goodwood were abundantly clear. Making their first appearance since victory at Le Mans, the C-Types had minor changes only and were determined to lead and win. The Aston team looked good, the DB3S cars each having differently painted grill surrounds, one red, one blue and one yellow. There would be only two classes in this race, 'Up to 2000 c.c.', and 'Over 2000 c.c.' The cars were lined up according to practice times and H.W.M.-Jaguar, which had been getting better and better, whereas the Grand Prix cars were not, was in the hands of George Abecassis and Graham Whitehead. The Salvadori/Poore and Parnell/Thompson Astons were in 3rd and 4th while Peter Collins and Pat Griffiths were down in 11th.

Moss, the perennial fastest starter in a Le Mans dash to the cars, was beaten to the car by Harry Schell but it was Moss in the C-Type in front at the end of the first lap. Salvadori was into the pit on only the third lap for some work on his steering but was quickly away. It was soon two C-Types in front from Parnell, Abecassis, a third Jaguar and then Peter Collins who was picking up places very quickly. The Jaguar plan was to break the opposition and it started to

This is the DB3S shared by Collins and Pat Griffith with which they finished second in the Nine-Hour race.
Photo - Ferret Fotographics

95

All about the boy!

work. Moss let Rolt take a stint in front and soon Salvadori had a hole in the crankcase and the first works Aston was out. Tyres were a much bigger problem for many cars than they were at Le Mans. Collins came in, changed all four after two hours and handed over to Pat Griffith. After the works Jaguars made their stops, the Coventry cars had 1st, 2nd and 4th with Astons in 3rd and 6th. At the half-way stage Moss and Peter Walker led. Shortly afterwards Parnell and Griffith were in 3rd and 4th, which looked good but they were still two laps down. Parnell had a tyre blow so he then lost 4th to another Jaguar.

Peter Collins had gotten back into the DB3S after dark and started to up the pace. He had taken over third and had reduced the gap to Moss to only a single lap. It became clear to those paying attention that Collins was really working, taking time off the cars in front on virtually every lap. Though the two leading C-Types had longish stops, Griffith, after he had taken over from Collins, also had to come in and lost a vital six minutes and third place with adjustments to brakes and lights.

With an hour to go, it all changed. Hamilton's C-Type came in for more oil and he went on his way. Then the Moss/Walker car appeared and all the oil was underneath it on the ground, a rod gone. Oil surge on the Goodwood corners was causing the problems. Then it was Hamilton's turn to quit, so Eric Thompson in the Aston was leading. With one C-Type between the two Astons, John Wyer slowed the leader and gave the Collins/Griffith car the 'faster' sign, to which they responded. As the Whitehead Jag was losing its oil pressure as well, under Wyer's careful guidance, Pat Griffith moved into second, so Parnell/Thompson and Collins/Griffith took 1st and 2nd to a huge reception. This rather made up for Peter Collins' disappointing year but with only one race left on the calendar for 1953, it was about to get even better.

September 5 - Dundrod Tourist Trophy

One of the interesting behind the scenes stories of the 1953 racing season centred on the Ulster Automobile Club's total lack of awareness of who was going to show up for their motor race on the Northern Ireland Dundrod circuit. September of that year was a time of both industrial and communications problems on the Continent and it was also the end of a hard season, so the organisers, until the teams actually showed up, had no clear idea of who was going to be there!

In spite of many non-appearances, there were sufficient Jaguars and Aston Martins to make a reasonable race, though all the teams were worried when the recently resurfaced track started chewing up tyres within a few miles. This race was run to a handicap format. The race was over 111 laps but each team was given a number of credit laps according to engine size and this effectively meant that the smaller cars were given a head start. It also meant that the Astons started with a one lap advantage over the Jaguar C-Types. Stirling Moss went round in practice in a stunningly fast 5 mins 2 secs and even more stunningly, this was equalled by Peter Collins in the DB3S, which made the Astons look good with a lap less to do than the Jaguars.

Not surprisingly Stirling Moss led the Jaguars away at the start, while Peter Collins got baulked by a few cars and dropped several places back. With the prospect of nine and a half hours racing ahead, the smallest cars, the Panhards, were in the lead and would be so on handicap for a number of hours, while the faster cars worked to eventually make up the gap. Within just a few laps, on scratch, Moss led the other C-

The racing career - The Grand Prix driver 1952-1955

Types of Rolt and Whitehead, with Peter Collins next ahead of Aston team mates Parnell and Salvadori. Tony Rolt was forced to retire the Jaguar he was sharing with Duncan Hamilton with gearbox failure after only five laps, a major blow to Jaguar hopes. Careful driving was the order of the day to save on tyre wear and Moss and Collins were lapping in near identical times. As some rain came down, tyre wear decreased but Moss went faster and established a new sports car lap record. After three and a half hours, Collins' consistency meant he had made the greatest improvement on his handicap and this was proving to be a very impressive drive. Dennis Poore managed to reduce the Aston team to two cars when he went to overtake Ken Wharton's Fraser-Nash and went off the road, damaging the car seriously. Peter Walker had taken over from Moss and was going even faster but then hit a bank and had a slow lap before he could come in to change a wheel.

At the five hour mark, Wharton now had the handicap lead from Collins and then Moss. Then another Jaguar gearbox failure eliminated Whitehead/Stewart. At six and a half hours, the leaders on handicap were beginning to unwind themselves and started to take over the lead on the road so the Parnell/Thompson DB3S was leading from Moss/Walker, Collins/Griffith and the Wharton/Robb Fraser-Nash. Collins increased the pace and shortly passed his team mate into the lead. Towards the very end of the race, with Moss lying second behind Collins, Moss replaced Walker and everyone thought he would start catching Collins but in fact he lost ground as Collins increased his speed. There was worry in the Jaguar pit about the third team gearbox and both Astons were now in front of Moss. When Collins had a three

Stirling Moss waits to cross the line knowing his Jaguar won't manage another lap; he acknowledges the win by Collins in the DB3S. Photo - LAT

97

All about the boy!

lap gap, Moss pulled up before the finish line knowing he would be unable to complete another lap. Collins, who had done the bulk of the driving, took a superb win from Parnell/Thompson and Wharton/Robb were third with Moss in 4th, his class win giving Jaguar a points lead over Ferrari who hadn't come to Dundrod.

Roy Salvadori thoroughly disliked the Dundrod circuit and his view of it being a 'driver's circuit' was summed up in his comment that any driver who liked it needed psychiatric treatment! Roy also noted that he did one more race that season, sharing Mike Sparken's DB3 fitted with the latest DB3S engine in a 12 Hours of Casablanca race on December 20. Peter Collins was initially down to share with Sparken but something else had come up and Salvadori took over, finishing 4th with privateer Sparken.

Collins was due to compete at the Italian Grand Prix on September 19 but he had already decided not to continue with H.W.M. even though the season was virtually at an end, so he wired John Heath that he would not be going to Monza. None of the three cars finished. When the new formula came into force for 1954, with Grand Prix races now running to Formula One rules, the engine capacities were 750 c.c. for supercharged cars and 2.5litres for unsupercharged cars. Lance Macklin did a few races over the season in the works H.W.M. and privateer Ted Whiteaway competed several times in his own car but H.W.M. was a spent force in Grand Prix racing in spite of its almost heroic efforts in the past. The team had certainly provided Collins with very valuable experience.

In early October, Peter Collins was on duty for Aston Martin at the Paris Motor Show, appearing on the stand of the French Aston distributor with his Dundrod winning DB3S.

Mike Hawthorn had established the clear lead in the contest for the annual British Racing Drivers' Club Gold Star award. He had a good points lead over Moss, winner the previous three years and the other runners were Peter Whitehead, Ken Wharton, Reg Parnell and Peter Collins. Gregor Grant, in his end of season report and preview of 1954, was unable to say what H.W.M.s plans were for 1954 as the team was still in dire financial straights. While he named the possible teams some drivers might be heading for, he was unable to speculate about Peter Collins.

1954

January 24 - Argentine 1000 Kilometers

The opening round of the World Sports Car Championship took place at the Buenos Aires Autodrome, or rather on a combination of the Autodrome and the surrounding roads. This included a stretch of dual carriageway with cars going up one side and down the other at very high speed.

The entry was not spectacular and the race provided a fairly easy win for the works Ferrari 375MM of Farina and Umberto Maglioli. There was a good fight for second between the Rosier/Trintignant Ferrari 375 and the Bonomi/Menditeguy 625TF but as fast as they were, they had mechanical problems which slowed them down. The race saw the first serious race appearance of the Marquis de Portago sharing a Ferrari 250MM with Harry Schell. Schell did the bulk of the driving and moved the car into an eventual second place.

Third was the Aston DB3S of Collins and Griffith which did not have the speed of the Ferraris but was consistent and just kept going. The other team DB3S of Parnell/Salvadori had ignition failure after 65 of the 106 laps and retired. A third works DB3S had been brought for Roberto Mieres and Carlo Tomassi and that

The racing career - The Grand Prix driver 1952-1955

also quit, the gearbox breaking on the 24th lap. A DB3 had been sold to Argentine-born Briton Eric Forrest-Greene and he was sadly killed when the car crashed in the very early laps of the race.

Roy Salvadori later commented on the disparity in speed between Collins and Pat Griffith. Collins was more than happy to have Griffith as a co-driver, though he was much slower and in terms of professionalism was nothing like Collins. It is interesting that Peter Collins was quite happy with this arrangement, but had been so adamant about not wanting to drive with Geoff Duke.

Roy Salvadori described how he had been on the flight out to the Argentine and was sitting with what he considered to be a rather scruffy looking person he took to be one of the Italian mechanics. Roy was surprised that this 'mechanic' spoke several languages and he later learned that he had been sitting with the Marquis de Portago!

It was not until later in February that Aston Martin made an official announcement of their drivers for the 1954 season and that these would be Reg Parnell, Peter Collins, Roy Salvadori, Pat Griffith, Dennis Poore and Graham Whitehead. There was still no inking of what Peter Collins' other plans were for the season, though in fact that was also true of several other drivers. The Aston Martin trip to South America had been an opportunity for David Brown to promote his agricultural equipment there and it is hoped that that was more successful than the racing.

One outcome of the race in Argentina was that Collins, who made a point of getting to know other drivers, came across Phil Hill and Carroll Shelby and introduced them both to John Wyer. This was a fruitful meeting, especially for Shelby who would join the team a bit later on.

March 7 - Sebring 12 Hours

In 1953, Aston Martin was the only European manufacturer represented at Sebring. They returned in 1954 but Ferrari, Maserati and Lancia also came and there was an impressive entry, backed up by a huge collection of good American-entered cars. In spite of the presence of the very fast Lancia D24s in the hands of Fangio, Ascari, Taruffi, Castellotti, Manzon and Villoresi, Sebring turned into the battle of the 'giant killer'. The Aston DB3S of Collins and Griffith went out on lap 26 with no brakes and Parnell and Salvadori disappeared two laps earlier with engine problems. Collins had been in 7th at the time and Parnell 8th. Roy later complained that when Reg, with a broken con-rod, pushed the car back to the pits he got a trophy for being 'Man of the Race'. Roy's complaint, thinking that Reg should have just looked under the bonnet, was that when he did the same thing at Goodwood he got 'harsh words' rather than a trophy!

The Taruffi/Manzon Lancia was nine laps ahead of the second place car which happened to be the Briggs Cunningham OSCA 1500 driven by Moss and Bill Lloyd. With an hour to go, the Lancia stopped out on the circuit and Taruffi pushed it back. Thus the little OSCA had steadily climbed through the field and took a most amazing win. It had been a serious mistake for Aston Martin to go all the way to South America and then straight to Sebring, as they really needed major rebuilds after South America.

May 2 - Mille Miglia

For the first time the Mille Miglia regulations allowed solo drivers in the event. Early in its history, drivers shared the time behind the wheel. Then came the period of more specialist navigating co-drivers,

All about the boy!

until drivers, wanting essentially to save weight in the car, could do the thousand miles single-handed. For 1954, Aston Martin chose the traditional route with Pat Griffith teamed up with Peter Collins and photographer Louis Klemantaski alongside Reg Parnell. Denis Jenkinson was making his first foray into sitting in a Mille Miglia car, this time going with George Abecassis in the H.W.M. Jaguar... which didn't last very long.

The two cars had been the ones which had raced in the two previous events, so had full rebuilds in a very short period of time. They were then tested at Monza by Collins and Parnell where they went quite well. Collins travelled out to Italy with Carroll Shelby who had showed up at Feltham and became a reserve driver. Going through Paris on the way out, they had a big lunch with Peter's 'boss' at Majestic Automobiles and then got done for speeding!

As at Sebring, both Collins and Parnell were well up the field enjoying close battles with Marzotto's Ferrari and Musso's Maserati. Farina had a big crash in his Ferrari 375 Plus and broke his arm and the first of the three competing Marzotto brothers, Giannino, went out in his Ferrari. When Parnell was in 5th spot, he missed a corner, went through a barrier and damaged the front end and Taruffi's Lancia retired after being in the lead at Rome. On the return run, over the Radicofani and Futa Passes, Ascari, Maglioli and Paolo Marzotto battled it out. Collins pushed by into third near Siena and was looking superb on the fast road sections. Just as suddenly the Collins/Griffith pairing was sitting beside the road with a broken Aston, as Ascari went on to win from Vittorio Marzotto. The Aston was hard to handle on Avons in the wet and there were a number of excursions. Then a blowout, caused by a broken De Dion tube, sent them into a ditch. They got back to Florence but when John Wyer saw the damage, he retired the car.

May 15 - Silverstone International Trophy Meeting

The fact that Stirling Moss had now joined Mike Hawthorn as the driver of a competitive Grand Prix car must have raised a number of issues for Peter Collins at Silverstone. Though he would race in the Aston works car in the sports car event, Moss was now in a works Maserati 250F and Collins was still out in the cold as far as a regular F1 drive was concerned.

Nevertheless, he set himself the task to do a good job in the sports car race and had his DB3S up behind Parnell who was racing the Lagonda, which had become his pet project. Salvadori and Graham Whitehead were also DB3S-mounted but they were in the new coupe versions. As the cars came to the grid just after the completion of the first heat of the International Trophy race, it had just stopped raining, though the track was very wet. One race report describes the contrast amongst the drivers waiting for the Le Mans start:

"There were thick, stocky fellows like Reg Parnell, Gonzales, Gould and Duncan Hamilton, tall ones like Peter Walker, George Abecassis and Roy Salvadori, athletic ones like Peter Collins, Ninian Sanderson and Lance Macklin." (*Autosport*, May 21, 1954, p.653).

The C-Type Jaguars got the jump on most of the field but it wasn't long before Gonzales was forcing his Ferrari between them. He equalled the fastest lap he had done in his Formula 1 heat as he took over the lead from Peter Walker. Parnell and Collins were 6th and 8th after the first half dozen laps. At one point Peter Collins was in 4th, ahead of the Lagonda but then he appeared to be struggling and Roy Salvadori was soon pressing him and got past into 7th. This

100

The racing career - The Grand Prix driver 1952-1955

meant a class 1-2-3 in the two to three litre group. Roy described the last few laps:

"The race was run in the wet, the coupe's cockpit misted up badly and it was a miserable drive, enlivened only by a dice between Peter Collins and me. This was, however, one of those rare occasions when I really went well in the wet and I closed up on Peter, uncertain whether I should have a go at taking him. I decided to press him fairly hard, he was getting slightly out of line under pressure and I was not surprised when he lost the DB3S at Becketts and spun in front of me. I kept clear of the spinning DB3S and moved up into seventh place, while Peter kept his engine running and rejoined the race some distance behind me." (Salvadori and Pritchard, 1985, p.51-52).

It was at this meeting that Tony Vandervell unveiled the much vaunted but little seen Vanwall Special, or Van-Wall Special as some journals first referred to it. Vandervell had been an early member of the organisation which was to produce the 'world-beating BRM' and he eventually became so disillusioned with BRM and 'building a racing car by committee' that he quit and went his own way. In fact, he was using the BRM lack of progress to do what he really wanted to do which was to build his own Grand Prix car. He was as patriotic as Mays and the rest and although popular legend has it that he allegedly wanted to beat 'those damned red cars', there is very little evidence that he actually said that or, if he did, really meant it. He worked very closely with Italians and with Enzo Ferrari and had a long-standing respect for Ferrari and his products. As the run-up to his own Grand Prix car, he bought and ran Ferraris as the prelude to being a constructor.

At the International Trophy meeting, Vandervell brought out the Vanwall Special, in temporary 2litre form, for Alan Brown to drive. The late Alan Brown told the author that not only did he do some of the testing but also thought, or at least hoped, that he would have a long-term arrangement with Vandervell. Brown, of course, from his days in 500 c.c. and F2 racing, knew Peter Collins well and had raced against him on many occasions. He said that he was not surprised to see Peter Collins spending time with Vandervell that weekend but had not realised that Collins' appearance in the team would come so soon and also be at his expense. In retrospect, when the author spoke to him in 2002, he believed that was the occasion when Vandervell invited Peter Collins to drive for him.

May 29 - Aintree 200

The opportunity came very soon indeed, only a fortnight later. *Autosport* of May 28, 1954 announced that Collins would be driving Vandervell's 4.5litre Ferrari 'Thin Wall Special' the following weekend at Aintree. So Collins wouldn't be getting into the prototype Vanwall but instead into the much used Ferrari and he would be facing opposition in the form of Ken Wharton and Ron Flockhart in the latest versions of the V-16 BRM. The race would be the Aintree 200, a Formula Libre event.

It has been argued that both Mike Hawthorn and Peter Collins were on Tony Vandervell's short-list for drivers for the Vanwall in Grand Prix races and that races in the Ferrari were something in the order of a test. If that was the case and it seems quite likely, then Collins did his chances a lot of good by putting the 4.5litre Ferrari 375 on pole position. The circuit was being used in the opposite direction to what was traditional at Aintree and the track was very wet, so Collins' achievement couldn't have been better timed. Collins was on pole with Reg Parnell on the outside in another Ferrari.

All about the boy!

Peter Collins on his winning way, beating Ron Flockhart with the Vandervell Ferrari Thin Wall Special. Photo - National Motor Museum

four until the end. Collins put in the fastest lap and nearly matched Hawthorn's earlier record with the same car. Hawthorn was not racing as he was still recovering from the painful burns he had received weeks earlier at Syracuse. The weekend ended on a tragic note, especially for Hawthorn, when his father Leslie crashed on the way home from Goodwood. He died from his serious injuries and that event had a big impact on Hawthorn and his career, though in fact it would be some time before people understood that.

June 12/13 - Le Mans 24 Hours

The performance of Collins at Aintree and especially at Goodwood was the main topic of conversation amongst the racing crowd at Goodwood and during the run-up to Le Mans the following weekend. The Aston Martin DB3S coupes had gotten a good deal of publicity so many would be watching to see what they could do. Not many of these people knew what Roy Salvadori felt about them after his earlier experience with the windows misting and being unable to straighten his neck against the low roof!

What should have been a victory in the 'Up to 3litre class' at least, turned to nothing less than disaster after a very good beginning. After much back and forth, Reg Parnell opted to drive the 'experimental' supercharged DB3S which he would share with Salvadori, while the one new 4.5litre Lagonda would be in the hands of Eric Thompson and Dennis Poore. The two coupes would go to Peter Collins and Prince Bira and to Graham Whitehead and Jimmy Stewart, the older brother of Jackie Stewart. Sadly Jimmy Stewart died during the time this book was written and thus the opportunity to talk about his time at Astons was lost. He was a much under-rated driver. Bira was in the team because Pat Griffith had been injured at Hyeres and was not fit for Le Mans. Carroll Shelby was sharing Paul Frere's own DB3S. Da Silva Ramos was in a DB2 with a DB3 engine.

At the start Moss was beaten across the road by a Talbot driver and three big Ferraris led at the end of the first lap. Parnell was the first Aston in sight, then a Talbot, three

Peter Collins and Prince Bira pose with officials and the Aston Martin DB3S coupe, which John Wyer referred to as 'DB3S saloon'. Photo - LAT

Cunninghams and then Peter Collins. As things sorted themselves out at the front the rains came and the leading group still had the Lagonda and Collins and Parnell attached to it. At the end of the first hour, Collins and Whitehead were engaged in a hard battle side by side. Stirling Moss put what was referred to in the press as the 'new' Jaguar into the lead...

the D-Type didn't get the D-Type tag until it had been around for a little while.

The Lagonda became the first Feltham casualty as Eric Thompson spun it in the Esses just before the 2hour mark and thumped the bank. He lost an hour extracting it and got back to the pits but with no rear lights it was retired.

Peter Collins behind the wheel of the DB3S coupe which was well up the leader board in the early hours of Le Mans. Here it is chased by the supercharged DB3S of Parnell and Salvadori. Photo - Ferret Fotographics

All about the boy!

At the end of the 4th hour, Collins and Bira had a healthy lead in the 'Up to 3litre class'. At nine-thirty in the evening Jimmy Stewart in one of the DB3S coupes hit the Talbot of Meyrat on the fast approach to White House. The Aston hit a marker stone and flipped onto its roof ending up on the other side of the road. Stewart had been thrown out before the car went over, and although he sustained a broken elbow and many bruises he was very lucky to escape.

The Moss/Walker Jaguar was pushed away after midnight and Collins and Bira still led the class and after ten hours it was 4th overall. The Shelby/Frere car broke a front hub housing and was out and Parnell was not far behind Collins. Sometime around 3.00 am, Bira was driving the coupe when he had an accident very similar to Stewart's very near the same place. He too was lucky to escape with minor injuries but both cars had been written off. Roy Salvadori later commented on the coupes:

"The new coupes proved disappointingly and inextricably slow and, although it was not fully appreciated at the time, suffered from a serious aerodynamic defect that caused the rear end to lift at high speed. In torrential rain both coupes crashed heavily." (Salvadori and Pritchard, op. cit. p.52). Roy subsequently hit the back of a very slow car creeping around the Dunlop Curve in the middle of the road. When he handed back over to Parnell, Reg came back in wondering why the headlights were illuminating the treetops...and he was very angry with his co-driver! They carried on until the head gasket went four hours before the finish.

The Da Silva Ramos car had also retired in the early hours of the morning. When the Parnell/Salvadori car went out, that was the end of a very big Aston effort and a big disappointment. In spite of what Roy said about the coupes, they had held the class lead for many, many hours. What it must have felt

The sorry remains of the Collins/Bira coupe. Bira was lucky to escape unharmed.
Photo - Ferret Fotographics

The racing career - The Grand Prix driver 1952-1955

Another view of the crashed DB3S coupe.
Photo - Ferret Fotographics

like to drive is difficult to imagine if the tail was lifting!

Victory finally went to the Gonzales/Trintignant 4.9 Ferrari, with Rolt and Hamilton two laps behind in the Jaguar, failing to repeat their victory of 1953 but doing a power of good for Jaguar.

June 19 - Crystal Palace Trophy

A large crowd turned out for the regular Spring meeting at the 'Palace' and there was a very good F1 field to contest two ten lap heats and a final. As expected, Reg Parnell in a Ferrari 500 entered by Scuderia Ambrosiana dominated heat one, though at first Les Leston made a huge effort to keep his tiny Cooper-JAP on terms with him. On the sixth lap, Peter Collins, having been invited by Rob Walker to drive his Connaught A-Type, tackled and passed the scrapping Cooper. Horace Gould had his Cooper-Bristol momentarily in front of Collins but at the end of the race the Connaught had closed the gap to Parnell to nine seconds.

A very interesting account of Peter Collins at Crystal Palace comes from the respectable Rob Walker. Collings, in 'The Piranha Club' quotes Rob Walker giving an insight into one side of the Peter Collins character:

"Tony (Rolt) was a gentleman driver and he drove like a gentleman; if someone who was obviously faster wanted to pass him, Tony would move over to let him through. Peter (Collins) was quite different. He was my first professional driver and he really opened my eyes to what the cut and thrust of what truly competitive driving was like. I remember one race at Crystal Palace, which was run in two ten-lap heats. In the first Horace Gould in a Cooper-Bristol got the drop on Peter at the start and then blocked him for the whole ten laps. During the interval, I heard Peter saying to Horace 'if you do that again, Horace, I'll push you off.' Horace did. And Peter pushed him off. And won. Peter had the most incredible will to win." (Collings, 2001, p.76).

This is indeed an interesting story but there are some problems with it. There is no evidence that Gould blocked Collins in any substantial way in this first heat nor in the final, nor that he was pushed off and Collins did not win this race. Peter Collins only raced three times at Crystal Palace and it hadn't happened in 1953. Collins did win in 1955 but Horace Gould wasn't there. So the incident may have happened in 1954 and Rob's memory was perhaps at fault when he recalled Collins as winning. Or is it another one of those 'mythical tales' which appear in motor racing? There is no doubt that Peter Collins had a fierce temper, as we can see from other sources and Rob Walker must have been well aware of this. Other references also quote Rob Walker but there remains little evidence that it actually happened!

Rodney Nuckey won the second heat in his Cooper-Bristol from Don Beauman's Connaught. Collins lined up next to Reg Parnell for the short final. At the flag, Leston desperately tried to hang onto Parnell but he didn't last a lap before the crankshaft broke. Peter Collins drove the Connaught superbly but couldn't get near the Ferrari which equalled the lap record Reg had set in the first heat. Collins finished five seconds behind with Beauman third.

July 12/15 - Alpine Rally

Tony Vandervell had decided to enter the Vanwall Special for Peter Collins at the French Grand Prix at Reims. As it happened, the entry was withdrawn as Vandervell was focussed on getting the larger

The racing career - The Grand Prix driver 1952-1955

2.3litre Vanwall engine ready and tested and this had not happened by the time the French race took place so he was concentrating on the British Grand Prix two weeks later. Reims witnessed the return of Mercedes Benz to Grand Prix racing and their streamlined car won in Fangio's capable hands.

Six factory Sunbeam Alpines had been entered for the 1954 event and this year it would be one day shorter, with an extra all-night run. There would be a 27 hour section over the most difficult mountain passes in Europe, so overall the event was expected to be much more difficult than in 1953.

The team cars before the start. Moss is in MKV 21 and Peter Collins again in MKV 23 with young Lewis Garrad. Photo - Rootes Archive

An impressive shot of the Sunbeam line-up. Photo - Rootes Archive

109

All about the boy!

Peter Collins and Lewis Garrad. Photo - Rootes Archive

Stirling Moss and John Cutts were together again, Peter Harper was in a car with Peter Miller, George Murray-Frame was again with John Pearman, and Peter Collins was back, this time with Lewis, the 17 year old son of Norman Garrad, the Rootes competition manager. Lewis was doing his apprenticeship at Rootes and it was thought that he might not be making such big demands of Peter Collins as Ronnie Adams had. Rootes dealer George Hartwell had replaced the now retired Leslie Johnson, and had Dr. Bill Dean as co-driver. Sheila van Damm was back with Anne Hall, hoping for another Coupe de Dames. Several of the team were after Coupes des Alpes and some after the Gold Cup for winning Coupes in three successive years.

Peter Miller reported Collins as being up to his usual antics before the start at Bandol and Marseilles, locking people in their rooms and using an air pellet pistol to shoot police in the back with when held up in traffic!

Stirling Moss and John Cutts in the mountains on one of the 'easier' sections. Photo - Rootes Archive

Peter Collins has the hood up as the weather was so unpleasant for most of the event. Photo - Rootes Archive

All about the boy!

Collins has his eyes firmly on the road during a difficult night section as Lewis Garrad checks his notes. Photo - Rootes Archive

Miller should have been used to Collins' tricks by now. After the Tourist Trophy victory at Dundrod the previous September, Peter Collins invited Miller to the Aston party and so Miller headed off to the Crawfordsburn Inn the next day. After the festivities with the Aston team, they were leaving on the night boat to Liverpool and Miller followed them down to the docks and went on board for a last drink, reassured by Collins and others that he would get a good warning before having to get off, as his car was still on the dock. Then the horn blasted, the engines started and the ferry pulled out. A steward came up to Miller and said the captain wished to see him. He was given a right rollicking for delaying departure and was taken down to a small boat and rowed ashore. Word had spread ashore that a stowaway had been found so a crowd turned out and Miller heard shouts from the ship. There was Peter Collins shouting and waving 'goodbye!' (Miller, 1962, p.45-6).

Weather was severe in the first stage to St. Moritz with 19 cars dropping out and half the 64 who got there had penalties, so the predictions were accurate. The Sunbeam and Renault teams were the only ones to get there with no penalties. The weather continued to follow the event across to Munich and then down through the Dolomites and by this stage only the Stirling Moss/John Cutts Alpine was still unpenalised from the Sunbeam team, a remarkable achievement.

The racing career - The Grand Prix driver 1952-1955

The weather was so bad that Sheila van Damm and Peter Collins had missed seeing the Innsbruck control which was subsequently cancelled. In fact some thirty crews didn't find that control. Harper and Miller had a big crash in the Dolomites and Peter Collins had the rear axle go at the bottom of the Stelvio Pass.

Only 37 cars got to the finish and only eleven Coupes des Alpes for getting through without penalties were awarded. Moss, having accomplished this in three successive events, was awarded the Gold Cup. George Murray-Frame missed the same achievement after being given a 1/5th of a second penalty at Munich. Sheila van Damm and Anne Hall again won the Coupe des Dames. Virtually every stage had sections cancelled or re-routed due to impassable snow, floods or landslides, making it the hardest event so far run. Moss told the author that he had lost second gear, so when it came to the final tests when the officials check the car is in order, he drove by shifting into overdrive and distracting the official so he wouldn't notice second gear was gone...very enterprising as usual!

Collins checks the time before leaving a control shortly before the car retired with a failed rear axle. Photo - Rootes Archive

All about the boy!

July 17 - British Grand Prix

As in 1953, Peter Collins had to hotfoot it from France back to Silverstone to practice for the British Grand Prix. A field of thirty-one cars was on hand and so were 100,000 spectators, though many of them wanted to see the Mercedes team which was making its first appearance in England since attending Donington in 1937. The Mercedes came with the all-enveloping body which had been suitable for Reims but was much harder for Fangio and Kling to handle at Silverstone. Nevertheless, Fangio broke Farina's lap record.

Gonzales and Hawthorn had their Ferraris on the front row with Fangio, along with Stirling Moss in the Maserati 250F. Peter Collins had got the Vanwall Special, now more regularly being referred to as the Vanwall, on to the third row of the grid. The car now had a rather unusual cowling over the external tube-affair radiator with which Alan Brown had raced at the International Trophy. This cowling was a simple alloy sheet ducting for better aerodynamics and it helped to concentrate the flow of cool air onto the tubing.

Collins had done an impressive job in his first drive in the Vanwall and he qualified 11th, 3rd fastest of all the non 2.5litre cars and ahead of several of the 'proper' F1 machines. In fact there were a full 21 cars behind him, though that was partly explained by the fact the Maseratis were late and all started at the back. Collins and the Vanwall had been very impressive from the start of Thursday practice. He was running well up the field amongst the bigger cars, getting past Kling into 8th and then about to pass Trintignant, until his 17th lap when a gasket failed, caused by a leak in a cylinder head joint, which caused some

The Vanwall is readied for practice at the British Grand Prix. Photo - John Pearson Collection

Above: A view of the new but odd cowling on the Vanwall radiator. Photo - John Pearson Collection

Below: Peter Collins to the left before the start as mechanics Burkinshaw and Pratt get the car ready. Photo - Anthony Pritchard/T.C.March Collection

During the race, Collins in the Vanwall chases the Rob Walker Connaught of Riseley-Pritchard

concern amongst the team and the parts suppliers. The engineers at Wills who provided the head gasket were of the opinion that the head might be moving on the pressure rings so set about making a thinner gasket for the future. Gonzales led Hawthorn home in the race. The press gave full recognition to the potential of the Vanwall and to what was referred to as 'Collins' enterprising driving'.

The crowds gave no sign of leaving after the Grand Prix as there was to be the F3 and sports car race for 'Over 1500 c.c. cars'. Leaving Silverstone in those days was not all that pleasant anyway, there being little point in sitting in traffic for often many hours. The crowd's patience was rewarded in the 25 lapper for 'Over 1500 c.c. sports cars'. There were several C-Type Jaguars and Aston Martin DB3S's for Salvadori and Collins, both right from the Grand Prix. Reg Parnell also had the team's 4.5litre V-12 Lagonda while Carroll Shelby was in the Paul Frere DB3S which he had been racing several times recently.

It was a good day for the Peter Collins Fan Club as it wasn't Rolt in the quickest C-Type which emerged first after the Le Mans start. The DB3S not only got straight into the lead but started pulling out a gap. All the time Collins had spent in speed events had really helped his starts and he had developed the knack of getting on the pace immediately. This also kept him out of trouble with a number of comings together behind the lead pack. Reg Parnell helped the Feltham cause by bringing the wailing Lagonda into second, though there was nothing he or anyone else could do as Collins just continued to pull away. At eight laps Roy Salvadori was in third and Shelby was behind him so it was a Feltham 1-2-3-4. By lap 15, Roy had passed Reg and the order remained this way until the end. Well, almost remained that way as the Lagonda lost a few cylinders and Shelby moved by. Collins had done a race average only three mph slower than Gonzales in the Grand Prix. David Brown of Astons was very pleased and Collins could not have chosen a better moment to turn in a virtuoso performance.

Roy Salvadori, remembering the previous Silverstone episode, recounts the end of the race:

The racing career - The Grand Prix driver 1952-1955

Collins totally dominated the sports car race at the Grand Prix meeting, winning easily in the DB3S. Photo - Anthony Pritchard/T.C.March Collection

"I began to pick up places but then I lost the DB3S at Copse, nearly hitting the bank. I kept going and was driving really well, pulling right up through the field to finish second behind Peter Collins. I was pushing Peter really hard and getting frantic 'easy' signals from the pit but there was no way I would have tried to pass him. At the flag I was a mere second behind Peter and set fastest lap." (Salvadori and Pritchard, op.cit.p.53).

July 24 - Fairwood Championship of Wales Meeting

The Welsh Fairwood Aerodrome was the rather unlikely follow-up to Collins' glory weekend at Silverstone. After a serious race for 500 c.c.F3s, there were a number of sports car races and one for 'unlimited' cars. While Michael Head dominated practice and the race in his Jaguar C-Type, Rob Walker had entered his Aston DB2 for Peter Collins, who ran as hard as he could and finished 4th behind Head and the Lister-Bristol of Archie Scott-Brown and Walton's Cooper-Bristol.

August 14 - Snetterton International

Tony Vandervell had decided not to enter a car at the German Grand Prix but would put in an entry for the Swiss GP. He then changed his mind and entered the Vanwall for Peter Collins at Snetterton the previous weekend. He changed his mind again and sent the Thin Wall Special Ferrari for Collins to drive in the Formula Libre race. Chris Nixon had made a comment that Collins wouldn't have been able to do the Swiss race anyway, at least implying he knew Collins had another engagement, though he didn't say what it was. (Nixon, 1991, p.143).

While Reg Parnell won the F1 race in his Ferrari 500 for which the Vanwall did not turn up, 29 cars had been entered for the 40 lap Formula Libre race. This should have been a pretty sensational field but practice and other

117

All about the boy!

incidents cut it down by half, though the front row of Collins in the Thin Wall, Flockhart in the BRM and Parnell in his Ferrari still looked promising. Collins dropped the clutch and the big green Ferrari just disappeared, leaving the BRM and the others in its wake. Flockhart struggled with the Bourn machine, running off the track and stopping at the pits with some brake problems. Reg's Ferrari had a blow-up. Collins went quicker and quicker, setting a new lap record in the process. Flockhart came back into 2nd but then ran off the road yet again. Rodney Nuckey's shirt had gradually come looser and looser and then disappeared! He still held second to the end in the Cooper-Bristol, coming in at the end with his helmet askew as well, with the BRM 3rd. Collins won by an amazing three laps.

September 5 - Italian Grand Prix

In the weeks preceding the Italian Grand Prix at Monza, there was speculation that Alfa Romeo would return to GP racing in 1955 and if that happened it was thought that Fangio would certainly join them. Much of the Mercedes success was credited to Fangio, so the question was, who would lead Mercedes? The current top drivers were seen, at least by *Autosport* as Fangio, Ascari, Gonzales, Farina, Behra, Villoresi, Moss and Hawthorn. With Farina injured, Villoresi aging, Gonzales possibly retiring, where were the new drivers going to come from? The others viewed as bordering on becoming stars were Trintignant, Wharton, Mieres and Peter Collins...so would one of them get the Mercedes drive? The

Peter Collins in the Monza pits with Tony Vandervell to his left and mechanic Norman Burkinshaw behind Vandervell.
Photo - Ferret Fotographics

The racing career - The Grand Prix driver 1952-1955

answer of course was no and there was never really a chance of Alfa returning at that time.

Meanwhile the Vanwall Special at Monza was entered by Vandervell Products Ltd. rather than the customary G.A. Vandervell and it had been hoped that the 2.5 litre engine would be ready for this important race. This 2490 c.c. unit was being tested at Maidenhead during August. At virtually the last minute, a valve failure on the test bed was catastrophic and it meant that the 2.3 would have to be installed for the Italian race. The 2.5 litre engine now had a bore of 96 mm with a modified combustion chamber. So the car went to Monza giving away a quarter of a litre capacity, not a good thing at the high speed circuit.

Collins qualified 16th, five seconds slower than Fangio on pole but he had impressed everyone by the way he had hurled the car around the track trying to compensate for having a smaller engine. The 2.3 was again able to compete on even terms, being fastest of all the cars with smaller engines. There were those who raised questions about the handling of the Vanwall but that was all down to how hard he had to drive it to be anywhere in the hunt. Most of the attention in the race was on the battle between Fangio, Ascari and Moss' Maserati. At 20 laps, Moss was lapping Collins who had moved up five places from the start but the Vanwall engine was running very smoothly and Collins was not over-extending it, conscious that he was in need of a regular Grand Prix drive. By 3/4 distance his consistent driving had brought him all the way up to 5th but on lap 63 he went into the Vanwall pit, as the cockpit had suddenly become flooded with oil from a fracture on the oil pipe to the pressure gauge - it was repaired by flattening the pipe. He had dropped back but then moved up again to finish seventh, as Juan Fangio put the seal on the 1954 World Championship. Collins had controlled his rather fierce practice pace and drove a smooth and mature race.

And it hadn't gone unnoticed that at one point

Collins got the 2.3 litre Vanwall up as far as fifth in the Italian Grand Prix. Photo - Ferret Fotographics

119

All about the boy!

in the race, all three of the British drivers...Moss, Hawthorn and Collins...were in the top six.

September 11 - Tourist Trophy

And like a top British driver, it was straight off to Northern Ireland from Monza for the 21st running of the TT. The officials had reassessed their handicapping procedure from the previous year, feeling that the small cars had had no chance. The revised handicapping was fairly generous and indeed the smaller cars went considerably faster than last year. That gave a victory to the 745 c.c. DB of Paul Armagnac and Gerard Laureau.

Gonzales had a very big crash in practice and was thrown from his Ferrari, being lucky not to be struck by another car. He went home and said he thought he would probably retire. Fangio also crashed but wasn't injured, Ascari was quickest, with Desmond Titterington second in a 3litre Ferrari. The Astons were in the three litre class with Parnell/Salvadori, Collins/Griffith and G.Whitehead/Poore, up against the Ferraris of Hawthorn/Trintignant and Titterington/Kelly. At the Le Mans start it was again Moss first across the road but Ascari was first to get his car going and head down the road. The Rolt/Hamilton D-Type was expected to be quick but it was not long before Peter Collins moved the DB3S alongside and then past it. Ascari in the Lancia was breaking the lap record repeatedly, touching just under 143 mph through the timing zone.

The pace set was a fast one and it began to tell. Peter Collins came walking in from Quarry after a universal joint broke before Griffith got in the car. It already looked like one of the DBs would win and a Ferrari might get second. The Parnell/Salvadori car hit a bank at Leathemstown and crawled back to retire. Ascari retired late in the race and at about the same time Moss came in to stop and wait for the finish.

So the DB won, Hawthorn/Trintignant were second on handicap and first on scratch and Whitehead/Poore were 13th, with Aston Martin only achieving a 3rd in class, disappointing after 1953. It was interesting that much later Roy Salvadori would say that the team's hopes were pinned on Collins who he said was "superb at Dundrod". Roy admitted his own problem in the race as having been relieved at being called in earlier than planned and that he lost concentration and side-swiped a bank, damaging the steering and suspension. It was only when he managed to get back to the pits that he learned that he was being brought in to hand over to Collins who was the quickest team driver at Dundrod. Roy felt very bad over the incident and thought that John Wyer must have realised this as he said nothing to him.

September 25 - Goodwood Trophy Meeting

Progress had been made in getting the 2.5 litre Vanwall engine ready and Vandervell decided to use the Goodwood Trophy meeting as a training and development session in preparation for the Spanish Grand Prix. The Vanwall would appear for Peter Collins to drive in the Formula 1 race, while Mike Hawthorn would be in it during the Libre race, where Collins would be handling the Thin Wall Special. For Vandervell, there was also undoubtedly an element of satisfaction in having both Collins and Hawthorn in his team at the same time.

There was a very solid British entry for the Goodwood Trophy F1 event over 21 laps, plus Louis Rosier and his 250F Maserati. Moss, Collins, Bob Gerard and Parnell made up the front row, though Moss was substantially quicker in qualifying in the 250F. For Collins

120

*Above: Collins on his way to a very impressive second place at Goodwood in the Vanwall.
Photo - Ferret Fotographics*

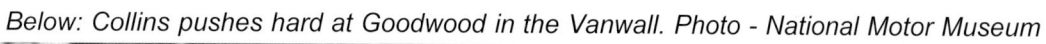

Below: Collins pushes hard at Goodwood in the Vanwall. Photo - National Motor Museum

All about the boy!

to have put Parnell and Salvadori behind him at Goodwood was a considerable achievement and though Parnell got the best start, Moss and Collins were soon in front. This was simply a battle between Moss and Collins...and a display of potential by the Vanwall. Collins had the crowd on its feet by driving on the very limit in his attempts to keep in contact with Moss. It didn't work but the performance got a star rating and it seemed that the Vanwall had come of age.

Collins then switched to the Thin Wall Special Ferrari and took that to a 16 second win over the BRM of Ken Wharton. Behind these two there was another fierce fight, this one between Moss in the Maserati and Hawthorn in the Vanwall. The Goodwood meeting was a fine showcase of Britain's best racing drivers and here they were having it out between themselves. Rumours after the meeting had not only Collins and Hawthorn signing for Vandervell for 1955 but Moss as well...though of course this was as much wishful thinking as anything. However, the predictions were not all that inaccurate.

Collins jumped from the Vanwall into the Ferrari Thin Wall Special to win the Formula Libre race in style. Photo - Ferret Fotographics

122

The racing career - The Grand Prix driver 1952-1955

October 2 - Aintree Daily Telegraph Meeting

The BARC organised a very full programme at Aintree, running the races the other way round from the season opening meeting. This didn't seem to make much difference to the competitors. Moss opened his programme by winning the hotly fought 500 race. He was also on pole for the Daily Telegraph Trophy race for F1 cars, his Maserati having Behra next to him, then Mike Hawthorn getting his serious trial in the Vanwall with the 2.5 engine. While Moss was pretty much in a class of his own, Hawthorn had his hands full with Harry Schell's 250F and towards the end Schell passed him, only to lose it and Hawthorn retook second place, the Vanwall out-accelerating the 250F.

In the sports car race, Peter Collins got the jump on Masten Gregory's 4.5litre Ferrari at the start and pushed the DB3S in front. Peter Walker and Reg Parnell were being left behind as Gregory used the power of the Ferrari to catch Collins and get past him. Collins hung on grimly to the tail of the Ferrari and could not find any means of getting back in front. So Gregory won by a small amount from Collins, Parnell and Peter Walker, with Salvadori not far behind.

Then came the Formula Libre race and again Moss was on pole, the Maserati being quicker than Wharton's BRM. Collins was the Thin Wall 'meat in the BRM sandwich' with Flockhart on the outside to complete row one. Mike Hawthorn was on row two in the Vanwall. It was Collins who took off into the lead which he extended on lap two. It was Moss who got on Collins' tail ahead of Wharton, Schell, Hawthorn and Flockhart. Schell and Wharton took each other out. On lap seven the Vanwall pulled in to retire just as Moss passed Collins in the slowing Thin Wall Special. Moss thus won his third race of the day, beating

The line-up at Aintree with Collins on the far side. Photo - Klemantaski Collection

All about the boy!

Mantovani's 250F and Flockhart's 3rd place was the last appearance of the BRM in this period. The Thin Wall engine was just in need of a rebuild and Hawthorn had spun the Vanwall, filling the oil radiator with rubbish which caused overheating and then the oil pressure disappeared.

The results were not overwhelmingly impressive for Collins...and Hawthorn for that matter but they had made it very clear to the British racing enthusiast that they, with Moss, were very serious forces to be reckoned with.

October 26 - Spanish Grand Prix

The Spanish race at Pedralbes was the final Championship round of the year. However, the British 'golden boys' did not end the season on the kind of note that they would have liked. First, the wonderful new Lancia D-50 appeared and Ascari put it on pole and that frightened a lot of people. In practice, Peter Collins just got caught out with the new Vanwall, taking a corner too quickly and managing to turn the car over, ramming a tree with the back end for good measure. There was too much damage to repair and the 2.5litre car therefore could not show itself in a proper Grand Prix as was the intention.

Then Moss seemed to have a rare moment of losing concentration, got his feet mixed up with the central throttle Maserati which was a works car and also crashed, though his car was repairable. Mike Hawthorn gave them both a hard time when they came back to the pits. This was a mistake as he did the same thing, crashing his new Ferrari 553 more or less in the same place. Fortunately his car was only lightly damaged and he then went on to win, while Collins sat on the sidelines and Moss retired on lap 20.

Tony Vandervell is thought to have referred to Collins as a "silly young fool" but on the whole he was philosophical about the incident. It did not shift his plans away from what he had in mind for the next season.

1955

The usual, sometimes amazing, predictions about who would go where in 1955 persisted but for some months, there were no 'official' announcements about where drivers would be. It has to be said that professional drivers were still a pretty rare commodity and motor racing professionalism had not developed to anything like it did a few short years later.

Alfa Romeo rumours were rife as usual and there were still those who said Fangio would be going to Alfa, though we now know that there was nothing resembling a Grand Prix car in the works at the time. Froilan Gonzales withdrew his intention to retire, though he had been deeply affected by the death of Onefre Marimon and by his own accident in 1954. Mike Hawthorn continued to have serious medical problems, having further surgery after his earlier Syracuse crash and then suffering a relapse at home. There were some detractors who saw this as an attempt to gain sympathy or publicity, or both. Again, much later, we have discovered that Hawthorn's physical ills were serious and he didn't do himself much good by his heavy drinking. Enzo Ferrari had announced that Hawthorn would be in the 1955 team but Hawthorn had made it known that he would have preferred to drive for a British team. This was not so much for 'patriotic' reasons as was Stirling Moss' motivation but primarily because he had responsibilities for the family garage business after the sudden death of Mike's father.

The racing career - The Grand Prix driver 1952-1955

Then, in the second week in January, the motoring and general press came out and announced that Mike Hawthorn had signed to drive for Tony Vandervell. *Autosport* made quite a fuss of this with an editorial and in a small note on the news page said that Peter Collins would be joining Hawthorn. The story behind the news was much more complex.

Tony Vandervell

Hawthorn was happy to sign for Vandervell as it meant he could stop living in Italy which he disliked and getting a Jaguar sports car drive also suited him and his programme for 1955. Tony Vandervell, to his own surprise, found it a much more difficult process to sign up Peter Collins. The reasons behind this remain very much uncertain and many people who knew Peter Collins made reasonable guesses. Collins never told anyone what his thoughts were when Vandervell asked him to drive the Vanwall. There was a long period between November and virtually the start of the 1955 season when Peter Collins remained out of touch, did not seem able to make up his mind or was saying he was just about to make up his mind. Several reasons for the delay were put forward such as contract conflicts with various trade organisations including fuel suppliers. Those who knew Collins well, including Neville Hay but also author Chris Nixon, felt that Collins was concerned about his status in the Vanwall team. His first contacts with Tony Vandervell had been cordial and promising and Collins is very likely to have assumed that Hawthorn was going elsewhere and he would have unquestioned number one position in the team. With the announcement that Hawthorn had been signed, this was all in doubt. The notion that Collins and Hawthorn were great friends did not apply to that period, as they had relatively little contact with each other. Even as late as March 1955, there were reports that Collins would be in the Vanwall at Pau. It remains unclear as to whether Collins ever contacted Vandervell to say what his plans were and that was in the character of Peter Collins to get into positions like that. Vandervell then had to hunt round for another driver when it was clear he wasn't going to get Collins and attempted to sign Robert Manzon, who had just signed for Gordini.

Peter Collins appeared in the *Autosport* portrait gallery on January 14, with his formal portrait done by the renowned Patrick Benjafield. The profile included the comment that Collins was not an up and coming driver but that he had very much arrived and his performance in the Thin Wall Special and the Vanwall in 1954 was the convincing evidence. For the second time, he was being mentioned as a very likely World Championship contender.

That same issue included mention of the number of racing drivers taking part in the upcoming Monte Carlo Rally. In addition to Collins in an Aston Martin, there were Ken Wharton and Willi Daetwyler (Daimler), John Claes and Reg Parnell (Aston Martin) and Cliff Davis (M.G.).

Collins on the way to victory in his first race for BRM, driving the V16 at the Goodwood Easter meeting where he won. Photo - AP

There was a short five-lap race for sports cars over 2 litres and this was clearly the province of Roy Salvadori in the works DB3S after Mike Sparken was given a 15 second penalty for a jumped start. The same happened to Duncan Hamilton and there was some feeling that the officials were being overly harsh. Collins and Rolt were having a thrilling nose to tail fight and Collins was again driving his own DB3S in this race.

Salvadori won the main Richmond Trophy race in the Maserati, a race where two Vanwalls had been entered, one for Hawthorn but neither appeared. The final event was the 5 lap Easter Handicap with slower cars getting a start according to earlier performance. Bob Gerard's Cooper-Bristol won this interesting contest but the day would be remembered for Peter Collins and the BRM which set off well behind the others and made it up to 5th at the end, setting the fastest ever lap at Goodwood by a BRM. Many people thought those last few laps were worth the price of admission.

Roy Salvadori, talking later about his own DB3S, said he preferred the DB3S with disc brakes which he felt were much better than drums for long distance races. He recalled that Peter Collins liked his with drum brakes and would convert a car back to drums for at least one race in 1956. Roy had done much of the testing on the DB3S over the winter, especially at times when Reg Parnell and

The racing career - The Grand Prix driver 1952-1955

This is Peter Collins' own Aston Martin DB3S which he ran in the sports car race at Goodwood and finished 5th. Photo - Ferret Fotographics

Collins were not available.

May 1 - Mille Miglia

When the press announcement came out detailing entries for the Mille Miglia, it pointed out that Collins would be driving a DB3S *with disc brakes* indicating that there must have been some discussion of the arguments over which was the best braking system. Paul Frere and Tommy Wisdom would be driving production DB2/4 saloons from the works.

The 1955 Mille Miglia pushed Stirling Moss into the category of legend, without a doubt. Mercedes finished five cars in the top ten and almost had the top three. Moss with Denis Jenkinson carved their way into history, leaving Fangio in second. Karl Kling was in fine form until he crashed and the Ferrari couldn't match Moss and Mercedes...simple as that.

The two Aston DB2/4s went out with clutch trouble and the much-vaunted Collins retired when the Aston engine let him down. Collins had had a puncture and in his haste to make up time, he overdid it and blew the engine. However, his Mille Miglia was more interesting than these bare facts indicate. Peter Miller, then working as John Wyer's assistant, kept a careful record of the event. He recalls arriving at Count Maggi's ancestral home at Calino near Brescia where the Aston team was based. Miller, Paul Frere, Tommy Wisdom and Peter Collins were among the first of many arrivals and were sitting at one of the tables in the large panelled dining room as a continuous supply of food appeared. Miller shared a room with Collins and they each had an ancient four-poster bed.

All about the boy!

Peter Collins in the DB3S which retired with a blown engine near Senigallia; it is seen here near the beginning of the Mille Miglia. Photo - Publifoto

Collins was up to his usual tricks, including waiting for Ron Flockhart to go take his bath and then rushing in, locking the door and stealing Ron's turn in the bath.

Miller provided some interesting insights into how Aston Martin tackled both the training and the Mille Miglia race itself. They would send, for example, Frere and Wisdom off in a lightweight DB2 training car, learning a third of the circuit in one day. Then Peter Collins, driving alone this year, would go and do the same route in a similar car on the next day, so the drivers were not on the same section at the same time. Then they swapped and Frere went off alone and Wisdom went with Collins.

Miller then drove the team's service vehicle, a Lagonda estate, towards Pescara with George Eyston. They broke down, to the amusement of Collins when Miller phoned him, as Collins had had the same experience. Peter, however, knew that the Lagonda had the same axle as that from a Jeep and thus Miller was able to get the car repaired.

Miller then went to set up the service point, once the event started, at Pescara and waited for the three crews which he expected to arrive in around four hours after the start. Collins, with number 702, was due in in 3 hours and 58 minutes by Aston reckoning but none of the cars appeared, all having encountered problems. Collins had a rear tyre break up at high speed and a large piece of rubber bounced off his helmet. Collins said he had spun five times down the road between the trees. He managed to bend the damaged bodywork back and changed the tyre. Soon after he set off there was a "big bang" and the engine seized. It turned out that the tyres had been running at a dangerously low pressure setting...28 lbs. instead of 45! (Miller, 1962).

The racing career - The Grand Prix driver 1952-1955

May 7 - Silverstone International Trophy

The Silverstone International Trophy meeting has always been a special event on the British racing calendar and it was more so this year as the British Grand Prix was moving to Aintree and that left only this one major meeting at the Northamptonshire circuit. It looked like the promised Vanwalls would finally make an appearance for Mike Hawthorn and Ken Wharton...and Peter Collins was definitely not in the team. He was indeed entered by the Owen Organisation but he was not driving a BRM because BRM didn't have a Grand Prix car for the 2.5litre formula...yet. What he did have was the Owen Organisation's Maserati 250F, chassis 2509.

It would be very easy to get side-tracked by the tale of Maserati 250Fs in the British manufacturers' teams. Vandervell also had a 250F though his was used entirely for study purposes and was not raced in period. BRM used their car in 1954 and 1955 because it was useful to study and because they wanted to race and didn't have a car. In those days it just wasn't that unusual though it is unthinkable now...unless you start to wonder how a Stewart turned into a Jaguar, a Jordan into a whatever it is this weekend, etc. What was significant was that this 250F was Peter Collins' Grand Prix ride for a good part of the season. The press preview the week before the race had only listed an Owen entry, not naming the car nor the driver, so it would seem that Collins' final deal with BRM came very late in the day.

The programme was an ambitious one. The sports car race looked to be a fight between Jaguar and Aston Martin and that alone would draw in a large crowd. While Hawthorn held pole position, he did not make the best of the Le Mans start in the D-Type and Parnell and Collins were initially 3rd and 4th, though Hawthorn got past them. There was a lot of shuffling round in the early laps and Wharton's

Peter Collins in the early stages of the race at Silverstone with the Owen Organisation Maserati 250F. Photo - Anthony Pritchard/T.C.March Collection

131

All about the boy!

DB3S stopped in the pits. Collins had dropped back several places but it was Parnell doing the hard work joined by Salvadori. They kept the pressure on Hawthorn until his radiator hose blew off and the Astons looked superior to the Jaguars on handling. Collins finished 7th overall with new team mate Peter Walker 8th.

Collins was driving his own car in this race, loaned back to the works team to be run under their umbrella. Salvadori, though he had his own car, was in a works machine. The Salvadori and Parnell cars were new, having been built up from the wreckage of the Le Mans coupes. Salvadori's car was on loan so that Peter Walker could drive it.

This was one of those meetings where some drivers were doing several races and Hawthorn, Wharton and Titterington seemed to be doing them all.

Hawthorn had put the new Vanwall on the front row of the grid for the International Trophy race for F1 cars, setting the same time as Roy Salvadori in the British-prepared Gilby 250F. Moss was up front with his own 250F and Fairman put the new Connaught up there as well. While Ken Wharton had the other new Vanwall back on row three, Collins had the Owen Maserati on the second row and the leading cars were all very close on time. This was a sixty lap race and it was Salvadori who took off first with Collins right on his tail. Roy led for some 25 laps as all the others struggled to keep up, Moss retiring on lap 10, Hawthorn in the Vanwall on lap 16 and Ken Wharton having a fiery crash on lap 22. Collins got past

Collins taking a very impressive win in the International Trophy race. Photo - Anthony Pritchard/T.C.March Collection

The racing career - The Grand Prix driver 1952-1955

and the next ten laps saw them swap back and forth every lap. Then Collins, now well settled into the well balanced Maserati started to ease away, finishing 39 seconds ahead of Salvadori. For Collins it was a major win in front of the 'home crowd' and did him a lot of good with his new team. Collins and Salvadori shared fastest lap of the race.

Several timely announcements were made over the next few weeks, one being that Collins would be driving a DB3S at Davidstow on the Whit weekend and was also confirmed as an Aston team driver for Le Mans, as was new man C.A.S. Brooks...who would soon be earning a name for himself. The Owen Organisation was being optimistic about the development of their new 2.5litre car. Progress had been delayed as designer Peter Berthon had had a very serious road accident. In the meantime, they would be running the Maserati 250F at several races. Within a few days it emerged that Collins would not after all be at Davidstow but would go to Crystal Palace with the Maserati and an Aston Martin. On May 22, one Vanwall went to Monaco for the Grand Prix which saw Alberto Ascari's famous plunge into the harbour. Motor racing was struck a blow a few days later when the Italian was killed at Monza in an inexplicable practice accident and one of the great but unassuming drivers of the era had gone.

May 28 - West Essex Car Club Snetterton

Just before the Snetterton race, the David Brown Automobiles Division who ran the Aston Martin racing effort announced that they had released Collins to be able to drive for the Owen Organisation in 'selected Formula 1 and Formula Libre events' during the remainder of 1955. It was indicated in the announcement that both teams wished to provide Collins with as much racing experience as possible. Presumably this agreement must have been reached before the International Trophy as Collins had already raced for the Owen team. It is also interesting that it at least implies the Aston Martin contract was exclusive, though Collins could only be racing sports cars for them.

No sooner had the announcement been made public than Collins was out at Snetterton duly driving for the Owen team. He was at the West Essex Car Club meeting to take part in the race for large sports cars and an expected duel between himself, Salvadori and Archie Scott-Brown. Roy could not start and Scott-Brown in the Lister Bristol more or less disappeared. Collins, in his own DB3S, could do little about his opponent and had to settle for second.

Salvadori won the F1 race but didn't look likely to challenge the Collins and Flockhart BRMs in the Libre race. Collins did fly into the lead and set a new Snetterton lap record. On lap seven he came up to lap Cunningham-Reid's Lister at the hairpin and the Lister moved over on him, touching wheels and inflicting a puncture on the BRM. Collins had a spin and was out and Roy came through to win as he had passed the not quite on-form Flockhart BRM.

May 30 - Crystal Palace Whit Monday

Quite a few of the cars which had been at Snetterton were to be found two days later in South London at the 'Palace'. While Salvadori had a grand day in Norfolk, things didn't go quite so well in London. He spun in the sports car race and the Gilby Maserati was showing signs of tiredness in the two-heat Formula Libre race. Roy has admitted that he had sometimes discounted Peter Collins' ability and had done so at the Silverstone meeting. It looked to be happening again, though perhaps the car was just not up to it this time. Collins was on pole for the first

All about the boy!

of the two heats and flashed away with Roy trying to keep him in sight. He dropped eight seconds behind the Owen Maserati to finish second to Collins who set fastest lap. This was all repeated in the second heat but this time Roy's engine let go and Bob Gerard took up the chase. Collins again set the fastest lap and won on the aggregate of the results of both heats. So now he had become a multiple winner in a Maserati 250F!

June 11/12 - Le Mans 24 Hours

Le Mans previews had announced the Aston Martin team as Collins, Salvadori and Peter Walker, with 'new boys' Tony Brooks and John Riseley-Pritchard also in DB3S and Parnell and Poore in the V-12 Lagonda which had been revised since last year.

The Astons being prepared for Le Mans.
Photo - Michael Green Collection

The racing career - The Grand Prix driver 1952-1955

The 1955 race was totally overshadowed by the huge accident involving the Mercedes of Levegh which catapulted into the crowd on the main straight. This accident had long term effects on motor racing in general and led to prolonged and difficult issues for the drivers involved, especially Hawthorn.

Practice was characterised by a lot of strategic foot-lifting so that teams would not give away their potential. It was clear that the Ferrari 4.4s, Mercedes, Jaguar D-Types and the Astons would all be very much in the hunt. A huge crowd appeared for the Saturday start and it was Roy Salvadori's DB3S which seemed to be making up the

well up the field.

Collins moved to the front of this trio after only a few laps and the Mercedes juggernaut started carving its way towards the front. Eventually Fangio caught Hawthorn and they both caught and passed Castellotti and one of the great all-time races in an endurance event took place, with Hawthorn and Fangio swapping the lead and the D-Type touching 280kph on the Mulsanne Straight. At two hours Parnell had got the Lagonda into 12th but the Feltham team seemed to be pacing itself, working rigidly to John Wyer's team orders and discipline. They couldn't have touched the leaders on speed so they had to hope for reliability.

Collins chases Roy Salvadori through the Le Mans Esses...they had some interesting moments. Photo - Anthony Pritchard/T.C.March Collection

most places, though Castellotti had the Ferrari in front as they all went up the hill and out towards the Esses. Ferraris led the first lap, then came a pack of Jaguars and the Mercedes team were all taking it very easily. The Astons were in the order Salvadori and Collins with Parnell's Lagonda between them and they were

The Levegh crash came at two and a half hours into the race and Mercedes did their driver changes and made consultations with Germany about withdrawal, a procedure which took many hours. At three hours Parnell/Poore were 9th, Salvadori/Peter Walker 10th and Collins/Frere 11th. Ivor Bueb took over the D-Type

All about the boy!

Early in the race, Peter Collins does his best to hang onto the tail of the ill-fated Mercedes of Pierre Levegh. Photo - LAT

The continuing battle between the Salvadori/Walker DB3S and Collins/Frere until the former retired. Photo - Ferret Fotographics

from a shaken Hawthorn and Moss relieved Fangio and Bueb managed to keep the Jaguar right with Moss in the Mercedes.

Darkness arrived and Collins was back in the car for his second stint and gaining ground on the Belgian D-Type. The Lagonda had dropped back but with Dennis Poore behind the wheel it was beginning to move forward again. The Castellotti Ferrari had long since disappeared and at quarter distance, 17 cars were out and Fangio/Moss had a two lap lead on Hawthorn/Bueb. Peter Collins then got past Swaters and Claes into seventh. The Brooks/Riseley-Pritchard DB3S then went out with a flat battery, without having made a significant impression, though Tony Brooks would soon be having an impact on the team. Then the Lagonda stopped and before halfway, Salvadori/Walker retired their DB3S so the pressure was now on Collins and Frere. Fangio had been timed down the Mulsanne at 181 mph, more than 25 mph faster than the Collins Aston. Anthony Pritchard reminded the author of the Aston battle than had gone on out of John Wyer's sight, which Pritchard had recounted in his book on Astons:

"For much of the early part of the race Collins

The racing career - The Grand Prix driver 1952-1955

and Salvadori (at the wheel of DB3S/7) enjoyed a furious dice all around the circuit out of sight of Wyer. Even after Levegh's crash these two drivers still battled furiously and full of fun when Salvadori spun, Collins waited for him to catch up - but then slowing off in accordance with Wyer's instructions to pass the pits at 50 mph." (Pritchard, 1991, p.58).

With the last works Ferrari gone, Collins/Frere were third at 4.0 0 am, as all the Mercedes cars were withdrawn on orders from Germany. Much of the fascination left with the team, though Hawthorn and Bueb were still a good five laps ahead of the second car.

Some six hours later, more cars had disappeared and Hawthorn was driving steadily, three laps in front of the Maserati of Musso and Valenzano but Collins was now on the same lap and the Maserati didn't sound good at all. One of the Porsches was leading on Index but the DB3S was second. An hour later and the Maserati pitted and never came out. The Aston was second, it was raining hard, the place was unpleasant and British cars finished in the top three spots. Frere was driving the Aston at the finish and he and Collins had done a mighty job for Aston Martin.

Prior to the Le Mans race, Aston's Peter Miller was involved in something that became known as Peter Collins' 'bucket and spade' routine.

Miller was staying with John Wyer, Roy Salvadori and Collins at the Ship Hotel in Brighton the night before the departure to France for the 24 Hours. On arrival, an exuberant Collins ran up and down the front shouting to Miller 'Have you got your bucket, Pete?' Miller replied 'Yes, have you got your spade?' In France Miller bought Collins a child's bucket and spade and Collins brought it to many races with him after that, right up to the time of his death according to Miller.

In the weeks after Le Mans, the press was full of related news, much of it concerning the cancellation of a large number of events, including the French Grand Prix and virtually everything in Switzerland. The latter was somewhat strange as Swiss citizens had been killed at several races at Bremgarten which was a highly dangerous and badly managed circuit, yet it took a French disaster for the Swiss to act.

In the midst of this, almost unnoticed, Mike Hawthorn had handed in his notice to Tony Vandervell, as Hawthorn was said to be very tired of the experience of either breakage or the car not showing up. He said he would 'free-lance' though the odds were that Ferrari would pick him up pretty quickly. They did.

In the days before Aintree, Peter Collins went over to Alcester Prep School for Speech Day after having lunch with Raymond Mays. They both made school officials happy as they mixed during the day with the boys and their parents and the school was impressed by how seriously Collins treated his relationship with them.

July 16 - British Grand Prix - Aintree

It must have struck Mike Hawthorn that having left Vanwall to go back to driving for Ferrari that he was now two rows behind Harry Schell in the Vanwall and Wharton in Mr. Vandervell's other car was just behind him. Whatever he thought, he must have been a lot happier than Peter Collins was. He had problems all through practice and was having difficulty making the Owen Maserati half competitive never mind a possible top finisher.

Before the Grand Prix came the sports car race and that was a shock for many, including Hawthorn. In the early laps of this 17 lap race,

137

The Aston Martin DB3S team was dominant in the sports car race at Aintree.
Photo - Ferret Fotographics

Peter Collins was second behind Salvadori and all the Astons beat Hawthorn's D-Type.
Photo - Anthony Pritchard/T.C.March Collection

Collins had a troubled practice in the Owen Maserati but went well in the race until the clutch gave up. Photo - Anthony Pritchard/T.C.March Collection

not one, not two but all four Aston DB3S cars got past the D-Type. Roy Salvadori was in superb form and led to the end. Collins moved in behind him in second and Parnell and Walker followed in 3rd and 4th, with Hawthorn 5th.

In the Grand Prix, with a magnificent field and all of the north of England there to watch, the silver might of Mercedes with Fangio, Moss, Kling and Taruffi streaked ahead, with only Behra's Maserati getting amongst them. Whatever had plagued Collins in practice seemed to be sorted as he took the Owen 250F up eight places on the first lap. Moss moved in front of Fangio and at ten laps Collins had gotten up to 8th and Behra was gone. Collins then fought his way past Hawthorn on lap 13 into seventh. Harry Schell also got by and was

John Wyer with Brian Turle of Shell Oil at the Grand Prix meeting. Photo - Cinelli

All about the boy!

setting out after Collins but the Vanwall expired when the throttle pedal fell apart. After an hour's racing Collins was closing on Musso and Taruffi and was about to go past when the 250F headed for the pits, its clutch having given up. This was probably one of Peter Collins' very best performances as he had mastered the 250F after only a few races with it.

August 7 - Swedish Sports Car Grand Prix

A strong sports car contingent travelled all the way to the Rabelov circuit near Kristianstad in Sweden. The Mercedes 300 SLRs for Fangio and Moss helped to bring out 75,000 spectators. Peter Collins had been going well in practice but a connecting rod broke with dire consequences and he had to sit it out as Fangio, Moss, Castellotti and Behra fought for 32 laps. Rumours were meanwhile circulating that Collins was going to appear in the Italian Grand Prix at Monza in a works 250F. As he was about to debut the new BRM, it wasn't clear at this stage how the rumour, which turned out to be accurate, had got started. Collins and Salvadori had brought their own drum-brake cars to this race as the works cars were being made ready for Goodwood.

August 13 - Snetterton Redex Trophy Meeting

While the Formula 1 race for the Redex Trophy was the main event at a wet Snetterton track, Peter Collins was a non-starter as the rebuild of the Maserati 250F hadn't been completed by the Owen Organisation, which was also working on the new BRM at the same time. The F1 race saw the two Vanwalls of Schell and Wharton finally beat some strong opposition, making Tony Vandervell very happy.

In the later Formula Libre race, Collins and Flockhart were out in the MKII BRMs and Collins was away first, the BRM engine screaming across the Norfolk countryside. But then the scream stopped before the cars got round at the end of the first lap and Collins was on the sidelines and Peter Walker's Connaught took a fine win.

Collins was then out again in Raymond May's personal car, a Ford Zephyr which had been entered in the saloon car race made up of four classes. The Zephyrs had been widely criticised for their handling but Collins proved that the car could be driven quickly. He managed to win his class comfortably, with few people realising that Collins had the advantage of practicing with customer cars from his father's Kidderminster Motors Ford garage...not that many of the customers knew either!

August 20 - Goodwood Nine Hours

Pre-event publicity was putting pressure on Aston Martin to reproduce their wins from the previous two years and they certainly seemed to have the means to do it. Parnell, Collins, Salvadori, Poore and Walker would be joined by Aston 'new boy' Tony Brooks. There would be no works Jaguars but plenty of privateers and Mike Hawthorn was in a Ferrari Monza with Fon Portago, an interesting combination.

When practice started on Thursday night, there was much more Jaguar works involvement than anticipated and Mike Hawthorn looked set to keep all the Brits on their toes. Hawthorn was quickest in both night and day sessions and Dennis Poore put in the best Aston time. Also quick were Salvadori and Tony Brooks who was co-driver to Collins. Stirling Moss was sharing a 550 Porsche in the smaller class but was not that much slower than the bigger machinery.

The racing career - The Grand Prix driver 1952-1955

There was the usual sprint during the Le Mans start at 3.00 pm on Saturday afternoon and although Les Leston had his sports Connaught moving first, Hawthorn was in front by Madgwick Corner. Moss stalled the Porsche and there was a lot of barging but they all managed to get away. The Ferrari led three Astons but within only a few minutes Reg Parnell came flying into the pits and discovered one of the wheel hubs had failed, which was a real blow to Aston hopes at this early stage. Meanwhile, Collins had disposed of team mate Peter Walker and moved up into second. When Hawthorn came in on lap 17 not being able to select any gears, Collins and Walker now led from an Ecurie Ecosse Jaguar. Hawthorn lost seven laps and Peter Collins was in command, though not by much. Fuel stops and driver changes started just after the first hour. Collins had all four wheels changed and Tony Brooks took over. Tyre wear was high and John Wyer had installed a small 'radio station' at the chicane so one of the team could keep watch over the tyre wear!

Brooks held the lead while the Walker/Poore car dropped to 6th and there was a struggle for the 1500 c.c. class between Moss' Porsche and one Colin Chapman in his Lotus. At three hours, Collins took over again but lost over three minutes in the stop and Titterington's Jaguar got a lap's lead, while Peter Walker moved the other DB3S back up to third. When Sanderson took over in the Jaguar it dropped back behind Collins. As darkness came, Hawthorn was the fastest car on the circuit, setting a new record two seconds quicker than his practice time but he was continually trying to make up lost ground from the Ferrari's long stops. Collins and Brooks kept up a high average and held onto the lead. Hawthorn was threatening Titterington for third but after six and a half hours the Ferrari's axle broke and he and Portago were out.

Then the leading Aston came in, the engine not running cleanly and there was some ignition problem that the Wyer team struggled to locate. Dennis Poore wanted to come in and change tyres but John Wyer waved him on. After the final stops, Walker and Poore led but had no second gear and the Ecurie Ecosse Jaguar of Sanderson/Titterington was catching them, while Collins/Brooks had dropped to third after leading most of the race. The winning Aston had done 309 laps, the Jaguar 308 and Collins/Brooks 305. During practice, John Wyer had calculated that a DB3S would do the race in 309 laps in nine hours one minute and 3.6 seconds. He was out by 18.6 seconds! Later inspection would reveal that Collins and Brooks lost the lead because the under bonnet lamp had a loose wire which was causing an irregular short circuit!

The Goodwood race was an occasion when Tony Brooks' attitude towards racing had something of an impact on Collins. On more than one occasion, Brooks would say 'I'm having an early night' and Collins would agree and go off for a decent night's sleep as well. Chris Nixon quoted Brooks on his view of Peter Collins:

"To me he epitomized what every 'Boys' Book of Motor Racing' pictured a racing driver to be. I never had any problems with Peter, never a cross word - it was a very genial relationship. We were quite often roommates and I thoroughly enjoyed his company. His attitude was not professional in the way that Stirling's was - he didn't eat, sleep and drink motor racing - but it was very much his life and he got a great kick out of it." (Nixon, 1991, p.154).

All about the boy!

August 20 - Oulton Park Daily Herald International

Although the Goodwood race was a major event, it was followed only a few days later by yet another significant race for sports cars, the Daily Herald International Trophy at Oulton Park in Cheshire. As this was an 80 lap race and would be run pretty much as a sprint, it looked like Hawthorn might make up for his problems down in Sussex and win. He set a new record and was on pole from Salvadori who was driving his own drum-braked car entered by Gilby Engineering and Reg Parnell was 3rd quickest in the only works Aston entered, this being the disc-brake car which was the spare at Goodwood. Masten Gregory was also in a Ferrari and that quartet made up the front row. Peter Collins was in his own DB3S with drum brakes with the Ferrari of Rosier beside him and then Peter Whitehead's Cooper-Jaguar. Both Salvadori and Collins, though entering their own cars, were getting works support at Oulton.

Parnell was more nimble than usual and got to his car first in the Le Mans start and led Gregory, Salvadori and then Hawthorn, while Moss in the Connaught, starting from the back of the grid, had passed over a dozen cars. Parnell came through next but Collins had sliced through the front row cars to pull in behind him in second and it looked like Astons might be having another good day. Roy lost 3rd gear and dropped back while Moss quickly got up to 9th overall. By lap 20, Hawthorn had squeezed past Collins and a lap later Masten Gregory did the same thing. After following Gregory at a reasonable and conservative pace, Collins retook 3rd on lap 33 so it was Parnell, Hawthorn, Collins, Gregory and Schell in the H.W.M. Reg went on to win, driving at his very best and Hawthorn could not get near him. Collins in his own car was a very good third, while Moss got to 7th and won the 1500 c.c. class. John Wyer was very happy.

September 3 - Aintree Daily Telegraph Trophy

For Peter Collins, the race at Aintree was to be the fifth of nine consecutive racing weekends and it was also to be a substantial anti-climax.

The new BRM, which people had known about generally but the details of which had been kept fairly secret, was announced as making its debut at this race with Collins behind the wheel. The car was unveiled to the press the week before Aintree and that was done in a low-key manner, so as not to repeat the setting up of great expectations as had happened with the V-16. It was made clear that the new 2.5litre car was running very much on an experimental basis for a few races and the engine still needed more development. Since the Owen Organisation had been running a 250F Maserati, many had expected the new BRM would be quite similar, though that was far from the truth. The engine was a very shallow four cylinder d.o.h.c. unit which sat very low in the chassis and allowed for a steeply raked front. It thus had a modern look and appeared to have been very well thought out. Peter Collins, it turned out, had done a lot of testing which had also been kept secret. Collins was quoted as saying: "...the power comes in everywhere, just where it's wanted and up to 120mph. It's quicker than the 1 1/2 litre blown V-16!" (*Autosport*, Sept.2, 1955, p.278).

Some people though that Collins was exaggerating the claim but in fact the torque from the new car was tremendous and the four-cylinder could produce very considerable power.

The cars came out for practice on Friday and

The racing career – The Grand Prix driver 1952-1955

Collins immediately turned in a respectable time but then an oil pipe came apart and oil sprayed everywhere including onto the rear wheels of the BRM. Collins was approaching Melling Crossing at the time and it slid wildly through a wooden fence, severely damaging the front end. Collins was shaken but not injured but BRM had made another rather inauspicious debut. Collins had found himself in a potentially very promising F1 seat and it was suddenly looking ominously like BRM might repeat the past.

Nevertheless, Collins was also down to drive in the Formula Libre race in the BRM MkII V-16. After Salvadori had unexpectedly won the F1 race on the last lap after Parnell's leading Connaught had faltered and died, there was a superb sports car race, with the Libre event last.

Collins raised the revs, dropped the clutch and was gone, Bob Gerard's Cooper trying to find its way through the haze with Salvadori next. Roy fell off and stalled at Melling and dropped to ninth though he started making up places very quickly. Collins in the BRM was a fantastic sight and sound experience for all, though of course most people knew that the car could go silent very quickly. It didn't this time and Collins went faster and faster, set the fastest time of the day and was a deserving winner. Salvadori fought back to 2nd after Gerard retired so Tony Brooks was 3rd in an A-Type Connaught.

September 11 - Italian Grand Prix

The Italian Grand Prix was in many ways an historically important race and Fangio put in a fine performance but it wasn't terribly exciting. It was important because Mercedes Benz had announced it was their last Grand Prix and because Lancia, after their huge financial disaster and the death of Ascari, had handed their cars over to Ferrari. However, Ferrari had not managed to sort out the tyre squabbles as the D-50s were using different rubber than that for which Ferrari was contracted, so they didn't appear. Castellotti was then in a works Ferrari Super Squalo with which he did a tremendous job. Collins put the works four-speed 250F Maserati in midfield while Horace Gould in a similar car was right at the back. The Vanwalls made an early departure and Collins went well until the gearbox broke on lap 22. Moss set fastest lap and retired on lap 27 when the Mercedes engine gave up, a rare occurrence and Fangio won from Taruffi's Mercedes and Castellotti.

Some accounts have this as an occasion of a rift between Aston Martin, John Wyer, David Brown and Peter Collins. Collins was invited to have a drive in the factory 250F and he was desperate to do this. He had thus gone to John Wyer who had indicated he wasn't happy about it and the Aston company lawyers said David Brown could 'slap a writ' on him preventing him from driving. Nevertheless, Peter decided he would do it and Astons were not about to take legal action. Reg Parnell went to Peter to wind him up, saying Wyer and Brown had arrived with the writ and he was in deep trouble, etc. etc!

Collins went straight to David Brown and John Wyer and they said, actually, they were there to see him race. John Wyer later told the author he remembered that because when the same thing happened with Pedro Rodriguez in 1971, he knew he should be saying "No". Well, Pedro like Peter was a racer and John Wyer found it very hard to stop a racer from racing. Wyer admitted he always regretted not stopping Pedro, because he was killed at the race at the Norisring while leading.

Peter Miller tells the story, repeated by Nixon, that John Wyer had dropped Collins from the Tourist Trophy team, seemingly as a

All about the boy!

punishment for going against orders. Carroll Shelby was going to take his place. All this was odd because it was to save Collins for the Tourist Trophy that Wyer didn't want him at Monza. When Peter showed up in Belfast as happy as could be, it struck some as a surprise. It seems likely that Wyer had to appear to be disciplining his awkward driver but the author believes that Wyer had probably convinced Collins he needed to play along with this so it looked like he had done the right thing.

September 17 - Dundrod Tourist Trophy

Mercedes may have departed Grand Prix racing at Monza but at the time it seemed as if the company would at least continue in sports car racing. This was confusing for those who thought Mercedes' departure had been triggered by the Le Mans accident...but that was a sports car race. Oh well, what did it matter as long as they continued. How final the decision to quit altogether was at that stage remains uncertain, though later it became clearer that those decisions were made entirely on commercial grounds, as Mercedes felt they had gotten what they wanted out of motor racing...for the time.

For drivers, the significance of this was who would manage to find what to drive for 1956 and the phone lines, as we will see, were very busy during this period.

Mercedes brought three cars and spares for the TT at Dundrod, while Aston had the same line-up as at Goodwood and there was only one works D-Type for Hawthorn and Titterington, with some supporting private Jaguars.

Dundrod always was an immensely dangerous circuit, being narrow, bumpy, slippery and lined with things to hit. The organisers went to a lot of trouble to make the unsafe safe for spectators. It was safer but the public were still very much at risk. What they couldn't do was make Dundrod safe for the drivers and three British amateur drivers paid the price in two separate accidents, one a serious multiple shunt. But those were the later days of open road racing. The Carrera PanAmericana was to go, the Mille Miglia would last only two more years and motor racing would experience a real change as a result. While there were drivers like Roy Salvadori who openly admitted his serious dislike of Dundrod, others said little and some still enjoyed it. For people like Hawthorn and Collins, it was still the great challenge and Hawthorn demonstrated this with immense speed against the Mercedes.

Fangio, Moss, Titterington and Hawthorn were joined by Collins in the DB3S as the only drivers under five minutes, with Tony Brooks just on five minutes. Brooks was noticed to be quicker than virtually everyone else on the fastest parts of the circuit.

Bob Berry's private D-Type got away first at the Le Mans start from Hawthorn and Moss, while Peter Collins and one of the Maseratis took ages to start and got away last of all. Berry was out on the second lap with a punctured tyre and Moss was out in front. Collins and Belluci's Maserati were making rapid progress and were quickly up to 12th and 18th places. As the cars came round for the 3rd lap, it was noticed that six cars were missing and a plume of smoke in the distance told a sad tale. Mayer's Cooper had gone off the road and hit the concrete road markers at Cochranstown, markers that other drivers had warned the organisers about. Several others crashed into the wreckage leaving Mayer and Bill Smith dead and others injured. Peter Collins had been flying and by the eighth lap he had moved all the way up to sixth place. Moss established a good lead on Hawthorn who had Fangio nipping at his hind quarters and all the attention

144

The racing career - The Grand Prix driver 1952-1955

was on that pair. Collins got past Behra's Maserati into 5th. The von Trips/Simon Mercedes was acting as a back-up for Moss and Fangio should anything go wrong there but they hadn't reckoned on Collins being faster than this pair as he hung onto the tail of von Trips.

When Moss pitted to hand over to John Fitch, Collins caught von Trips and set a lap time some ten seconds faster than his practice time. Titterington had taken over the Jaguar and was now leading Fitch and then Collins went past Fangio's co-driver Kling into 3rd. This was getting to be embarrassing to Mercedes. It is not unlikely that Collins was thinking about a Mercedes drive if the company was going to continue in sports cars. Unfortunately, when Collins came in two laps later, there was oil soaking the distributor and the team lost five minutes working on it. Brooks went out with the engine misfiring and was back in within two laps to finally retire after a great performance by Collins. A con rod bolt was found to have broken.

After 84 laps, much of it in pouring rain, Moss had established himself as a fine wet weather driver and won from Fangio as Hawthorn dropped out just before the end. Walker/Poore were 4th in the DB3S and Parnell/Salvadori were 7th. Salvadori later would acknowledge that the Collins/Brooks Aston was the team's only real hope for a good result on this dreaded circuit.

September 24 - Oulton Park Gold Cup

The teams and drivers left a soggy and rather sad Dundrod back to go back to England for a day's rest and the F1 crowd headed to Oulton Park for its premier event of the season, the Gold Cup. If you read *Autosport* the week after the Oulton race you would have thought BRM had won the World Championship, such was their praise for the team. There was even an announcement that BRM would run three cars in 1956 and the rumour was that Collins and Moss would be in the team. It was a rumour!

To be fair, the BRM mechanics were very deserving of praise as they set to work after practice to repair a very damaged engine and worked through the night. The BRM's handling in the hands of Peter Collins was very positive but the overall impression was not outstanding. That was largely because the engine problems intervened followed by a broken prop shaft. All of this had followed 140 laps of testing before official practice so the car had already had a severe work-out. This meant Collins was only on the 4th row of the grid, seven seconds slower than Hawthorn. Hawthorn was in one of the Ferrari team's 'new' Lancia D-50s, its first appearance in the UK, Castellotti was in the other one. Desmond Titterington was making an F1 debut in the Vanwall as Wharton had been injured again, at the TT and Harry Schell was in the other green machine for Tony Vandervell. Fangio had been offered the Vanwall as had Farina but they declined.

Moss led the race which would be 55 laps of the sweeping Cheshire circuit but the surprise was coming from the middle of the grid. Collins had started on row 4 with twelve cars in front of him. The BRM was now sounding healthy and on the first lap Collins got all the way up past Schell's Vanwall into 5th. On lap 3 he out-manoeuvred Castellotti into 4th and one lap later had passed Hawthorn's Lancia into third. He was now closing on Musso's Maserati for second when on the 10th lap the BRM's oil pressure disappeared and Collins was forced into the pits. The P25 had made a stunning start and showed that it had the potential to be a force in racing in 1956. However, the reality was that it was a BRM - a team fraught with difficulties and it took much longer to

All about the boy!

The first lap of the Gold Cup with Castellotti, Hawthorn, Moss, Musso and then a flying Collins back in 7th spot.

demonstrate just how good it could have been. The irony was that the oil pressure was fine but that the gauge had broken with all the vibration.

Moss went on to win from Hawthorn and a remarkable Titterington in his F1 debut was 3rd in the Vanwall.

October 1 - Castle Combe International

The BRM P25 was entered for the Avon Trophy race for Formula One cars at the Wiltshire circuit but it was down for Flockhart, not Collins, to drive. The car was then withdrawn anyway and Collins appeared in the Owen Maserati 250F for which he had been entered.

Collins, it seems, didn't manage a recorded qualifying time and was at the back of the grid. It didn't seem to matter much as he was soon up into 4th place but it was Harry Schell's day in the Vanwall which led the race from start to finish. Collins moved into second behind Schell and held that spot until the 13th lap when poor handling signalled that a de Dion tube had broken and Collins' retirement saw the end of any challenge to the Vanwall.

The night before this race, Peter Collins had had a very serious row with Raymond Mays, with whom he never seemed to feel comfortable. This was partly about the preparation of the BRM P25...or lack of it...and also something with Collins being uncomfortable with Mays. Mike Hawthorn would share this discomfort. Some people, like Tony Rudd, tended to side with Mays over this issue, seeing him as a 'real gentleman' and Collins and Hawthorn as, he called them, 'a pair of roughs'. The actual events around this row, however, remain unknown. It was to be Collins' last drive for the team.

The racing career - The Grand Prix driver 1952-1955

October 16 - Targa Florio

Ken Gregory, acting as manager for Stirling Moss and later for Collins, had been given the task of finding a co-driver for Moss and together they chose Collins, as described earlier in this book by Robert Edwards.

Peter Collins, of course, had never done the Targa Florio, so it would be a severe and realistic test of the theory that his early racing had trained him to cope well with narrow and tree and rock-lined roads His car control was already evidently skilful to a significant degree, as was his ability to learn a new course or circuit. But the Targa in a strange car would really test him as a road racer at the level of Moss.

The Mercedes team took the event very seriously and all drivers did dozens of laps in road and race cars over the 72 kilometer Madonie circuit. Moss and Collins, Fitch and Titterington and Fangio and Karl Kling were the pairings, with Hans Herrmann as back-up and relief driver. Ferraris were to be driven by Castellotti/Manzon, Maglioli/Sighinolfi, Franco Cortese, Shelby and Munaron and there were Maseratis for Luigi Musso and Gigi Villoresi and also for Musso's brother Giuseppe and for Bracco. There were a total of 47 cars to start and the entry was somewhat smaller than usual as it was late in the year, though for the first time it was a round of the World Championship, which was why Mercedes was taking it so seriously.

When the cars set off at 7.00 am at thirty second intervals, an Alfa Ti saloon was first away. The cars came past at the end of the first lap and several cars had made progress but none as much as Moss who had come round in 44 minutes, a new record and that from a standing start. Castellotti's Ferrari was next fastest so was second, with Fangio 3rd some 50 seconds further back. Moss's driving was nothing less than sensational and the reports of the event

Pre-Targa testing. Left to right: John Fitch, Stirling Moss, Hans Herrman, Peter Collins. Photo - Daimler Benz

147

All about the boy!

Above: A formal photo of the Mercedes drivers: Fitch, Titterington, Collins, Moss, Fangio and Kling. Photo - Daimler Benz

Below: Peter Collins before the start. Photo - Daimler Benz

describe it as something that Sicily had never witnessed before. He took almost a further minute off the record. *Autosport* described Castellotti as "wild", Fangio "indecisive" and Maglioli as "subdued".

After three laps the first of the pit stops began, with driver changes and Moss was suddenly overdue. He had slid on mud, missed going over a drop, hit a wall and then fell ten to twelve feet into a field. Many minutes were lost before enough spectators could be gathered to help get him back onto the road. His radiator had boiled and he had lost his helmet, which he stopped to retrieve. The mechanics set to work to check the mangled 300 SLR and Peter Collins finally set off for his stint, now not hopeful of a good position. But this was the end of 1955 and he did not have himself a drive yet for 1956. Without knowing that Mercedes were going to quit racing altogether in 1956,

The racing career - The Grand Prix driver 1952-1955

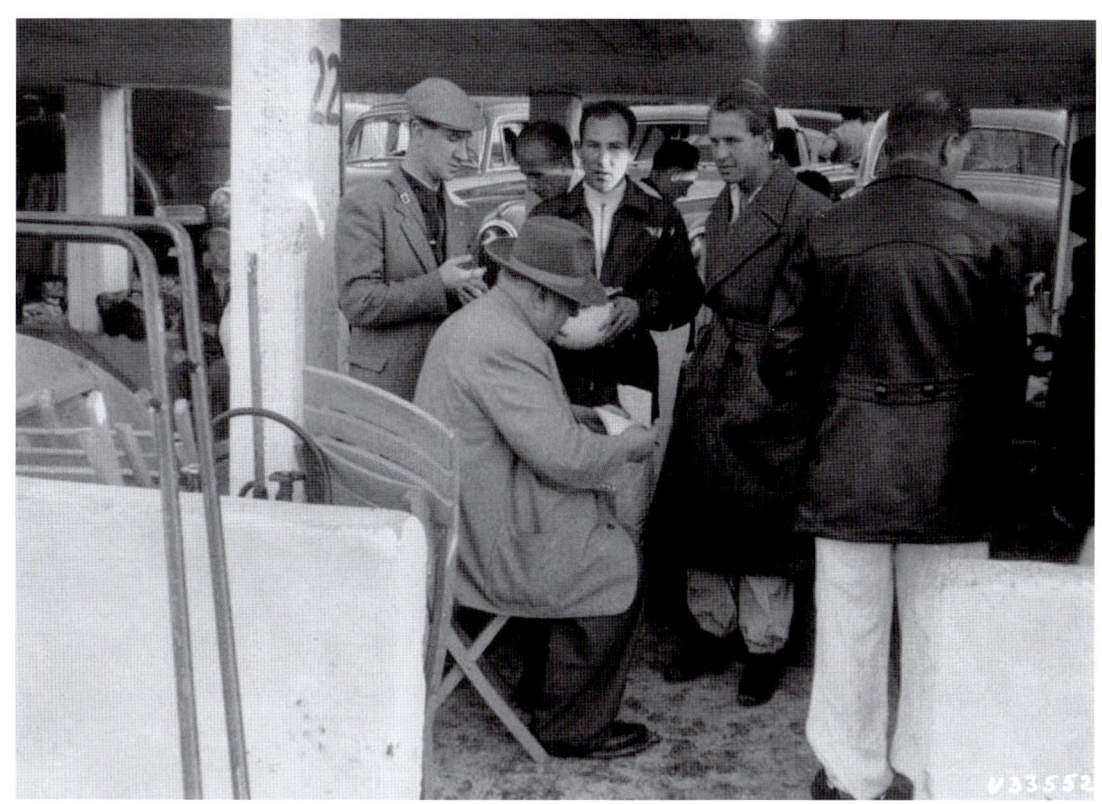

A final briefing with Mercedes' Herr Neubauer before the start. Photo - Daimler Benz.

Moss passes the pits having inflicted some damage on the 300 SLR. Photo - Daimler Benz

All about the boy!

Above: Stirling Moss has had his big excursion off the road. Photo - Daimler Benz

Below: Moss has come in, some repairs are made and Collins takes over. Photo - Daimler Benz

The racing career - The Grand Prix driver 1952-1955

the chance of a Mercedes drive must have been a significant motivator for him...if he needed one.

Including the pit stop, Collins set his first lap at 47 mins 50 seconds and he was already moving in on Juan Fangio, who now seemed to have been given the role as the driver who would reap the reward when the 'rabbits' faltered.

Collins out in the Sicilian countryside. Photo - Daimler Benz

A rear view of the winner with Collins at the wheel. Photo - Daimler Benz

When Collins came around the next time, it was abundantly evident that the Targa was a test that he was clearly passing! He had put in a lap 21 seconds slower than Moss' quickest, and had become the second person after his co-driver to record an 100 kph lap. After five laps and the driver changes the order was Fangio/Kling, Castellotti/Manzon, Moss/Collins and Fitch/Titterington.

Collins joined the 'wall-smackers' brigade on his sixth lap but he lost little time and was now ahead of Kling on the road and gaining on time and Fitch also managed to remove some Mercedes rear bodywork. While some cars had dropped out, Collins was the dominant force on the circuit and moved into the lead, working to build a gap so that Moss could do the final section while still in front. In spite of the 12 minutes lost when Moss went off the road, Collins brought the car in and when Moss came round at the end of his lap, he was in the lead. Ferrari had made a miscalculation and put Castellotti in the car too early, so he had to stop again and that allowed all three Mercedes to get ahead. Castellotti caught the Fitch/Titterington car for 3rd but it was not enough to secure the Championship which went to Mercedes. While Alfred Neubauer went off to send a telegram to thank David Brown for releasing Collins from his Aston Martin contract to drive for Mercedes, the celebrations had begun. Gregor Grant would point out in his later reflections on the race that Collins was regularly turning laps 50 seconds faster than Fangio and this was meant as a considerable tribute.

A jubilant Collins and Moss. Photo - Labruzzo

Stirling Moss himself commented on the Targa and his arrival back at the pits after being off the road:

"Back at the pits, Neubauer, Peter and the crew had virtually given me up for lost until I came hurtling in. They checked the car very quickly and Peter took off with the bit firmly between his teeth to stage a brilliant recovery drive. Under the regulations no driver was allowed more than five consecutive laps unrelieved. Our plan now was for Peter to do three, then for me to take over for the final five and despite hitting a wall along the way - which he said 'wasn't a very good wall, it simply seemed to crumble away before me' - the SLR again survived and when Pete brought it back in he was leading from Fangio - who had led briefly - and Castellotti!" (Moss, 1987, p.126).

Immediately after returning from the Targa Florio, Mercedes Benz arranged a ceremony at Stuttgart to celebrate their attainment of the World Drivers, the World Sports Car and the European Touring Car Championships. Fangio, Moss, Kling and Collins were amongst the Mercedes drivers present when the surprise announcement came that the company was making a complete withdrawal from motor racing, stating that the aims had been achieved and the engineering focus would be on passenger cars. It was interesting that the

Moss and Collins enjoying their great moment. Photo - Daimler Benz

*Moss and Collins get the rewards for a great drive.
Photo - Daimler Benz*

The Mercedes competition entourage back at Stuttgart for more celebrations. Photo - Daimler Benz

announcement coincided with the reporting of Tony Brooks winning the non-championship Syracuse Grand Prix, thus becoming the first British driver in a British car to win a Grand Prix since 1923. His win in the Connaught raised hopes that, with Mercedes out, British cars might have a more optimistic future. This was well-placed optimism and though Brooks would share in it, it would not be in a Connaught.

In November, when it had become obvious that Mercedes were now not going to be around in 1956, it became clear that there was a degree of 'casting' around for drives by some very significant people. It was reported that Stirling Moss would be "almost certain" to be driving for BRM and in America, Tony Parravano was said to be putting together a big team with Ferraris, Maseratis and Astons and that he had approached Moss, Brooks and Collins to drive for him. Apparently Carroll Shelby, Masten Gregory, Ken Miles, Cesare Pedisa and Giorgio Scarlatti would also be in his team! Moss went as far as to fly to Italy to test some of Parravano's new acquisitions. At a BARC awards dinner in London, Moss received a BARC Gold Star with all the luminaries present, including Peter Collins who was seen in a jovial conversation with Raymond Mays and Peter Berthon of BRM.

To add fuel to the BRM rumours, Moss tested the BRM P25 at Oulton Park on the weekend

The poster announcing Mercedes' Championship win.

155

All about the boy!

of 13/14 November but he also drove a Vanwall. Stirling brought his own Maserati 250F along and Peter Collins did a number of laps in that car.

Discussions and disagreements over contracts continued into December. While Collins was being confirmed as a Parravano driver at Nassau in a 3litre Maserati (it never happened), Mike Hawthorn was having difficulties with Ferrari and reports now said that earlier assurances that he had signed for Ferrari were inaccurate. Hawthorn wanted to be free to drive Jaguar sports cars and this was not agreeable to Ferrari. He had had a trial with Maserati in recent weeks and was also testing for BRM. Stirling Moss received another Gold Star, this time from the BRDC and Collins and Salvadori were rewarded for their fastest laps at Silverstone.

In the second week in December Stirling Moss, after calling a 'dinner party/press conference' to discuss what he should drive in 1956, announced that he had signed to drive works Maseratis in Grand Prix races. The next three weeks were something of a continuity nightmare for those trying to work out who was really going where. On December 16, *Autosport* states that Fangio was definitely not going to Ferrari but would be at Maserati and a few pages later says that he will be driving for Ferrari! The last issue of the month confirmed that Peter Collins had indeed signed for Scuderia Ferrari and would be team mate to Fangio. Hawthorn was still seen as a possible for BRM...as was Ivor Bueb!

What only emerged some years later were the details of what was going on behind the scenes between drivers, teams and occasionally managers, as well as an understanding of what had been fairly normal practice for people like Enzo Ferrari though it was private information at the time.

Ken Gregory, having been friendly with Moss and Collins for some years and having acted as manager for Moss - although Stirling says he was more of a public relations officer - began to take on a similar role for Peter Collins and this grew out of acting on his behalf to secure the drive at the Targa Florio. Because Gregory had been instrumental in getting Moss the contact to drive for Maserati, he was also making enquiries about Peter Collins. A very serious misunderstanding arose out of this. At the time, Colin Davis, son of veteran driver S.C.H. 'Sammy' Davis, had himself been talking to Maserati, mainly about buying a sports car. When the people at Maserati received Gregory's request, they thought he was talking about *Colin* Davis rather than Peter *Collins*. Given that Davis had had limited experience, they turned down the request for an F1 drive! Given the leaks in the teams at the time, Ferrari would have known that Collins was talking to Maserati. After all, he had driven in the Italian Grand Prix for them but Ferrari didn't know about the mix-up. Thus Enzo Ferrari, as stated by Neville Hay, was doing the hiring and the firing and he decided to get Peter Collins onto his side. As Collins had no other offers, he signed, though not on very favourable terms as far as money was concerned. But he was, at the end of 1955, a full-fledged Grand Prix driver for Ferrari.

Stirling Moss recalled the period for the author, describing the day on which he had tried all the British contenders:

"The first car I drove for Vanwall had been the Cooper-designed car and I must say I thought the handling was quite good but I wasn't so impressed by the engine. It seemed to be flat below about 4,500 to 4,700 rpm

The racing career - The Grand Prix driver 1952-1955

and at higher revs it had a misfire. I thought the car had potential but overall it wasn't that good. I drove a BRM on the same day which was considerably quicker. Ten days later a test of all three British-made cars was arranged at Silverstone. I really wanted to drive a British car if it would be competitive. Cars came from Vanwall, BRM and Connaught and I drove them all on both Dunlop and Pirelli tyres. The BRM was quicker than the Connaught, but the Vanwall was quicker than both by several seconds, and wasn't much slower on full tanks, which we tried as well. I was very impressed with the Vanwall and with the team. I later decided that I would join Maserati for 1956 but I told Mr. Vandervell that I would drive for him when my other commitments allowed and he was happy with that." (McDonough, 2003, p.84-85).

Thus Moss had managed to 'sign' for two teams! As a result Vanwall took on Harry Schell, with others to get occasional drives and these included Maurice Trintignant, Froilan Gonzales, Colin Chapman and Piero Taruffi. BRM would have Hawthorn, Brooks and Ron Flockhart.

Collins, Moss and Parnell (5th from left) at a charity event at the end of the year.

157

All about the boy!

THE RACING CAREER
The Ferrari years 1956 - 1958

1956

Early in the New Year came the announcement that, somewhat surprisingly, Stirling Moss would not be driving Jaguar sports cars in 1956 but would go with Targa partner Collins and join David Brown's Aston Martin team. That meant that Astons had considerable strength with Salvadori, Brooks and Parnell as well. The team would make their season debut at Sebring and it seems odd now that the reports didn't question how Collins had managed to sign for Enzo Ferrari but was still part of the Aston Martin team. It was, however, public knowledge that Ferrari was sending five Grand Prix cars to Argentina for the Argentine GP on January 22, for Fangio, Castellotti, Musso and Collins and possibly one for Olivier Gendebien. Collins and Gendebien were photographed together waiting for their fog-delayed flight to the Argentine from Rome.

It later emerged that there had been series of discussions over driving arrangements for 1956. Hawthorn had wanted to drive Grand Prix cars for Ferrari and sports cars for Jaguars but Ferrari wouldn't agree. As Hawthorn had not yet signed for Jaguar at the time of these talks, he had a free choice. Peter Collins was already contracted to Aston Martin and Ferrari wanted a similar all or nothing deal but Ferrari knew about the existing contract. Collins asked David Brown if he could drive exclusively for Ferrari for two years and then go back to Aston Martin later. David Brown wouldn't allow that and Enzo Ferrari agreed to Peter driving for Astons in sports cars. There was a view that David Brown should have let him go as he was 'disenchanted' with Aston Martin. That seems logical though there is not a lot of first hand evidence for that theory. While some say he wanted to go to the more competitive Ferrari team, it could be later argued that he wanted to go back. Peter was changeable and he was open to influence and he liked to please as well. That was at times a difficult combination of attributes to carry around, especially as he was likely to keep those things to himself.

January 22 - Gran Premio De La Republica Argentina

The programme of races for 1956 was distinctly different than that of the previous year. A number of factors had combined to bring about changes. The former F2 cars which had competed in F1 races in 1955 were fewer in number as they could certainly not compete with the improving F1 cars. As a result there were six F2 races, all in Britain, down for 1956 against only one in 1955. However, the programme for F1 events shrunk somewhat and a number of sports car races had disappeared, or certainly looked to be likely to be run differently as a result of the Le Mans tragedy.

On first glance, the Argentine race was entirely between Maserati and Ferrari, as all but two cars were works Ferrari or Maserati entries. The exceptions were the Owen Organisation entry for Mike Hawthorn, though even this was in the team's 250F rather than the BRM and the private Maserati A6GCM of Alberto Uria.

All about the boy!

Works' Maseratis were in the hands of regular team drivers Moss and Behra with other cars for Menditeguy, Piotti, Landi and Gonzales. Scuderia Ferrari had the Lancia D-50s they had taken over after the demise of the Lancia Grand Prix team for Fangio, Castellotti and Musso, while the Ferrari Super Squalo 555s were on hand for Collins and Gendebien. There was talk that there had been trials with the Lancia engine in the Ferrari and vice versa and the D-50s had been modified. Fangio's had the fuel tank in the tail and while retaining the side pods, these were now empty. Castellotti was said to have a similar car but was not as quick, while Musso's remained standard. Collins had the 'regular' 555 while Gendebien got one with the Lancia engine, which must have been difficult because it had been designed to fit into the D-50 chassis at an angle! Contemporary reports suggest Collins would have preferred the punchier Lancia engine but his brief from Ferrari was to give the Squalo a proper test in race conditions, which he certainly did.

While Fangio, Castellotti and Musso took the first three places on the front row with Behra 4th, Peter Collins was doing a competent job in getting the Ferrari to run quickly in his Ferrari debut, turning in a qualifying time some three seconds faster than Gendebien, who it has to be said was not nearly that experienced in single seaters. Fangio was surprised when his car just wouldn't run cleanly and he was quickly relegated as first Gonzales led and then everyone gasped as Menditeguy went to the front. He held station for some time with Moss second ahead of Castellotti and Gonzales. Fangio took over Musso's car and Menditeguy was fantastic until a half-shaft broke on lap 42. Collins moved the somewhat ungainly Ferrari steadily up to 5th by the halfway point. Some eight laps later he was moving up to lap the Italian Luigi Piotti. Piotti was given the blue flag and apparently panicked, jamming on the brakes and Collins ran straight into the back of the Maserati, breaking its fuel tank and the Ferrari's suspension. The Fangio/Musso car won and Moss retired before the end with an engine failure. Thus Behra got second and Hawthorn was a surprised third.

January 29 - Buenos Aires 1000 Kilometers

The first significant sports car race for 1956 was due to take place on the combined Autodromo and dual carriageway combination in Buenos Aires. Ferrari had entered two 4.9litre Ferraris for the Fangio/Castellotti and Collins/Musso pairing. This was to be a long race in hot conditions. The two big Ferraris were fastest of all in practice and they led the race for the first two hours, right up until it was time for driver changes. Castellotti and Collins set out where their team mates had left off, with the Moss/Menditeguy Maserati 3litre in pursuit. When Castellotti's car ran into trouble, Collins was leading in a Ferrari for the very first time in his career. The 4.9 was very quick and Collins established a new record, though Moss was pressing hard and eventually went by. Castellotti was catching up as well. Then a bit of South American drama intervened. Musso had burnt his arm on the exhaust and therefore Collins now knew he would drive the rest of the race solo. He seemed to ease off, as Castellotti went by but then Eugenio hit one of the many dogs which wandered about the circuit so Collins was back in second. Then Collins' Ferrari's differential broke so he was suddenly out. Fangio had replaced Castellotti in the repaired car and had set out like a demon to make up time. He eventually was in front again, only to have the transmission fail, leaving Moss to win from the new Ferrari 'boys', Gendebien and Phil Hill.

The racing career - The Ferrari years 1956-1958

There was relatively little appraisal of the performances of new drivers in new teams in the period but several of the drivers, especially Collins, Hill and Gendebien had done quite well in the 4.9 which was something of a handful.

February 5 - City of Buenos Aires Grand Prix

This race was something like having the Aintree Grand Prix in Southampton, as the race the week after the sports car event was held in Mendoza which is hundreds of miles from Buenos Aires! The conditions were incredibly hot, delaying the start for some time. The field was the same as for the earlier F1 race in Buenos Aires. This time Fangio was headed by Castellotti but when he and Musso retired, Fangio had to fight off the whole Maserati 'platoon' with only Collins to attack them from behind. Collins again had started on row three, drove a good though out-paced race in the same Ferrari 555 and eventually survived to finish 5th, a lap ahead of Gendebien, also in the same car he had driven two weeks previously. It was pretty clear that the Ferrari 555 was not going to be competitive and although Collins had driven very hard throughout the race, he could not get on terms with the Maseratis.

Reports in the motoring press in mid-February carried the news that the Belgian Johnny Claes had died after being ill for some months. He had been in the H.W.M. team and was a well known sports car driver as well. It was also noted that Aston Martin's 'Dickey' Green, whose notes appeared earlier in this book, was moving to California to take up a post doing competition work. At the time this book is being written, he is still there in California after a long and active career.

March 24 - Sebring 12 Hours

Peter Collins was back in an Aston Martin for Sebring and his partner behind the wheel was Stirling Moss, both drivers splitting their loyalties as far as Grand Prix and sports car drives were concerned.

Ferrari was the big favourite for victory with a full team of its best drivers but Jaguar were serious too and had no less than nine D-Types in the entry list, headed by Mike Hawthorn. Aston Martin came with three cars and though the DB3S was now in its fourth season, few people would discount the Moss/Collins pairing. Hawthorn and Titterington led the first 25 laps in the D-Type though the Musso/Schell Ferrari was in front at the end of the first hour. Moss had the DB3S right behind them and stayed in second spot for over two hours but the car retired before it went much further. He had handed over to Collins and both drivers had made the aging Aston go very quickly. The engine seized at the back of the circuit and Collins came back as a passenger of the local sheriff.

Fangio and Castellotti led most of the rest of the race. Salvadori and Shelby were highest placed Aston drivers in 4th and Parnell/Brooks retired as well. Peter Collins would probably have been in the second placed Ferrari with Musso if he had not been driving the Aston. However, his moment was to come soon.

April 8 - Giro de Sicilia

"The wonderful victory by Peter Collins (Ferrari) in the Tour of Sicily has confirmed the view that this young man is one of the finest exponents of mountain racing in the world"...the words used in brilliant praise of Collins in Sicily by *Autosport* of April 13, 1956. After his victory in the Targa Florio only a few months before, Collins' popularity

All about the boy!

in Sicily was enormous. The words reflected the recognition Collins was finally getting, though it has to be said it was the British press in praise of a British driver.

Ferrari entered three 3.5litre cars for Musso, Castellotti and Collins, the first two having V-12 engines but Collins getting the four cylinder. Musso decided to do the single lap of the 671 mile circuit solo while Castellotti and Collins had 'co-drivers'...who wouldn't drive. Peter Collins had the well-known photographer Louis Klemantaski beside him, whom he had known for sometime and who of course had already done two Mille Miglia events with Reg Parnell. Collins had already planned to have 'Klem' with him on this year's Mille Miglia in a few weeks time. Some practising had been going on in the week up to the event but very little of that had been possible at high speeds.

The cars set off at one minute intervals and the early lead was taken by Castellotti who led Taruffi's Maserati and Collins. Musso went out in the early stages but Castellotti had established a healthy six minute gap over the Maserati at the halfway point with Collins going quickly but putting less wear and tear on the Ferrari a further five minutes back. Before two-thirds distance Castellotti fell victim to a failing axle and although Piero Taruffi was still in front, his brakes were worn so he eased off. In fact it seems that Maserati slowed him, thinking Collins couldn't catch him and he was immensely disappointed to discover that Collins was driving like a man possessed over the last two hundred miles. Taruffi arrived at the finish, ahead of Collins on the road but then the Ferrari came flying into Palermo having taken 53 seconds less and had set a new course record of 65.86 mph. This, of course, was Peter Collins' first victory as a Ferrari driver and the beginning of what would be a very rewarding season for him.

A famous and characteristic Louis Klemantaski photo of Collins driving in the Giro di Sicilia in 1956. Klemantaski seemed unaware of the speeds they were going. Photo - Klemantaski Collection

The racing career - The Ferrari years 1956-1958

*Collins with Klemantaski as passenger fly to the finish to beat Taruffi by nearly a minute.
Photo - LAT*

April 15 - Gran Premio Di Siracusa

The Siracusa race had been moved from its usual date to coincide with the Giro di Sicilia and attract both competitors and holidaying spectators to the island. Ferrari sent four, now somewhat modified, Lancia D-50s for this race for Fangio, Castellotti, Musso and Collins, the latter in the car Castellotti had raced twice in Argentina. This was probably the least changed of the D-50s, though it seems the Lancia badge had disappeared in favour of a 'prancing horse'. Jean Behra had more or less forced Maserati to send a car for him and he therefore put pressure on the Ferraris. Fangio was fastest from Castellotti who at this stage wanted to beat Musso at everything. Behra was third and Collins didn't find the Lancia quite as easy as he had hoped for, qualifying on row three, some four seconds behind his team leader.

All about the boy!

Collins stops the Ferrari just before it touches the flag of Ferrari mechanic Parenti at the second refuelling stop. Photo - Klemantaski Collection

Moss was already finding the 350S not to his liking. In fact, at one quarter distance, von Trips was in front in the coupe. Castellotti regained the lead and then von Trips crashed out. All this time, Peter Collins was using a nice smooth approach to increase his speed, his partner 'Klem' seeming to be very content to just sit there and take occasional photos. Shortly before Rome, Collins had moved up past Reiss on the time sheets and was now in second place. At the country village of Antrodoco near Rieti, Moss came down a hill through a series of swerves and the Maserati got away from him in the wet and was left hanging over the edge of a precipice. The author has been to visit this spot and understands why Moss didn't like the 350S that much! Towards the end, the Collins' Ferrari had developed an oil leak, so that oil was spraying into the cockpit, forcing both driver and passenger to have to remove their goggles in order to see. Whether Collins could have managed to catch Castellotti is doubtful, though he did pull out a gap of over thirty minutes on Musso.

Though people have always said the 'leader at Rome never wins', it wasn't true in 1955 nor in 1956 and the same has been the case in the past. Castellotti was at his best for this race, staying on the road all the time for once and he took a great victory.

A blow for Collins, after his fine second place, was to later learn that his former employer John Heath, had died of his injuries when his sports H.W.M. crashed. It was first thought that Heath was on the mend. John Heath had given both Moss and Collins their first opportunities in a 'proper' Grand Prix team and he had, against the odds, kept the British flag flying in seasons dominated by Ferraris.

The challenge of driving a 160 mph sports car in the wet. Photo - Klemantaski Collection

May 5 - Silverstone International Trophy

It is odd, on reflection, to realise that when the Mille Miglia finished, the season for many top line drivers, including Collins, was already one third over and May had yet to arrive!

The return to the UK was not as glorious as perhaps it should have been for Collins who had done amazingly well over the last few months. He was in the DB3S again for the Aston Martin team in the 'Over 1.5litre sports cars' race on the day before the F1 event. At the Le Mans start Moss and Salvadori in Astons led Jaguars of Hawthorn and Titterington, with Parnell and Collins next. Then Titterington spun, Collins drove straight into the side of him and Parnell and Ninian Sanderson also went off, so four of the top cars and drivers were out. Salvadori and Moss were left to fight it out when Hawthorn also dropped out, though Moss could not catch Roy's faster car.

For the International Trophy, again there was an impressive entry. Ferrari sent the Lancia D-50s, 0007 again for Fangio and 0001, Musso's car at Siracusa, for Peter Collins. Castellotti and Musso had been sent to have their own private battle at Naples, where neither finished. The Ferrari, Maserati, BRM and Connaught opposition was, however, overwhelmed at Silverstone by the speed of the new Vanwall, with Moss on pole followed by Harry Schell. Fangio was next ahead of Hawthorn in the quick new BRM, Collins, and Salvadori in the Gilby Engineering 250F.

Hawthorn showed the potential of the BRM once again by leading Fangio and behind them were the Vanwalls and Collins. Hawthorn went out at 13 laps followed by Schell's Vanwall on lap 19 and Fangio with clutch trouble the next lap. Peter Collins was now second to Moss in the Vanwall but then team orders intervened and Peter was called in to hand over to the acknowledged team leader. But that didn't gain

Above: Collins along the harbour on the approach to the Gasometer Hairpin. Photo - LAT

Below: Collins powers out of the old Gasometer Hairpin, what is now Rascasse. Photo - LAT

led the Ferrari team cars of Fangio and Castellotti. Schell got a Vanwall amongst them briefly but on lap two Collins had moved from 9th to 5th, a lap later he was right behind Castellotti, then the next time round he had gotten past him. Then Fangio spun at St. Devote and incurred the wrath of many by regaining the circuit in what was described as an

The racing career - The Ferrari years 1956-1958

'inconsiderate' manner. Musso and Schell were forced into the bales and were out. During his recovery Fangio forced his way past Castellotti and then got by Behra and Collins, though they tended not to argue with him quite so much. Collins held him off for two laps but then let him through.

This was all rather futile as a rather battered car came into the pits on lap 41. Fangio was reported as having hit a wall...at least once, possibly twice but he later denied this. Anyway, Moss led from Collins and after 14 laps in the pits, Fangio got Ferrari team manager Sculati to call Collins in to hand over to Fangio. Meanwhile, Castellotti, who had retired, got into Fangio's car and set off. He actually managed to get this car to the finish, though some laps behind but was credited with 4th. Thus, Fangio himself could have done the same thing, not losing time with the stop and finished in third behind Collins.

Collins and Fangio in good humour after the race, Collins not appearing to regret handing his car over.
Photo - Motor Racing/BRSCC Archives

But life at Ferrari was, as always, strange. This was another season when Enzo Ferrari refused to name an official team leader and that Fangio was acknowledged as such by the others. It was not helpful when a quick decision had to be made. It says much about Peter Collins' character that he obeyed the signal to come in and hand over while in a secure second place. It was too early in the season to calculate any likely outcomes from this action and it was in Collins' nature to 'do the right thing'.

Peter Collins ended up sharing second place and the Championship points with Fangio, who did a good job in cutting the gap to Moss but without that pit stop and change over, there was at least the possibility that Collins himself might have caught and passed Moss. This was perhaps the one race where Fangio gains less points for being the 'great man', although that may in fact underestimate how powerful he could be in any team and how hard he worked to give himself an advantage.

Certainly, Collins didn't deserve this treatment. He was reported as having left the circuit and gone off to his hotel, clearly unhappy about it. However, there are photos where he seems to be in an affable enough mood with Fangio. Fangio did later express his gratitude to Collins, as well he should have as second place gave him 3 points and the extra point for fastest lap. After two races, Behra led the World Championship from Fangio and Moss.

An interesting sidelight to the race is the fact that Stirling Moss had introduced him to an American girl named Louise King at a pre-race gathering at journalist/photographer Bernard Cahier's villa. According to Moss, Louise was friendly at the time with Donald Healey. Peter and Louise met again during the weekend at the Monaco beach but they had no further contact until they met again the following year.

May 27 - Nurburgring 1000 Kilometers

It has been said and it is probably true, that this race marked a growing distance between Collins and the Aston Martin team. His performance at the Ring was criticised by

All about the boy!

John Wyer about this race and it was evident at the time that Collins' experience in the Mercedes and the Ferrari sports cars now made the Aston look like much harder work, as it was well down on power in comparison. Criticism of Collins, though, has often been in the face of fairly limited evidence and perceptions of the situation many years later were often highly speculative. Some of the same people who spoke and wrote about Alfonso de Portago were those who were judgemental about Collins and very few people were ever accurate about Portago, as it turned out. And, of course, Collins had come fresh from a brilliant drive at Monaco which he had taken away from him, to face his own Ferrari team mates in faster cars while he honoured his Aston contract. In context, perhaps his less than 100% commitment was not too surprising. Peter Collins was now an established Ferrari driver, capable of being at the front with Moss and Fangio. There was more of the man than the boy about him in this period and by now he could sniff a World Championship.

Having said that, Collins put in the quickest of all the Aston Martin times in practice, while

*The Peter Collins/Tony Brooks Aston DB3S finished 5th, here passing behind the pits.
Photo - Bill Bean*

three Ferraris were at the front, ahead of Moss' Maserati 300S, some 26 seconds quicker than the Aston. More humiliating was the fact that the 1500 c.c. Porsches were also quicker. As usual the 'star sprinter' Stirling Moss was first to his car and first away, followed immediately by Hawthorn's Jaguar and Collins in the Aston Martin and behind them came Portago, Fangio, Musso and the huge pack. Fangio had the lead briefly but Moss was in front at the end of the first of many laps. It wasn't long before Portago was in the bushes and Musso rolled his Ferrari, breaking his arm. Collins had thus moved up into 4th ahead of Phil Hill. On lap five, Collins rushed into the Aston pit to report that the engine was misfiring. It took a long time for the team to discover that a fly was blocking one of the main jets on the carburettor. An entire lap was lost, putting the car down to 18th. Collins had brought it back up to 14th when he came in to hand over to Tony Brooks. Nixon (1991) concludes that this incident caused Collins to lose heart and give up, in spite of the fact that he was pulling in cars regularly before he stopped.

It was shortly after this that Hawthorn was flagged in and warned about overtaking on the inside! In spite of the fact that many other cars were doing the same thing, it later led to Hawthorn being refused entry to the German Grand Prix. This became a *cause celebre* in some of the British press, with many very strong anti-German sentiments being freely expressed!

At half-distance, Moss had retired and Behra took over Schell's Maserati. Fangio and Castellotti led from Portago/Gendebien, as the Spaniard had been disqualified so he took Phil Hill's seat, Behra/Schell were third and Hawthorn/Titterington 4th. The Aston Martin was in 8th place and after 23 laps Collins got back in. Moss also rejoined the Behra/Schell team and held the lead after Fangio stopped

The racing career - The Ferrari years 1956-1958

for some more fuel. With only a few laps left, both the Jaguar and Salvadori's second Aston were missing, the DB3S having had the De Dion rear axle break.

According to Nixon's summary of John Wyer's notes, Collins was making no progress so after eight laps was brought in and Brooks took over again. Collins was said to have complained that the shock absorbers were not working properly, though Brooks was then credited with some very fast times, prompting Wyer to express his disappointment in Collins and hope for the future in Brooks. Brooks had done a lap some 17 seconds quicker than Collins had done in his second turn at the wheel.

It is interesting that John Wyer, in his book 'The Certain Sound', doesn't make reference to these issues other than to say that Collins had complained about the handling of the DB3S at the Ring, feeling that this was due to the additional unsprung weight as a result of having disc brakes. He therefore asked for his car at the forthcoming Rouen race to have drum brakes, which Wyer agreed to. As we will see, Moss thought this modification was so good that he opted to drive that car in the race. So, perhaps the handling was poor at the Ring and this would serve to show that Collins recognised it and that Brooks managed to drive around it!

June 3 - Belgian Grand Prix

"*Peter Collins has now added his name to the British drivers who have won a major Grand Prix. His performance at Spa-Franchorchamps last Sunday was one which thrilled all present and showed that he must be regarded as one of the great drivers of the present time. It must also have been most satisfying to him, following on his Monaco experience when he was ordered to hand over his car to Fangio, with World Championship points at stake. Now that he shares the lead with Stirling Moss, the politics underlying changes of drivers may have to be drastically changed in Scuderia Ferrari.*" (*Autosport*, June 8, 1956, p.569).

If Collins' performance in Germany had been viewed as lack-lustre, Spa was indeed something else. Much of what was said about the Ring was said in retrospect and there was little of this negative sentiment picked up in the reports at the time. When it came to the Belgian Grand Prix, there are further hints at a kind of weakness in the Collins' character, as his times in the first practice sessions were not unduly impressive. However, in context, the reality was somewhat different and perhaps reflects a sentiment at the time and by some writers that somehow Hawthorn was the slightly more 'golden' of the 'golden boys'. Nixon refers to Collins as 'foolish', saying that he should have been doing more practice laps, even though the cars had been given to Fangio to do most of the practice driving.

Scuderia Ferrari again sent four D-50s to Spa, Collins again in 0008 which he had driven at Siracusa and Musso raced at Naples. Musso of course was nursing his broken arm, so journalist Paul Frere was co-opted into the team to join Fangio and Castellotti. A fifth car was painted in yellow Belgian colours for Andre Pilette to drive.

With some repaving of the circuit having been done, times were expected to be faster. This was an understatement. Ferrari only ran two cars on Thursday and Fangio had most of the time in the cars, while Castellotti was having problems in his, so Collins missed the first day. Fangio then took ten seconds off his Mercedes time from the previous year, eight seconds under Castellotti's fast practice time in 1955. Moss went very quickly but then Fangio set

Peter Collins on his way to a fine win.

The French Grand Prix at Reims took place the day after the death of Enzo Ferrari's son Dino. Collings noted that "...the drivers, Fangio, Collins, Castellotti, Portago and Gendebien, were each wearing a black armband. Collins, for whom the Old Man had a soft spot, won." (Collings, 2001, p.47) Collins' win at Reims coinciding with the death of Dino Ferrari brought Collins and Enzo Ferrari closer together on purely sentimental grounds, helped also by Collins' standing now as a world class driver.

Brock Yates commented on this relationship:

"If there was a favourite driver among this youthful retinue, it surely was Peter Collins. This garrulous. totally loyal Englishman had endeared himself to Ferrari by turning his car over to Fangio at Monza (slightly later in the season-EM) and for a while it seemed he was being groomed as a replacement - at least in an emotional sense - for the much-lamented Dino. Collins was given the use of a villa Ferrari had purchased on the Abetone road a few yards north of the factory and as the months passed it became an extension of the Ferrari household. Enzo stopped there periodically on the way to work and Laura, chauffeured by the loyal Pepino Verdelli, would travel regularly to do Collins' laundry and tidy up his quarters. At the time the likeable bachelor was between girl friends, which suited Ferrari perfectly. Women (other than his own) were not welcome members of the retinue. Ferrari considered them a distraction, not only to the drivers but also to the mechanics and the entire operation." (Yates, 1992, p.290).

July 8 - Grand Prix of Rouen

In spite of its title, this race was a sports car event, not a Formula One Grand Prix. Nevertheless, there was as much tension in the Aston Martin team, it seems, as there might be at any major F1 race. Collins had asked John Wyer to give him a DB3S with drum brakes for Rouen which Wyer agreed to. It is said that he didn't accept the Collins' theory about the weight of the disc brakes, but it was very much

The racing career - The Ferrari years 1956-1958

*Collins chases Behra at the start of the Rouen sports car race, where Collins retired.
Photo - Motor Racing/BRSCC Archive*

unlike Wyer to do something he didn't feel was right.

Astons had entered two new DB3S models for Moss and Salvadori and two older ones for Collins and Brooks, one having drum brakes. Collins was just slower than Moss in practice and Moss thus asked Wyer if he could try Collins' car. He went very quickly in it and so asked to drive it in the race, to which John Wyer had replied that that was alright if Collins agreed. Moss seemed to have talked Collins round. The two of them had left the standard Aston housing arrangement to be in Rouen centre. In spite of their friendship, Collins was described as being very angry over this, though in retrospect it does seem characteristic of him to be annoyed by something but not say or do anything about it, keeping up a smiling front for those around. This is very difficult to be certain of, because there is no one, including Moss, who can really verify Collins' thoughts.

In the race, however, Collins seemed to let his driving do the talking. He and Moss shot off at the start to chase Perdisa's Maserati. Collins was soon in front of Moss and by lap six he had taken the lead. But it was Jean Behra who was determined to win, or at least lead, his home race and he worked his way to the front. On lap 16 Collins was right behind Behra and Perdisa and then didn't come round. Eventually the DB3S trickled into the pits, the rev counter stuck some 1300 rpm above where it should have been. This did, indeed, seem to signal a serious problem to the Aston Martin camp as far as Collins was concerned. John Wyer had described Collins as being "understandably bad

185

All about the boy!

tempered." (Wyer, 1981, p.82).

Castellotti eventually won from Moss' Aston and Behra, and Colin Chapman won the separate 1500 c.c. event in his Lotus. It was interesting that Chris Nixon quoted Peter Miller's account of the Aston team at Rouen, indicating that the presence of Moss in the team had something to do with the disappearance of the usual happy atmosphere. There is an implication that Moss and Collins were getting too professional and that Collins took his frustration out by breaking the Aston's engine. However, this account left out Miller's reporting of Collins coming into the pits to tell the team that he had over-revved the engine.

July 15 - British Grand Prix

In a matter of a few days, all the F1 teams and drivers and the supporting groups were back in the UK for the British Grand Prix at Silverstone. The entry of 12 Maserati 250Fs, four Ferrari-Lancia D-50s, four Connaughts and three Vanwalls was enhanced further by the presence of three BRM P25s. Hawthorn put his on the front row behind Moss but ahead of Fangio and Collins, who was having his third consecutive front row start. As the flag dropped, Brooks came through to join team mate Hawthorn and the two BRMs led for five laps, before Fangio got past Brooks, with Collins next, leading Moss. When Fangio had a spin the BRMs again led but Hawthorn stopped on lap 24 and Brooks had a huge accident on lap 39, the car flipping and Tony being hurled onto the road. His famous quote after this was that "the car did the decent thing and burnt itself out."

All the Vanwalls retired as did the BRMs. At 40 laps Moss and Salvadori in Maseratis led, with Fangio, Collins, Portago and Behra behind. Twenty laps later, it was Moss, Fangio and Collins and then Collins had his oil pressure disappear but he got to the pits, taking over Portago's car. Moss made a quick stop and resumed in second, Fangio leading him, Behra and the fast moving Collins. Collins then

Stirling Moss and Peter Collins before the start of the British Grand Prix.
Photo - Motor Racing/BRSCC

The racing career - The Ferrari years 1956-1958

passed Behra and was flying in pursuit of Moss and Championship points. Castellotti damaged his suspension and came in but Portago just jumped in the car and continued. Collins pushed himself hard and passed Moss on the 94th lap, at which time poor Stirling's car ran out of fuel. Thus Peter Collins had managed to get a share of second place, three points, while all Moss had was one point for fastest lap.

July 28/29 - Le Mans 24 Hours

Le Mans regulations were late in coming, having been rewritten after the 1955 disaster to restrict prototype engines to 2.5litres. This had a serious impact on Aston Martin which had been developing the new DBR1 but the new rules only gave them enough time to complete one car for Parnell and Brooks. The two 'newer' DB3S cars which had been at Rouen would be there for Moss and Collins in one and Salvadori and Peter Walker in the other.

Fangio, Collins and Portago discuss their chances. Photo - Fodisch Archive

Peter Collins retired Chassis 0008 but then took over Portago's car to share second place. Photo - Anthony Pritchard/T.C.March Collection

All about the boy!

Production sports cars would still have an unlimited capacity and there would be a fuel consumption rule which set maximum consumption at just less than 11 mpg. The DBR1 was entered as a prototype and the DB3Ss as production sports cars, which made a nonsense of the rules of course. Jaguar and Aston Martin had told the organisers that each had built more than 50 D-Types and DB3Ss, which was a significant untruth! The Jaguars, however, would have a harder time with the fuel rules than the Astons and many teams were also hindered by higher windscreens. In the wet, visibility was very difficult, and therefore it was more rather than less dangerous.

It was wet at the start and within three laps two Jaguars and one Ferrari had crashed at the Esses and Hawthorn was in the pits. Flockhart led initially but the Moss/Collins Aston soon took over. As night came on, Peter Walker crashed the other DB3S and Flockhart was back in front, with Moss and Collins in second, driving at a steady pace. Tony Brooks was driving in the morning when the DBR1 had the axle break when he was well placed, though the car was slower than the DB3S. As the rain stopped and the circuit dried, the advantage fell to the Ron Flockhart/Ninian Sanderson D-Type and in spite of the pace of Moss and Collins, the Aston was in no position to take the lead, though they only finished a lap down. The Trintignant/Gendebien Ferrari 2.5 was third.

In his book, *The Certain Sound*, John Wyer paid tribute to the driving of Moss and Collins:

"Moss and Collins were greatly superior to the Jaguar drivers, particularly when it rained but, unfortunately for us it did not rain quite often enough." (Wyer, 1981, p.85).

The Moss/Collins Aston leads the winning Flockhart/Sanderson Jaguar just before heading onto the Mulsanne Straight. Photo - LAT

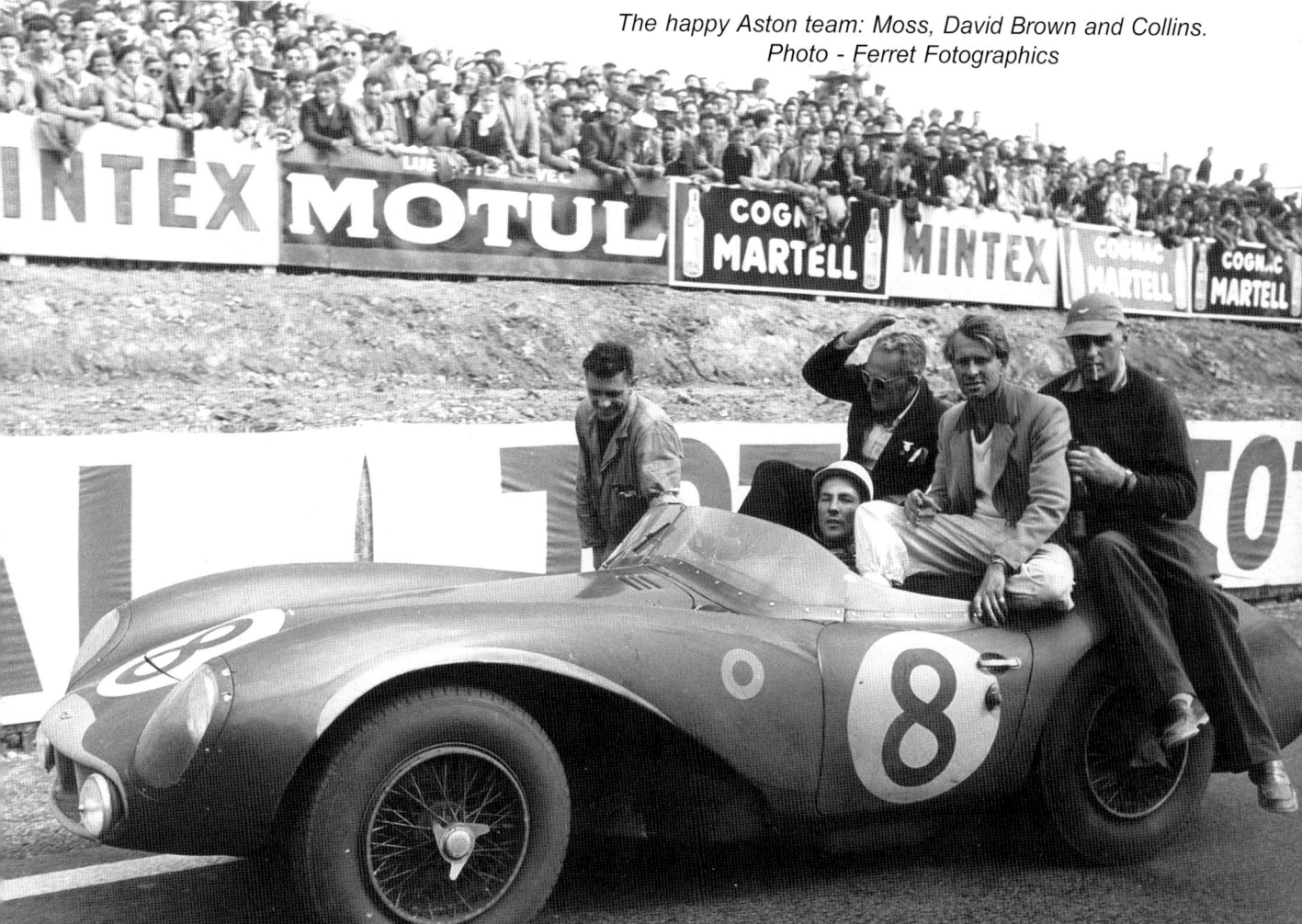

The first and second place cars just after the end of the 24 Hours, with Collins on the right. Photo - Chris Bayley

The happy Aston team: Moss, David Brown and Collins. Photo - Ferret Fotographics

All about the boy!

Wyer also summed up the issues which were around regarding Collins, as Le Mans was Collins' last race with the team:

"In response to a personal letter from Enzo Ferrari to David Brown we had, in 1956, released Peter Collins to drive for Ferrari in Formula One, while retaining his services for sports car racing. It was not a happy arrangement. It might have worked if we had not been competing against Ferrari in sports car racing but, as we were, comparisons were inevitable and were encouraged by Amarotti, the Ferrari team manager. Peter left us at the end of the year to drive for Ferrari full time." (Wyer, op. cit. p.85).

August 5 - German Grand Prix

With Le Mans over, the 1956 season was now rushing towards completion. Peter Collins had taken advantage of the affection which Enzo Ferrari seemed to have for him and sought some reassurance that he would not have to hand over his car to Fangio again. This seems to have been forthcoming, though that is not by any means certain, as Fangio seems to have stepped up a gear after Silverstone and might well have sought the opposite assurance from Ferrari. Collins now seemed focussed on the Championship though there is very little evidence that he spoke openly about it and would have kept his thoughts to himself. While wanting to beat Fangio, he would have remained somewhat in awe and in deference of him.

However, at the Nurburgring, Collins again did his talking on the track. Ferrari sent five D-50s for Fangio, Collins (0008), Castellotti, Portago and the returning Luigi Musso. While Fangio was clearly on his best form, so was Collins and the two were the centre of much attention as Collins was just three tenths of a second slower than Fangio in practice. Castellotti was three seconds slower than Collins and Moss no less than twelve seconds behind the D-50 in his works Maserati.

The race grid was made up entirely of Italian cars except for the two Gordinis in the hands of Manzon and Milhoux. There wasn't a

Collins with Senora Fangio before the race. Photo - AP

Collins with the Ferrari mechanics before the start. Photo - Walter Bauemer

single British car in spite of the fact that Vanwall, BRM and Connaught had all been showing promise.

Fangio and Collins left most of the pack behind at the start, only Moss remotely in the hunt. This trio all managed to break the old Hermann Lang 1939 circuit record but it was Fangio who went the quickest. He and Collins drove a tremendous race but at the end of lap nine, Collins wasn't there and slowly trickled down the pit lane. He had held the car's hand-brake at the start and the cable had then jammed against a fuel line, wearing a hole in it. The fuel leaked into the cockpit and Collins was nearly unconscious when he arrived in the pits. He recovered fairly quickly, or so it seemed and he took over Portago's car and rushed out again with a good chance of still earning some points. On lap 14 of 22, having got back up

The start of the German Grand Prix. Collins (2), Fangio (1), Moss (7), Castellotti (3). Photo - P3 Motorsports

All about the boy!

to third, Collins lost the car on the tricky section between the Karussel and Schwalbenschwanz and was down in a ditch.

So Fangio took the points, with Moss second and Behra hanging on in third. This put Fangio in a clear lead for the Championship on 30 points, with Collins and Behra sharing second on 22 and Moss fourth on 19. The three points he might have gained for third place would have changed the complexion of the title fight considerably but he still had a mathematical chance of winning.

As ever, there were interesting antics and side shows in the Ferrari pits:

"After the race it was revealed that when Collins had come in, Castellotti thought it was Musso's car and was surprised to find that he had jumped into the wrong car. It didn't slow him down as he was then hopping aboard Musso's car when it arrived. Portago argued after the race that Collins should have pushed the car back onto the road and continued. The two took a road car, Collins' road-going Ford Zephyr, and went to collect it. It turned out that it required a tow and the assistance of many people to get it out of the ditch, so Portago withdrew his argument, still bitter about not being on the podium. But Collins was still in the Championship hunt so he would also have been aware where the priorities were." (McDonough, 2006, p.118-9).

August 12 - Swedish Grand Prix

As at Rouen, this Grand Prix was for sports cars and although it was a Championship round, Ferrari had already clinched the sports car series, something which contributed to the Ferrari team morale, as they looked to be heading for the F1 Championship as well.

This situation is very interesting as some reports at the time and later had the two teams going head to head in Sweden. Nixon (1991) clearly states that the title fight was still on and thus implies that the team drivers were thus very much in competition to gain points for their own team. This is inaccurate as, on the basis that the four best results counted, Ferrari already had 55 points and Maserati only 25, so there was no way Maserati could have won. This of course doesn't mean that the teams and drivers wouldn't have been out to win but the mood would have been quite different in that situation.

In spite of the Championship situation, Maserati and Ferrari both brought a strong contingent of cars, Maserati sending the new 4.5litre eight cylinder which practiced but didn't race.

Collins and Hawthorn were originally to share a car but Hawthorn wanted to be in a four cylinder so he was with Portago in the 860 Monza, where Duncan Hamilton also had a place. Collins was then teamed with Gendebien in a 290 MM and Fangio and von Trips were also in a 290 MM, as were Trintignant and Phil Hill. Castellotti had another 860 Monza. As it turned out, almost everybody drove everything at some point during practice and the race and how the officials kept track of who was doing what is hard to understand. Moss' Maserati was quickest in practice followed by Collins and several Ferraris.

Again, Moss won the race for the Le Mans start and just led Collins away from the other 25 cars for this 153 lap, 621 mile race on the Rabelov circuit, four miles long and somewhat modified from the previous year. Collins got in front and was moving away from Moss and a bit of rain started on only the sixth lap but it didn't last long. Collins drew away as a lot of driver swapping started in the Maserati camp

The racing career - The Ferrari years 1956-1958

as various cars ran into trouble. At quarter distance, Collins had lapped everyone but the next five cars but on lap 47 he came storming into the pit and the following group got past before Gendebien was on his way. After further stops, Fangio/Castellotti led from Moss and Behra and then Collins who had now gotten into the von Trips car. Collins was soon back into the lead and when his 'first' co-driver came in, he handed over to Robert Manzon, who soon ran off the road in tandem with the Trintignant/Hill car. The latter recovered but Manzon was out. Fangio was chasing Collins just as Collins himself went off-road, hit a sandbank but then came round in third spot. Moss had also changed cars and then his original, with Behra still driving, caught fire and that was out, so Fangio now led Portago, Collins and Trintignant...all Ferraris. Moss' surviving Maserati blew up and Fangio handed over to Castellotti and he then retired out on the track. Thus Trintignant and Hill, perhaps the only pair who stayed in their own car, won from Collins/von Trips and the third Ferrari of Hawthorn/Portago and Hamilton. Collins had also had a short spell in this car as well so he was credited with a second, a third and a dnf...a busy weekend!

In addition to the results of this race, the contemporary motor sport press had Collins down as a likely entry in the Tour de France...it didn't happen...though Portago entered his private Ferrari and won!

September 2 - Italian Grand Prix

Nelson 'Vick' Vickers ran the Washington Hotel on Curzon Street in London and then later the Westbury Hotel. He was one of Collins few close friends. Chris Nixon discovered that after the Swedish race, Collins had contacted Vickers and asked him to come out and meet him in Denmark and then go to Italy with him. Collins, Hawthorn and Hamilton took the ferry from Malmo to Copenhagen where they managed to get themselves into some mischief, tying a tourist's Cadillac bumper to a railway wagon on board. Collins and Vickers then met, and spent a few days in Stuttgart, where they visited the Daimler Benz Museum before going on to Milan. Vickers then had to be back in London so he wasn't present at the Italian Grand Prix. (Nixon, 1991, p.193).

The Italian Grand Prix was absolutely full of excitement and anticipation. Fangio was the clear favourite to win another Drivers' Championship. There were six Lancia D-50s for the usual crowd and also one for von Trips who had made it into the Scuderia Ferrari F1 squad. Collins was in his 'usual' 0008. There were many Maseratis, three Vanwalls for Schell, Trintignant and veteran Taruffi, Gordinis and Connaughts but no BRM.

Ferrari was in serious trouble from the start. The Engelbert tyres were not up to the pounding they were taking on the Monza banking and they were losing treads after very few laps. Von Trips had a big practice accident from which he was lucky to escape. In true Ferrari fashion, his protestations that something had broken were dismissed and the blame was put at the door of his own inexperience. Had Ferrari checked their cars, they would have discovered that a steering arm had broken and two more of these would break in the race.

The grid saw Fangio, Castellotti and Musso in front, then Taruffi's Vanwall valiantly leading all the Maseratis, with Collins back on row three. The D-50s of Castellotti and Musso shot into the lead and their total lack of foresight had them in changing tyres in four laps! It was unbelievable. Harry Schell had gotten the other Vanwall into third so when the two impetuous Italians were in the pits, he had a short spell in the lead. Portago's tyres went on lap six but he

All about the boy!

Fangio leads, Schell, Behra behind Schell, Collins and de Graffenried early in the race.

slid into a barrier and the suspension was damaged and he was out. At the front, there was a slip-streaming group of Moss, Fangio, Collins and Schell while Castellotti again wrecked his tyres after five more laps, this time ending in a wall and out.

Collins came in on lap eleven for new tyres and Schell led Moss until it rained, when Moss went by. Musso had worked back up to third which was when Fangio had the steering arm on his D-50 break and he trundled into the pits, so Moss, Schell, Musso and Collins led and were the only cars on the lead lap and Taruffi had had a long stop in the Vanwall after his promising start. Fangio's car was repaired in the pits but it was Castellotti who drove in it, his third attempt to stay in the race. At thirty

Castellotti just stays in front of Collins, before Collins handed over to Fangio. Photo - Bagalini

laps it was Moss, Musso and Collins; Collins driving very smoothly and seemingly watching Musso's tactics and thinking he could catch Moss and take the lead if he could keep the car going.

When Musso came in for the expected tyre change, Fangio had been sitting on the pit counter, waiting for the chance to take over. Musso would not get out of the car and set off after Moss. Very shortly afterwards, Collins was called in for a 'tyre check'. Amarotti asked him if he would hand the car over to Fangio. Without hesitating Collins did as he was asked, Fangio patted him on the back according to Gregor Grant's report in *Autosport* and off Fangio went. Moss ran out of fuel on lap 45 but fortuitously privateer Luigi Piotti was coming by just in time to give Moss the shove he needed to get to the pits from the Lesmo corner!

Musso then went into the lead, wore out another tyre and again had a steering breakage so his refusal to hand over to Fangio had not paid off. Moss was also in some tyre trouble and eased off but Fangio soon knew this and

AUTOSPORT

SEPTEMBER 7, 1956

1/6

EVERY FRIDAY
Vol. 13   No. 10

BRITAIN'S MOTOR SPORTING WEEKLY

IN THIS ISSUE

GRAND PRIX OF EUROPE: FULL REPORT

*The cover of Autosport showing Collins handing over to Fangio.
One might guess from this photo that Fangio appears to be expecting to take over,
which is different from some accounts of what happened. Photo - LAT*

was now setting new lap records in pursuit. He got to within five seconds but Moss took a great win and amazingly Ron Flockhart had worked the Connaught up to third. Fangio and Collins thus shared second place points, giving Fangio the Championship. Fangio had 34.5 points overall and after dropping low scores ended up with 31.5, Moss was second on 28/27 and Collins third with 25/25. If Fangio had not taken over his car and Collins finished 2nd, he would have scored more than Moss and if he taken fastest lap as seems likely as Moss' tyres were wearing out, he would have outscored Fangio and become World Champion.

195

All about the boy!

Why did he give it away?

The Collins gesture at Monza is one that everyone discussed at the time and it has been retold and re-analysed endlessly. Timothy Collings, in *The Piranha Club*, analysing team strategies, saw it as, essentially, just another tactic for winning. He quoted Enzo Ferrari:

"Musso and Collins stepped down for the sake of Fangio, obviously with my consent. Had Collins not handed his own car over to Fangio twice, he would with mathematical certainty have become world champion that year, as he well deserved. Instead, Collins and Musso met their deaths without ever being able to win this coveted distinction." (Collings, 2001, p.29).

Of course, this Ferrari quote is inaccurate as Musso didn't hand over, at Monza. *Autosport* Editor Gregor Grant told what happened at the pit stop where Collins handed over:

"Pete came in for a quick tyre change, when he was in third place, about 70 secs behind and with a reasonable chance of winning the World Championship. Amarotti, Ferrari's technical chief, suggested that Fangio should take over. The Argentinean also wanted to do so, in order to make absolutely certain of the Championship and to try to catch Moss. Peter, with a cheery grin, waved Fangio into the seat, saying that he was perfectly content to wait another year." (*Autosport*, Sept.7, 1956, p.300).

Collins' move was universally greeted as a great act of sportsmanship and there was very wide coverage of his generosity and good will.

But what had happened to the assurance that he would not have been asked to hand his car over to Fangio? Was it possible that it was clear that Collins would defer if asked, given his nature and the way he viewed Fangio? It is speculative of course but Fangio represented something of a rather benevolent father-figure to Collins, possibly in a similar way that Enzo Ferrari did as well and Peter Collins might well have found it very difficult not to do what they wanted. If this was an act of sportsmanship, then why was Fangio not the one to be the sportsman and step aside? The answer to that is, of course, that he was ultimately competitive in a way that Collins wasn't. Journalist/photographer Bernard Cahier was one of few people who ever seemed to have asked Collins about why he did it and got the response that he felt he was still young, perhaps too young to take on the responsibility that Fangio would have to carry as World Champion. Cynics might also ask if there was a reluctance to ask either Castellotti or Musso to move aside in front of their home crowd.

Towards the end of the year, two short announcements appeared in the motoring press. One was that, as negotiations between Ferrari and Juan Fangio over 1957 contracts had broken down, Peter Collins was to be the Scuderia's number one driver for 1957. What would have happened at Monza if Ferrari had known then that Fangio was likely to leave for a place at Maserati? Ferrari's Championship winning driver was deserting to another team. If Collins had won, of course it would have meant that Enzo Ferrari again had a reigning World Champion in his team.

The second bit of news was slightly less earth-shattering: Peter Collins had bought a scooter but discovered that his road license didn't cover it and he would have to have an 'L plate'!

This cartoon by Sallon appeared towards the end of 1956.

1957

January 13 - Argentine Grand Prix

This was certainly the earliest start in any year that Peter Collins had been driving in a competitive event. He had done some early rallies, but nothing quite this early. It is very difficult to say how Collins saw the season ahead. He was nominally the lead driver for Ferrari but that had relatively little meaning as Ferrari would not clearly designate him as such. He now had Mike Hawthorn, giving up on British cars, in the team with him. Sir David Brown had been quoted as overhearing Collins telling Mike Hawthorn that there was still a place in the Ferrari team and that he should contact Enzo Ferrari, which he did. Ferrari told Hawthorn, contrary to what he had said to Collins, that there would be no number one driver until after the first three races. This is interesting in the light of informed views that Collins was not keen to be in a team with Hawthorn, not for personal reasons but because he wanted to be number one to Hawthorn. Collins had been voted Guild of Motoring

197

All about the boy!

Writers' Driver of the Year for 1956, so he was, theoretically, in a position to argue more strongly about his position at Ferrari but it is doubtful that he did. He had earned something like £20,000 in 1956, a fair amount of which was from Ferrari so he was looking towards an increase in 1957 as he would not be driving for Astons where the pay was 'not good'. However, money seemed not to be an incentive for Collins.

Collins was also up against the impulsive and not always consistent pair of Musso and Castellotti. For the Argentine race there were also Hawthorn, who had obviously signed for Ferrari, Gonzales and Perdisa but all in the now aging Lancia D-50s. These had been 'developed' somewhat but were not looking likely to be too competitive against the opposition. Fangio had gone to Maserati, where he would be joined by Moss until the Vanwall was ready and then Moss would lead the Vanwall attack. Other drivers would also be signed to be part of the Ferrari force to try to take the Championship again.

The Maseratis were quicker than the Lancias in Buenos Aires, though Moss got caught out at the start, bent the throttle linkage and lost any chance of winning. Behra took the initial lead and then Castellotti took over. Collins moved neatly past Fangio, then Castellotti and Behra and was now in front. He stayed there and started to pull out a gap on the others, until lap 13 when the clutch started to slip badly and he came in to retire. Collins took over Perdisa's car with which he could do little and eventually handed it over to von Trips.

Fangio, driving for Maserati, was having his first race of the year. Ferrari, with all their strength in depth, could only salvage 5th place with Gonzales and Portago sharing a car. Moss set fastest lap but only finished 8th after his long pit stop. Hawthorn didn't make much of an impression in his return to the Scuderia.

January 20 - Buenos Aires 1000 Kilometers

The 1000 Kilometers was being run on the Costanera circuit, somewhat east of the city and where racing used to take place before the autodromo was constructed. Essentially it was a high-speed and dangerous run up one side of a dual carriageway and down the other, with a chicane in the middle. Ferrari sent several cars and again, everybody drove everything! Unlike Ferrari, Maserati had both their regulars and some local drivers, while two Ecosse D-Type Jaguars came but Flockhart wrecked one in practice. Roberto Mieres shared the other with Ninian Sanderson. Mieres recently told the author "it was so great to be asked to drive a D-Type Jaguar...I couldn't believe they knew me and Ninian Sanderson was a great gentleman!"

Moss and Fangio were sharing the 450S Maserati and they were straight into the lead. Castellotti hit a kerb on lap one and was in to be replaced by Musso. Masten Gregory was in a Ferrari 290 MM and held second from Portago's similar car, with Mieres in 4th, soon to be passed by Behra in the 300S which he

Peter Collins took over Cesare Perdisa's car when his own failed and that eventually finished 6th. Photo - Whitefly

198

The racing career - The Ferrari years 1956-1958

would share with both Menditeguy and Moss. It was staggeringly hot and this affected virtually all the drivers. Castellotti was sent in to replace Gregory, Collins for Portago and von Trips for Musso. Moss handed over to Fangio and when the big car's clutch went he continued until the gearbox broke altogether and Moss started swapping round too.

Collins shared the third place Ferrari with von Trips amongst others. Photo - Fodisch Archive

In the end the Castellotti/Gregory/Musso car won from Behra/Menditeguy/Moss and Collins/Portago/Castellotti and von Trips were third...it was a bit difficult to follow! Had Portago not been called in to hand over he would have been second and he let his feelings be known to the Ferrari manager Sculati, who told him he would not be needed for the race the following weekend!

January 27 - Buenos Aires Grand Prix

The third race in as many weekends was back in Buenos Aires, though it was to use a different version of the circuit than had been employed a fortnight before. It was again very, very hot for the race.

The British motoring press carried both the race report and the announcement that Castellotti and Collins would be driving 4.2litre Ferraris at Indianapolis in May!

The race was to be run in two 30 lap heats, a good thing considering the sweltering conditions. Fangio, Moss and Behra had Maseratis on the front row again, though Hawthorn squeezed in between Moss and Behra, and Collins was on row two between Castellotti and Musso. Fangio stormed away to win the first heat and Moss and Collins were made quite ill by the heat, Moss stopping on lap 24 and Collins' car being taken over by Gregory in his first F1 drive. Both Moss and Collins recovered sufficiently to drive in the delayed second heat. Gregory stayed in the car he had driven the first time and Collins took over Musso's car. Peter Collins drove superbly to win the heat and Behra held off Fangio for second. Moss handed over to Menditeguy and went to hospital to recover. Fangio won overall on the aggregate from both heats with Behra second and Collins/Musso third. Collins' drive was very gutsy as he fought off heat exhaustion in the second heat and set fastest lap, equalling Fangio's best from the first heat.

February 24 - Cuba Grand Prix

Peter's plan after Buenos Aires was to fly to Miami on the way to Kansas where he was going to stay with Masten Gregory until it was time for both of them to fly to Havana for the up-coming sports car race. The stop-over in Miami meant that Collins had the chance to look up a young woman Stirling Moss had introduced him to at Monaco the previous year, who he seemingly hadn't remembered at all. The next few days changed everything in his life and by the time he was on his way to Cuba he was a married man.

All about the boy!

There had been serious stories of another whirlwind romance in Buenos Aires around the time of the Argentine Grand Prix. Peter had met the wealthy heiress Eleanora Herrera and according to her story in a London paper, they had become engaged. Collins later denied that this had been a serious relationship and he seemingly ducked out of Buenos Aires without a word.

In Miami, Collins 'looked' up' Louise King, and the details of what followed are recorded elsewhere in this book. Louise was a year younger than Peter, born in Indiana, daughter of Andrew and Dorothy Cordier. She was a model before becoming a successful stage actress. At eighteen, she married John Michael King, but this did not last very long. In 1953, she began her interest in sports cars, and acting appearances around the country gave her a chance to do some rallies and meet a lot of Sports Car Club of America notables.

When the teams and drivers arrived in Cuba, they immediately had serious doubts as to whether they had made the right decision in coming. It was apparent that the organisation of the first important international race in Cuba was not up to the task. There was extremely poor communication between the organisers and the shippers of cars from the USA and Europe and lack of awareness of a dockers' strike in New York had already put the whole enterprise at risk. Fourteen cars arrived in New York from Italy aboard the freight ship Independence and the strike meant the Ferraris, Maseratis and Gordinis couldn't be unloaded. The Cuban race was delayed 24 hours in an attempt to get more cars flown into Cuba from the USA.

When the event started a day late Stirling Moss was not in a Scuderia Madunina Maserati 300S but in Chimori's 2litre Maserati. Castellotti was said to be taking over Portago's spare 3.5litre Ferrari, the first time anyone was aware that Portago had been allocated a spare car! Harry Schell was in a Brazilian Maserati 300S, several well known drivers didn't have anything at all to race and Peter Collins took over Howard Hively's Ferrari, a 2litre Testa Rossa. Peter's new wife, having an acting engagement, joined him on the second day of practice. She later mentioned that this was the only night in their eighteen months of marriage that they were apart.

Fangio had been fastest in practice but the star of the event was undoubtedly Fon Portago, who took the early lead with the 2litre Maserati of Moss behind him, chased by Castellotti, Schell, with Fangio 7th. Portago led for 15 laps and Fangio had moved up behind him. Moss retired and Peter Collins led the two litre brigade with Masten Gregory next, though the Kansas driver had a failing gearbox so was no threat to Collins. Portago refuelled and Phil Hill was waiting to take over but the Spaniard didn't get out of the car and dashed back out onto the circuit. Portago looked to be in complete charge when he had a fuel leak and lost two laps making repairs, which handed the race to Fangio, though Fangio was generous in saying later that it was truly Portago's race.

Collins was very much unnoticed during all this drama and he had moved up to 4th overall and took the 2litre class with ease, finding the Ferrari very comfortable to drive on the tough Havana road circuit. Carroll Shelby was second and Portago had managed to retrieve third place. Louise Collins was there to rub shoulders with the international set which included Gary Cooper and his wife. Linda Christian was also there, accompanying Portago and she remarked on her own meeting with the 'glamorous Collins pair'.

The racing career - The Ferrari years 1956-1958

March 24 - Sebring 12 Hours

For the first time since Sebring became an important race, no Aston Martins were sent over and that freed Roy Salvadori to join Carroll Shelby in what was turning out to be a shrinking effort by Maserati. The Moss/Schell 300S looked the most likely to take the fight to Ferrari, which had four works entered cars. There was a 290 MM for von Trips and Phil Hill and one for Gregory/Lou Brero, and two of the 3.7litre 315Ss for Collins/Trintignant and Portago/Musso. There was a cloud over the Ferrari camp as Eugenio Castellotti had been killed testing a 315S for Sebring at the Modena Autodromo only ten days before. Castellotti was a vibrant character and his tense rivalry with Musso had become characteristic of the Scuderia team at a race meeting. Musso now carried the responsibility for being the leading Italian driver. Enzo Ferrari, at the time and later, fuelled speculation that Castellotti did not have his mind on his work and was spending too much energy on his relationship with singer Gia Scala. This led to the development of another set of myths which Ferrari helped to perpetuate through books written about him by a number of his minions. Nevertheless, Ferrari was known to express his cavalier opinions about women fairly freely and, given his cultural and family background, that was in context for his age and time. He, however, didn't necessarily apply the same restrictions to himself.

Back at Sebring, no one was surprised at the speed of Fangio and Behra in practice with the new V8 450S Maserati but they all knew it wouldn't last. Both Fangio and Moss tried out the new Corvette SS in practice, Fangio going as quick as the regular drivers, Taruffi and John Fitch.

Peter Collins made the best start and was off into the lead for 20 laps, when the Behra/Fangio 450S came past. The Corvette was already in the pit and out of contention and several notable cars failed to meet the minimum fuelling distance. The Collins/Trintignant car had some minor problems and dropped down to finish sixth, while the 450S kept on going for the full twelve hours. Moss and Schell were 2nd, Hawthorn/Bueb in the D-Type 3rd and Gregory/Brero 4th. The Ferraris were just outpaced, so it wasn't a happy debut for new Ferrari team manager Romolo Tavoni who had taken over from Sculati.

Barratt Clark and Bill Grauer were at Sebring. They had been making one of their series of motor racing recordings for Riverside Records, this time on Alfonso de Portago. Among the people they talked to about 'Fon' was Peter Collins, who provided a rare opportunity for people to hear, today, the sound of his voice. It was all a little bit patronizing:

"He is a man who is devoted to sport whether it is skiing, bobsleighing, water skiing, swimming, fishing, hunting, whatever it might be but as far as motor racing is concerned, he has got tremendous enthusiasm, a great deal of ability and as soon as he learns to moderate his ability - he knows how to drive well and fast...but he does tend to go off the road and my own opinion, and he obviously won't agree with me on this, but he does tend to fly off the road and you can't go off the road and win motor races. I think once he can arrive at a decision which can only be with himself that he will drive slower than he wants to drive and he knows that he can and stay on the road and become reliable, then he will be one of the best drivers there are in the world. I hope he continues to drive like he did today because, in my opinion, on his form today, if he goes on driving like that in sports cars and Grand Prix cars, he will be up among the world champions tomorrow." (Riverside Records, 1957).

Above: A mesmerizing Klemantaski photo from the 335S with spectators barely inches away. Photo - Klemantaski Collection

Over the Futa Pass in the wet. Photo - Klemantaski Collection

The racing career - The Ferrari years 1956-1958

Padua and was averaging over 120mph. By Rimini, Ron Flockhart brought the D-Type Jaguar into 5th behind Portago. Though Taruffi got by Trips, Collins had opened up a gap of over four minutes by Rieti. On the mountain section to Rome, Collins widened the gap and he was now under Moss' record from 1955 and driving superbly.

Collins' position looked even stronger when Taruffi was delayed by a stop to check the rear axle and he had eight minutes on his team mate which was extended to eleven minutes by Bologna. Trips was two minutes further back, Gendebien another eleven minutes down and Portago 18 seconds behind him.

Enzo Ferrari was present at the Bologna service stop. There have been many tales of what he had said to who at that stop. He is reputed to have goaded Portago for being behind Gendebien and although Portago knew he had a bent wheel, he stopped a mechanic from changing it and rushed off. Ferrari was also said to have both cautioned his drivers and urged them on. Collins knew the rear axles were now suspect and his was noisy, as was Taruffi's. Collins only got as far as Parma…his had broken and he drove several miles on one shaft before being forced to stop with a new circuit record in his grasp. Taruffi soldiered on to win, Portago had his crash, so von Trips was second and Gendebien third…and the Mille Miglia was about to end forever.

Louise Collins King later recalled that she and Peter had had dinner the night before the Mille Miglia with Portago, Nelson, von Trips and others. Portago had said that 'life must be lived to the full'. Louise said she had no idea how Portago managed all his conquests of women and had time to race! She also recalled Peter's great disappointment at not winning the Mille Miglia, as he thought he could and would. She said that the drivers' mood after they heard of Portago's death was strange, shocked, but not

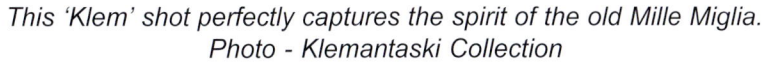

This 'Klem' shot perfectly captures the spirit of the old Mille Miglia.
Photo - Klemantaski Collection

All about the boy!

unexpected. Several of them went out for dinner and ended up dancing...that was how it was then.

May 19 - Monaco Grand Prix

While the press, both national and motoring, continued a long and often irrational and uninformed debate about the Mille Miglia, road racing and racing in general, the teams themselves buckled down to another event, this time the Monaco Grand Prix. Even Monaco's continuation as a venue was discussed in some quarters, so how influential must the forces who wanted to continue have been to ensure that is still going today, 51 years later. As has often been said, if race organizers at other circuits did what they did at Monaco, they would be banned immediately. Yet the Monaco Grand Prix goes on in a place now wholly unsuited to it.

The 1957 race proved the circuit to be as potentially dangerous then as it is today. The

Above: Hawthorn and Collins walk back to the pits after the crash.

British 'golden boys'...Moss, Hawthorn and Collins...tarnished their crowns a bit by throwing themselves off on the fourth lap. The fight at the start had been terrific with Moss, Fangio and Collins getting off in that order. Collins passed Fangio and was trying to do the

*The early race crash with the Hawthorn and Collins Ferraris hanging over the harbour.
Photo - LAT*

The remains of the Collins (26) and Hawthorn(28) Ferraris. Photo - Ferret Fotographics

*Below: Peter shows Louise and others the wreck and explains what happened.
This is the day after the race. Photo - Ferret Fotographics*

All about the boy!

Peter Collins offers up his explanation. Photo - Ferret Fotographics

The racing career - The Ferrari years 1956-1958

same to Moss. Moss in the Vanwall came out of the tunnel and the brakes seemed to be locked as he arrived at the chicane. He went straight on scattering poles and bits of barrier which bounced onto Collins' car. Hawthorn was trying to pass Tony Brooks, bounced off him damaging suspension and losing a wheel and ended up on top of Collins car hanging off the edge of the road over the water. The three drivers had to walk back to the pits.

All of this was a shame for Collins who had driven very well throughout the first practice session, only to have to lose the car at the chicane and he only just avoided going into the sea. Louise Collins described Peter's attempts to get himself wet in her letters home and somewhat minimized just how potentially serious his two crashes were.

Collins had been asked by Rob Walker whether he would give the 2.2litre Cooper a practice run as regular driver Jack Brabham was late arriving:

"We had never tried the car and Jack had never seen Monte Carlo and of course only 16 cars qualified out of 23 entrants. Every moment was vital. When Jack had not turned up halfway through the practice I got Peter Collins, who had driven for me before and was there as a works Ferrari driver, to do a few laps with the car. He said that he thought it was alright but obviously he did not want to push it. Jack never did turn up during this practice but arrived about an hour later." (Collings, 2001, p.80).

Jack then managed to have a fairly large practice shunt himself but the car was repaired. There is no indication whether anyone asked Ferrari about Collins driving the car. It seems a spur of the moment decision and he just got in and did it. It must have impressed him as there were later thoughts about driving a Cooper in 1959. Tony Brooks gave Vanwall their best Grand Prix result so far by finishing second to Fangio. Brooks drove brilliantly, his hands red raw with blisters from dealing with the awful Vanwall gear shift. Masten Gregory was 3rd and Stewart Lewis-Evans fourth. The race marked something of a 'decline' for Collins, as just when he had demonstrated that he could run easily with Fangio and Moss, he just couldn't win and 1957 would become a tough season for him, especially in Grand Prix events.

May 26 - Nurburgring 1000 Kilometers

If Peter Collins' departure from Aston Martin had been regretted, then Tony Brooks' arrival had been enthusiastically welcomed. He had quickly proved to be a very, very fast driver. In the wet practice at the Ring, Brooks took the Aston Martin DBR1/300 round fastest of all and when it dried, only Fangio was quicker. What, again, was expected to be a Maserati vs. Ferrari duel was soon to turn into an Aston Martin-beats-everyone affair.

At the end of the first lap, Brooks, in a car he shared with Noel Cunningham-Reid, was in front. Collins was sharing his 315S with Olivier Gendebien and was third behind Schell's Maserati. On lap six, Moss forced the 450S Maserati past Collins and Schell and on lap eight past Brooks...and on lap nine...a wheel came off and he hitched a ride back. He and Fangio then took over the Schell/Hermann car. Fangio held 2nd for a time in the Schell car but eventually both Collins and Hawthorn went by. He was back in 3rd on lap seventeen when Collins handed over to Gendebien and Hawthorn to Trintignant. When Moss took over from Fangio, the oil tank split so that car was out, though Moss then got into the Scarlatti/Bonnier machine.

209

*Peter Collins sits studiously on the pit counter with female company, while Hawthorn chats to Tavoni, in grey suit and von Trips with his back to the camera.
Number 6 is the Hawthorn/Trintignant 315S. Photo - Klemantaski Collection*

Collins and Hawthorn and their co-drivers swapped back and forth between 2nd and 3rd places, with Collins/Gendebien finally finishing four minutes behind the Aston and two in front of Hawthorn/Trintignant. The Aston had been averaging 2 kph quicker than Collins, who was 2 kph faster than Hawthorn. Hawthorn had provided some amusement at

*Peter Collins plunges the Ferrari 335S through the Karussel.
Photo - Klemantaski Collection*

The racing career - The Ferrari years 1956-1958

the start for those in the pits. He had jumped into the car, turned the key, pressed the starter. He heard the engine and lifted the clutch…to go nowhere. It was Collins' engine he had heard and he hadn't gotten his started yet! When the race was over, Collins was amongst those at the Aston pits to congratulate his former team.

June 23/24 - Le Mans 24 Hours

With the cancellation of the Belgian and Dutch Grand Prix events June was an empty month until it was again time for Le Mans, a full month after the Nurburgring 1000 kms. The two Grand Prix races were lost because the organisers could not or would not meet the starting money demands of the teams, particularly Ferrari and Maserati. This triggered the establishment of the UPPI (l'Union des Pilotes Professionels Internationaux) to protect the interest of drivers. Moss, Hawthorn and Collins were the British representatives. This was around the time that arrangements were being made to run the Race of Two Worlds on the banked circuit at Monza with Grand Prix and Indy cars. The UPPI protested this as too dangerous and Collins was very much against it, though he was not a public spokesman. It did run, was very successful and the Grand Prix drivers changed their position the following year.

Ferrari and Maserati were both determined to set things right at Le Mans after the Nurburgring loss to Aston Martin, so they both had strong entries, Ferrari recruiting Stuart Lewis-Evans to the fold to assist in getting a good showing. Except, this time it was Jaguar who would manage to disrupt their plans.

For Ferrari, Hawthorn was with Musso, Collins with Phil Hill in a 315S, Gendebien with Trintignant and Lewis-Evans with mechanic and sometime test driver Severi. Collins made the quickest and most effective dash to his car and headed off in the lead, which he held as they came around the first time, with Brooks and the Aston threatening him. The second time it was Hawthorn in the lead and Collins down to 10th and the Ferrari sounded sick. He soon made a pit stop and several more attempts to continue running but the car was retired with a broken piston before two hours were up. Meanwhile a Grand Prix was going on at the front which would wear out several more cars. Ron Flockhart/Ivor Bueb led a string of four

Peter Collins takes off in the lead in the 335S but the engine expired on the third lap. Photo - LAT

All about the boy!

D-Type Jaguars to the finish, with new boy, Lewis-Evans and Severi next in the first Ferrari home.

The Hill/Collins car had some problems with water circulation and it had been worked on and tested the evening before the race by Phil Hill. He remembers asking Peter to take it easy for a few laps and when he saw Collins coming around at the end of the first lap with a three second lead, felt a sense of apprehension...justified. Was the fact that there was Tony Brooks in the Aston that got the usually cautious Collins to 'let it rip'? Was there still something to be settled? We just don't know.

After the race, Collins and Louise, with Peter's sister Tricia, set off back to Kidderminster.

July 7 - French Grand Prix

The French Grand Prix moved to the Rouen circuit for the first time in 1957, the previous year the Rouen GP being for sports cars only. Although some of the drivers had been there before, many in F1 cars hadn't. Tony Brooks was recuperating from his Le Mans crash and Moss was down with sinusitis. As Lewis-Evans wasn't going to get a Ferrari drive, he was available for Vanwall and Salvadori took over Brooks' car.

Maseratis had the upper hand in practice, all the works drivers trying the V12 but settling for the six-cylinder with Fangio a second quicker than everyone, Behra's Maserati next, Musso's Ferrari, Schell in a Maserati, then Collins, Salvadori and Hawthorn. While Collins was just a fraction behind Musso, he had more than two seconds on Hawthorn and looked much more assured through the fast downhill sweeps after the pits.

Behra managed to get away after a lot of fuss on the grid with engines refusing to start, the Frenchman moving some two seconds before the flag finally fell! Everyone, though there were only 15 runners, went with him. Collins was in 4th on lap two when Fangio shoved Behra and got into second behind Musso. Brabham bent the Cooper-Bristol front end trying to avoid a locked up Horace Gould and Flockhart rolled the BRM on some oil and was off to hospital. Collins had been on the same oil, got well tweaked up but with hands

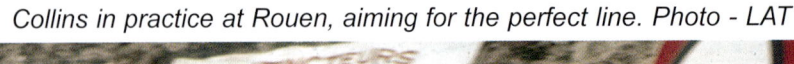

Collins in practice at Rouen, aiming for the perfect line. Photo - LAT

The racing career - The Ferrari years 1956-1958

twirling at the wheel had kept the power on and the car on the road. So, there were now only a dozen cars left. With Fangio pulling away, Collins started to close the gap to Musso. He stayed on his tail for some laps and on the 15th tour got by into second. He then broke the lap record but this had taken its toll on the brakes, allowing Musso back into 2nd. Hawthorn had moved up to 4th and even though Collins was taking it very easily on the brakes, Hawthorn wasn't running fast enough to catch him. By 44 laps there were only seven cars still running, with most of the British entries out.

With ten laps left, Musso started to charge and was catching Fangio whose tyres were by now well worn. But Musso had a spin and lost the ground he had made up, Collins was third and Hawthorn eventually a full lap behind the leader, Juan Fangio, now leading the World Championship by 18 points from Behra, with Collins in 6th on 4.5 points.

Above: Collins chases Musso in the early laps at Rouen.
Photo - LAT

Left: Collins flings the Scuderia Ferrari D-50 through the Nouveau Monde hairpin. This is still chassis 0008 though now much modified.
Photo - BRDC Archive

All about the boy!

July 14 - Reims Grand Prix

Ferrari had a generally successful weekend as the teams went back to Reims for a non-championship F1 race, as well as F2 and sports cars. Trintignant took the F2 race, Gendebien and Frere the 12 Hour sports car race and Luigi Musso had a convincing win in the F1 event. The F2 race saw the death of Herbert Mackay Frazer, the American who had been doing so well in a Lotus and had been superb at Rouen in the works BRM. He had been signed to drive the BRM at Aintree in the British Grand Prix. Bill Whitehouse, a former 500 c.c. F3 driver, was also killed in the F2 race.

In the second practice there was some spectacular driving as race director Toto Roche said he would give 100 bottles of champagne every time the circuit record was broken. Thus Fangio and Lewis-Evans got 300 and 200 bottles respectively having done the deed five times. Salvadori, Schell and Collins were on row three. Lewis-Evans in the Vanwall had the initial lead over Fangio with Hawthorn and Collins arguing for 4th and 5th. Then on only lap three, Collins was in the pits with a serious misfire. He went out and did another slow lap after the mechanics checked the engine but it was clear something serious was wrong and that was that. It turned out that there was no water remaining in the system. Nixon says this car had a 'Ferrari chassis' but it was still the D-50 chassis 0007 and it seems unlikely that there would be a new chassis referred to by the name of the old car! Musso eventually went by Lewis-Evans and so did Behra and Fangio but Fangio retired leaving the Vanwall in third.

July 20 - British Grand Prix

The British Grand Prix, also running as the Grand Prix of Europe, is of course remembered for Vanwall finally providing a Grand Prix victory for a British

Collins, sitting low in 0007, was trying hard but to no avail. Photo - LAT

The racing career - The Ferrari years 1956-1958

car and driver…or drivers. Stirling Moss took over Brooks' car when his was in trouble and they shared a magnificent victory.

Fangio had been relegated to row two of the grid by the Vanwalls and Behra's Maserati and Hawthorn was quickest of the Ferraris, ahead of Collins, Trintignant and Musso. The Ferraris never had the pace of the Vanwalls or Maseratis. After ten laps, Moss led Behra, Hawthorn and Collins, who had made up a number of places. When Moss took over Brooks' car he was back in ninth but started a sensational charge through the field. At 30 laps Behra led Hawthorn and Collins and Moss was 7th and then was behind Collins on lap 40. Then Lewis-Evans and Moss both got by the Ferrari and on lap 53, with water leaking from the radiator, Collins came in and retired. Moss, of course, got to the front and shared the famous win with Tony Brooks, with Musso second and Hawthorn third. Collins' season was getting worse as each race went by.

August 4 - German Grand Prix

Only two weeks after the memorable Grand Prix at Aintree, the Nurburgring provided the venue for another of the 'great races'. There are still people who were at Aintree and the Nurburgring and there is no doubt that even over fifty years later, they are convinced they saw some of the greatest, most spectacular and most skilled motor racing of all time. Unfortunately most of those fans who watched GP races in the last thirty years didn't see those of the 1950s so were never able to compare them. It would be interesting to see what consensus there is on the most exciting races of the last three decades and consider how they compare with their earlier counterparts. 'Experts' say you can't compare drivers and races from different times. Those who were there in the '50s, however, say that some of those classics were easily the best and they have watched the later races.

The start, with Collins closest to the camera, then Behra, Hawthorn and Fangio on pole.
Photo - P3 Motorsport

As the field charges down to South Turn, Hawthorn leads from Collins, Fangio and Behra.

It has always been a matter of conjecture as to whether Fangio drove his best race that day in Germany. Being the kind of person he was, he was unlikely to be anything other than modest and he does give other examples as possibly his best events. Nevertheless, what he did at the Ring was staggering.

Because the circuit was so long and the F1 field rather small, it was decided to incorporate an F2 field into the same race. The Vanwalls were not at all suited to the bumpiness of the Ring and were well off the pace, though Brooks was some five seconds quicker than Moss.

Before the race, the lap record had stood at 9 mins 41.6 secs, so when Fangio reduced it by sixteen seconds to set pole time, everyone knew the 46 year old was still in fine form. The first seven cars were under the old record and there was a spread of nine seconds covering the front row. The Maseratis of Fangio and Behra would start on half fuel so it was clear that there would be a pit stop, while Hawthorn and Collins in the D-50s, Collins in 0008 again, would attempt to run without stopping. Though they

Collins looks grim as he heads out into the country.
Photo - P3 Motorsport

Collins has taken the lead from Hawthorn, not worried about Fangio at this point.

would never underestimate Fangio, they would have felt the battle would be between the two of them.

Hawthorn led Collins across the line at the end of the first, long lap, somewhat surprising in light of the Maseratis' lighter weight. It took Fangio three laps to take the lead. Behra had stayed in 4th and came in for fuel on lap ten and Fangio did the same the following lap, having a gap over Hawthorn and Collins of 27 seconds. Hawthorn and Collins had been passing each other for the lead and seemed to be enjoying a race they thought they would win. The lap record was down to 9 mins 29.5 secs by this time. Fangio had a longish stop and when the Ferraris went by, he rejoined in third nearly a minute behind with Schell,

Hawthorn went back in front not knowing that Fangio was closing.

All about the boy!

Musso, Moss, Behra and Brooks next and Lewis-Evans had crashed his Vanwall through some hedges.

At first Fangio did nothing dramatic with full fuel tanks and new tyres but then it started and he began to take six seconds a lap from the leaders. He simply went faster and faster, reducing the lap record by no less than 24 seconds, getting down to 9 mins 17.4 seconds!

He caught the pair on lap 20 and then went past. He made a pretty forceful move on Collins taking him up the inside. Collins fought back and repassed Fangio. A bit later, Fangio again charged past, hurling stones and gravel into Collins' face and breaking his goggles. It was not entirely 'gentlemanly'! Collins was then having trouble with his clutch and eased off, Fangio beating Hawthorn by 3.6 seconds, with Collins 32 seconds behind. Mike Hawthorn in his book said that he and Collins thought Fangio was in trouble and that Collins had signalled him that he was happy to finish second and that they wouldn't race each other. Was this another indication of Collins hesitating when he could have taken charge? Much was made of Collins' handing over his car to Fangio in 1956 and possibly giving away the World Championship but little has been said about this incident, if it were true and Mike Hawthorn wrote about it as a fact. Perhaps as Fangio was already so far in the lead in 1957, it didn't matter so much in Championship terms, though competitively it again raises the question of Collins' determination to win. This relaxed approached to winning, in combination with an absence of signals on the long Nurburgring lap, certainly helped them lose the race. Had they kept the pace up Fangio was unlikely to have caught them. But then, we wouldn't be celebrating this as one of the great races.

August 11 - Swedish Grand Prix

Now the teams travelled north to Sweden to Kristianstad for the Championship sports car round. As the Championship status of the Venezuelan race

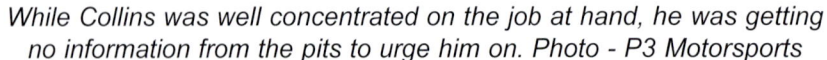

While Collins was well concentrated on the job at hand, he was getting no information from the pits to urge him on. Photo - P3 Motorsports

Collins and Phil Hill discuss the finer points of the Ferrari engine in practice at Kristianstad. Photo - Ferret Fotographics

later in the season had not been confirmed, this was a crucial race which could decide the Championship.

Peter was sharing a 315S with Phil Hill and though it was a Moss/Behra 450S Maserati on pole, it was Hill who took the initial lead in this six hour race on a very bumpy, difficult circuit. Hawthorn and Moss then went to the front and after some laps Moss and Behra, in another 450S though he was also sharing the Moss car, had the two lead spots. There was a great deal of tough racing down through the top ten, as the Ferrari drivers knew that they had to push the Maseratis to breaking point if Ferrari were to win the title. Well into the race, it was Peter Collins in the Ferrari who was taking the race to Maserati. He cut the gap to the leading Behra/Moss car and when he came in for more fuel, he stayed in the car and carried on the pursuit. Hawthorn had dropped back to fourth and Moss had taken over the 300S Maserati which had also been driven by Bonnier, Scarlatti and Schell. After 145 laps it was the Behra/Moss 450S which won but the fine effort by Collins and Phil Hill had earned Ferrari enough points to win the Championship. Counting the four best results Ferrari had 28 points to the 25 of Maserati with Jaguar 3rd on 17. The work of Collins and Hill was very much recognised by Enzo Ferrari.

As the Dutch and Belgian Grands Prix had been cancelled, the race at Pescara was given Championship status. In the post Mille Miglia furore, where Enzo Ferrari felt the finger of blame for the Portago accident was being pointed at him, Ferrari had said he would not race on an Italian road circuit again. This was like many of the threats he had made and would make over the years and as often happened, he backed down, this time when Musso pleaded

219

All about the boy!

for a car for himself at this Italian race. Perhaps Ferrari should have been uncomfortable over the Portago accident but what he did at Pescara was to fail to send cars for his regular and more competitive drivers, Collins and Hawthorn. If there was ever really a 'mon ami mate' bond between these two, then incidents such as these helped it along.

England as they wouldn't be going to Pescara and were based at Dartmouth, spending most of the time on the boat Genie Maris. This was not the boat they used at Monaco but another one kept for use in the UK and it suited the 'newlyweds' to be able to spend their time together on the water. Pat Collins had bought this larger boat some years before and the

This photo of Musso at Pescara epitomizes what Grand Prix racing on real roads was like. Photo - De Amicis

Musso looked promising for this race over the very long, 15.9 mile circuit, longer than the Nurburgring. However, Fangio was 15.4 seconds quicker than Musso and ten quicker than Moss but it was Moss in the Vanwall who beat Fangio by three minutes, while Musso retired after nine laps. As Collins and Hawthorn had still been in the hunt for second place in the World Championship, their absence did indeed seem strange. Were Hawthorn and Collins being punished for losing at the Ring? If so, what about Ferrari's lack of information from the pits?

Peter Collins and Louise had returned to

Collins family tended to spend at least one weekend a month on it. It was fully fitted and had a full-time captain to look after it and it was largely responsible both for Peter's love of sailing and travel by boat but also his skill in doing so.

September 8 - Italian Grand Prix

The race at Monza was marked by the absence of any non-Italian cars...with the exception of three Vanwalls and they sat on the front row of the grid with only Fangio's Maserati scraping in on the outside of the row. Stuart Lewis-Evans shocked many

220

The racing career - The Ferrari years 1956-1958

Collins at high speed in Chassis 0008, a car he had driven many times. Photo - LAT

when he took pole from Moss, Brooks and Fangio and the now apparent relative reliability of the Vanwalls made the Italians very worried.

While Fangio stuck with the six cylinder Maserati, Behra was to race the V12 but it was not as fast as either the six or the Vanwalls. Collins, in 0008 again, was fastest of the Ferraris with von Trips, Musso and Hawthorn next on the grid. At the start it was the Maseratis and the Vanwalls running away and the Ferraris were definitely in the second group with Harry Schell's Maserati to fight with. Collins remained the fastest of the Ferrari drivers until a cracked block on lap 62 forced him out. The slip-streaming battle at the front continued for many laps, until Brooks made a stop and Lewis-Evans retired. Moss then pulled away from Fangio and finished well ahead of him, with von Trips getting third after persisting and surviving!

September 22 - Modena Grand Prix

After Monza, the Collins' stayed in Italy before going to Modena for the next race. The Spanish Grand Prix had also been cancelled in 1957 so there was rather more time than usual for leisure than in most seasons and of course testing was much less a feature of both Grand Prix and sports car racing in period, never approaching what it is today.

Modena was hosting an interesting non-championship race, interesting from the technical perspective in that Ferrari wanted to try out their development of the 1.5litre F2 car. This new Dino 156 with a V6 engine of 1860 c.c., designated the 196 engine, was really a preview of what was to come in the near future and cars were sent for Collins and Musso. The race was run in two 40 lap heats on a circuit just under three miles in length.

Behra was fastest in practice and duly gave the

221

All about the boy!

Maserati V12 its first win in Heat One, while Musso showed the new Ferrari was quite quick. Collins struggled in practice but made up for it in the heat and was fourth. In the second heat, Behra led from start to finish but there was a 40 lap tussle between Musso, Schell and Collins and they finished literally nose to tail, a good showing for the new car with a smaller engine. Musso had equal fastest time with Behra in the first heat which made an interesting comparison between the two cars, the 250F having been around now for some years.

Stirling Moss was not at the Modena race. He was back in the UK and getting ready to get married to Katie Molson, part of the Canadian Molson brewery family. The wedding was lavish, in total contrast to Peter and Louise's own wedding but they went to London and Peter was one of Moss' ushers along with Hawthorn, Peter Jopp and Jo Bonnier, with Ken Gregory as best man. There was a dazzling array of motor racing and other famous folk in attendance, some 500 invited guests as well as a huge throng who showed up outside St. Peter's Church in Eaton Square.

Peter and Louise had been settling into life in Italy at the time they made the trip to England for the wedding. The Moss wedding seemed to trigger some thinking about the future on Peter's part, as Nixon (1991) reported that on their return to Italy, he and Louise spent considerable time discussing a future without motor racing. This included the possibility of building a new house for them near Shatterford Grange. Louise had said they had some land there, though this may have been part of the Collins' family land. Several business possibilities were discussed, one of which was a Nassau-based boat construction company with Donald Healey, and arrangements were made for Peter to compete at Nassau and have meetings with Healey later in the year. Of course, that would have been at odds with other plans Peter had already discussed with his father to set up a performance car sales business near the existing Kidderminster Motors as Pat Collins already owned enough land there to build a showroom.

Gregor Grant of *Autosport* did his annual rating of the top 12 Grand Prix drivers of 1957, giving Fangio and Moss each five stars, Behra four, and Hawthorn, Collins, Musso and Brooks three. He saw Hawthorn as having 'flashes of brilliance' and Collins as having suffered more from Ferrari unreliability than the others, though Grant felt himself that Peter was driving better in 1957 and he saw Collins as a driving 'artist'. This is interesting in the light of comments over the years that Peter Collins was off-form in 1957, though the evidence is fairly speculative. Neville Hay is of the view that Peter, in 1958, changed his technique of driving the Ferrari and consequently improved considerably.

October 27 - Moroccan Grand Prix

The cars were immediately shipped off to the race in Morocco which was the country's test race before a championship round would be run there in 1958.

For the Casablanca circuit, Musso was left out of the team as Collins and Hawthorn had been at Pescara. This time, Collins would have chassis 0012 and Hawthorn would use 0011. There was another substantial difference and that was that Collins now had an engine enlarged to 2.4litres and Hawthorn had a 2.2litre unit and these would run on aviation fuel rather than alcohol-based fuel as used by the rest of the teams. The cars would thus be lighter as they were F2 chassis anyway and would be able to carry less fuel. Stirling Moss had been quickest in the first practice session

The racing career - The Ferrari years 1956-1958

but a wave of Asian Flu attacked the race personnel and Moss was so ill he flew home without taking further part. Fangio, Collins, Hawthorn and Schell were also affected but attempted to carry on. Brooks, Behra and Lewis-Evans had the front row sewn up but at the start it was Collins with less fuel on board who took advantage and shot into the lead.

Collins led until lap eight when his worsening health prompted a spin into the hay bales lining the circuit. This was a busy lap as Hawthorn decided he was too ill to continue so pulled in and Jack Brabham went into the paddock with a seized gearbox. This was replaced in the paddock and he went out again but was later stopped as this was an infraction of the rules. And then eight laps further, Collins again spun, this time causing some damage and decided it was time to quit. Behra went on to win in the Maserati from Lewis-Evans and Trintignant.

Fangio himself had had a spin and received outside assistance to restart. When the black flag went out for Brabham, Jack and Fangio were side by side, so Fangio thought the flag was for him and in he came. He was told to continue and his drive back up to 4th while suffering from the flu was indeed impressive and as determined as his effort at the Nurburgring, though it has been rather overlooked as one of his great drives.

November 3 - Venezuela Grand Prix

Flying off to Venezuela with a severe bout of the flu to take part in a race that only a few weeks earlier looked unlikely to take place or have any significance must have been something of a surreal experience for the participants. Nevertheless, the Grand Prix of Venezuela had been given status as the final round of the World Sports Car Championship. The Swedish win for Collins and Phil Hill had not been as decisive as it seemed and the fight had to start again. Maserati needed to win this race and keep Ferrari out of the points scoring positions, so Maserati had a lot at stake but they had no idea of the price they would pay.

Peter and Louise Collins and Mike Hawthorn flew from Morocco to Spain to pick up a connecting flight to Caracas. The Spanish driver Francisco Godia was going to be one of the Maserati drivers but complained that the pay was insufficient. Maserati wouldn't increase the payment so Godia cancelled his flight. It was a good decision as the plane he was to fly on crashed.

Collins and Phil Hill were teamed in the 4.1litre Ferrari 335S, as were Hawthorn and Musso. Von Trips and Wolfgang Seidel would share a 250 Testa Rossa as would Trintignant and Gendebien. There were also two 500 Testa Rossas as private entrants, one being driven by Piero Drogo. Maserati was out in force with a works 300S for Bonnier and Brooks, two 450S open cars for Moss, Behra, Brooks and Schell, while American Temple Buell brought a Maserati for Masten Gregory and Dale Duncan. There was a works Porsche RSK and some private 550 RS Porsches but it was clearly going to be a battle between the Maserati and Ferrari teams. The two 450S Maseratis were quickest in practice, not surprisingly on this very high speed circuit. The circuit, when first seen by the drivers, was universally hated. It had long straights interrupted by very tight bends and at some points the circuit changed direction as the main road carried on and there was no way of telling at first where the turns were. Thus Phil Hill drove several kilometers into Caracas traffic before he realised he shouldn't be there. Complaints were made and assurances were given that improvements would be made. Phil Hill described these 'improvements':

"There was a very brave fellow who stood at

All about the boy!

the end of one straight, waving two large yellow flags. Now on this stretch you'd be doing perhaps 170 mph and this intrepid man provided the only clue that, so far as racing was concerned, you were at the end of the straight and should turn right. The road carried on, die-straight, for another 15 miles and this little character simply placed himself in the middle, waved his flags and hoped you'd turn." (Nolan, 1996, p.95).

Hawthorn and Musso were 3rd quickest, Collins/Hill 4th, the Bonnier 300S 5th, Gregory 6th, von Trips 7th and Trintignant 8th. The Le Mans start was bizarre. Hardly anyone could get their engines started, until one of the American-entered Corvettes spluttered into life but that was quickly overtaken by Masten Gregory. What happened next is etched in the author's memory from the time he first saw reports and photos of this race in *Automobile Year*.

Masten Gregory was only just starting the second lap on this 6.1 mile course in a race that was 1000 kilometers long when he glanced back to see where the Hawthorn and Collins Ferraris were. This was enough for him to clip a kerb and roll the Maserati from which he escaped, as he always seemed to, more or less intact. Collins and Hawthorn then alternated the lead for some laps until the big 450S of Behra rumbled up behind them. Then an America-entered A.C. swerved across in front of Moss and the Maserati cut the A.C. in half, though the driver, Dressler, survived and Moss walked back to the pits. Two big Maseratis were out. When Behra came in for his fuel stop, the fuel caught fire and the crew had to work quickly to put it out. Moss was back by then and he jumped in and drove off, returning the next lap hopping up and down as the seat was still alight. Harry Schell then got in for a try. He shouldn't have bothered.

As Hawthorn and Collins held 1st and 2nd, Bonnier was 3rd in the 300S and Schell was catching him. But Bonnier had a tyre blow with Schell alongside and the 300S slid into the 450S. Bonnier struck a lamp post which fell on the car as he jumped out and Schell hit a wall, was thrown out and the car again caught fire. There were unforgettable photos of the burned and tattered Schell and the bleeding Bonnier looking like they never knew what hit them. What hit Maserati, of course, was the devastating realisation that all their cars had been destroyed. Already in deep financial trouble, this had an even bigger impact on the company.

In the midst of all this, Collins and Hill drove superbly, knowing they had clinched the Championship...again...but wanting the win. They pulled away into a full lap lead over Hawthorn and Musso. The other two Ferraris completed the top four and Huschke von Hanstein and Edgar Barth brought the Porsche RSK in to 5th.

A few weeks later, James Tilling was at the party in Dartmouth described below and he cornered Collins and got him to describe the race in Caracas:

"Once we got to know the proper way round and which way to go, the circuit itself was fairly good. The surface was concrete - very slippery in the wet. On the first day of practice it was very wet but gradually we got to know it, if not like it. It was neither one thing nor the other, yet it was very fast on the straight section but the big snag was the existence of big, high curved stones, with no indication as to turning left or right. In the heat of the race - or battle if you like - people were apt to send them back to hit someone else. This did, in fact, happen several times on race day."

Collins described an incident in the race that

The racing career - The Ferrari years 1956-1958

didn't seem to appear in many reports:

"A Porsche shot off the road, hitting some sandbags and spilling them all over the track. I couldn't go round behind the Porsche because there just wasn't enough room. So over the sandbags I went and tore off my exhaust pipes. I stopped after 34 laps of the 101 to be completed. However I was scheduled to stop after 37 laps. Phil Hill took over the car." (*Autosport,* Nov.15, 1957, p.639-40).

Peter Collins gave a hint as to the depth of his mechanical knowledge when he commented that, after the exhausts had lost seven inches of their length on each of the four pipes, the revs available went up from 6800 rpm to 7200. He said this " will be sorted out by Ferraris as it seems to mean something or other". He also commented that the race in Caracas should never have been given Championship status.

Over the years, relatively little attention has been paid to the Drivers' Championship within the World Sports Car Championship. The manufacturers, not surprisingly, advertised their wins in the Marque Championship, which in 1957 was won by Ferrari from Maserati, Jaguar and Aston Martin. But the Drivers' Championship went to Peter Collins with 68 points from Moss (58), Behra (55), Hawthorn (49), Musso (49), Gregory (37), Gendebien (37) and Phil Hill (35).

Castellotti had taken this title in 1956 and though Moss had the same number of points, Castellotti had more wins. Collins was only two points behind in 1956. Moss had won in 1955 with Collins sixth, so his progression as a world class sports car driver was abundantly clear. Though then, as now, much more attention was paid to the Grand Prix Championship, Collins had clearly risen to the level where he was officially a World Champion and in terms of skill was at the top of the table with the very best sports car drivers of the time. By comparison, Fangio had been 6th in 1956 and only 11th in 1957, preferring to concentrate on winning the Grand Prix title.

December 8 - Nassau Trophy Race

After the race in Caracas, Peter and Louise flew back to London. They had decided to travel to Dartmouth where they had organised what was a belated wedding reception and a birthday celebration for both of them, as Louise's birthday was on November 16 and Peter's had been ten days earlier.

There was a cocktail reception at the Royal Dart Yacht Club and then the party moved to the Queens Hotel. There were a fair number of serious 'pranks' going on and Peter was presented with a hefty bill for damages. The party continued next day aboard the Genie Maris. The party even rated a report in Autosport, not surprising as Gregor Grant had been at the party and had contributed to the damage!

It is difficult to tell whether Peter Collins went to Nassau to discuss a possible business deal with Donald Healey and got a race, or whether he went there to race and the business came up because they were there. Louise had already known Donald Healey so there was a door waiting to be opened. In any event, it seems that Ken Gregory had a hand in this and is 'credited' with giving the idea to Donald Healey that it would be an attractive proposition to have an Austin-Healey that had a substantial power improvement. Donald Healey had bought a Ferrari 500 and it was the 2.5litre engine from this which was shoe-horned into the Healey. This was said to be the ex-Monaco winning 1955 car but actually was the ex-Portago car, a 500 which had been updated to 625 specifications. The chassis was an Austin-Healey 100-6 competition chassis

All about the boy!

Peter and Donald Healey have a 'business meeting'. Photo - Louise Collins King Collection

with the Ferrari De Dion rear welded on.

There is little recorded about the details of this endeavour. Collins was due to start in the five lap heat for the Governor's Trophy on December 6 but the car didn't start. It then did appear in the 50 lap Nassau Tourist Trophy two days later. In spite of high oil consumption and a down on power engine, Collins managed to finish 10th overall and first in his class. Collins had managed to beat some impressive Ferraris and Porsches, including Greenspun's Ferrari 315S and 18 other finishers. The race was won by Moss in a Ferrari 290 MM. Peter Collins had reported in a letter back home that Moss was happy enough that his works Aston had been crashed by American Ruth Levy as he thought it wasn't much good anyway! The same letter home had revealed that Peter was

A rare photo of Peter Collins at Nassua in the Healey-Ferrari. Photo - Terry O'Neil

The racing career - The Ferrari years 1956-1958

surprised the Healey had lasted the 250 mile race but said most of the cars he had beaten were 'junk'!

Peter and Louise left Nassau on the way back to the USA to spend Christmas with Louise's family on Long Island, New York. They stopped in Florida on the way to make arrangements for his trip to Cuba for the race scheduled for February. He thus missed the Ferrari end of year 'celebrations', unfortunate because Ferrari's success with sports cars had managed to overshadow the poor season in Grand Prix races. Ferrari announced his drivers for 1958 as Collins, Hawthorn, Musso, possibly von Trips and Phil Hill and Olivier Gendebien in sports cars.

Louise and Peter enjoying Nassau in December 1957. Photo - Louise Collins King Collection

All about the boy!

1958

January 19 - Argentine Grand Prix

The 1958 season got off to a rapid and hectic start, as the race in Argentina had not been confirmed as a Championship round until quite late. The British teams protested this very strongly saying they did not have enough notice to get the cars prepared, though indeed the race had been a title event the previous year.

Other changes included the move to use of aviation fuel rather than alcohol, though the 2.5litre formula was to be retained until the end of 1960. Race lengths were to be reduced and of course that meant that the smaller cars might now be able to run the full distance without refuelling. In addition to the technical advances made with cars such as the Cooper, with the engine behind the driver, this last change effectively meant that front-engine cars would become less dominant. Maserati's departure from competition made it seem that this would easily be Ferrari's year, as they had been gearing up for the new fuel regulations and thought Vanwall would take some time to catch up. With no Vanwalls or BRMs going to the Argentine, the only works cars were the Ferraris...and an OSCA for Colin Davis and that never made it and a Rob Walker Cooper for Moss but that wouldn't be competitive against the Ferraris!

Most of the teams flew to Buenos Aires, though Peter and Louise Collins, now enamoured with travel by boat, chose to take that method of transport from New York to South America, a trip of over two weeks in those days. Originally the idea was to travel on to Cuba, but while they were in Argentina Peter decided to skip the Cuban race, interesting in view of the fact that an entry must have already been made.

Musso, Collins and von Trips were down to drive the Dino 156 chassis with 2.4litre engine and Hawthorn the new 246 chassis with the same engine. Trips' car wasn't finished so he didn't get a chance. There were surprises in practice as Fangio was delaying his retirement and had a 250F which he put on pole as the Ferraris were not running as smoothly as expected. Nevertheless, Hawthorn and Collins (chassis 0012) were 2nd and 3rd quickest with Behra next in another dated 250F and Moss was three places further back.

It was all over for Peter Collins when a drive shaft broke before the first lap was over. This meant Hawthorn led until Fangio took over. The Maseratis started to overheat as they had not adapted very well to the non-alcohol fuel and then Hawthorn went in to have his oil pressure checked, though he came out again. All this meant that the slow starting Moss in the little Cooper T43 with a 1.9litre Coventry Climax engine was in the lead, with Musso behind. Then came the famous collective 'Ferrari double take' as Musso and the team waited for the Cooper to go in for fresh tyres. Musso had made his stop so fully expected to win as he was close behind. Then the penny dropped...Moss wasn't going to stop. Even though the tyres were worn to the canvas, it was too late for Musso to do anything about it. The Rob Walker team had cleverly wheeled out a set of new tyres for Moss which fooled the Ferrari team altogether and Cooper got a famous win, Musso disappointed in 2nd and Hawthorn 3rd. This was Rob Walker's first Grand Prix win and though not many people realised it at the time, was the significant sign of change for F1 racing.

January 26 - Argentine 1000 Kilometers

Peter and Louise had started off in Buenos Aires in the same hotel with the Ferrari team but after an invitation from an old friend, Tito Reynal, they moved to his suburban home for the time in Argentina. They also had

Peter Collins and Phil Hill opened the 1958 season with a fine win over their team mates in this Ferrari 250 Testa Rossa. Photo - Whitefly

a trip to Uruguay with Mike Hawthorn accompanying them, where he managed to get so sun-burned that he was confined to bed and missed the first practice for the following weekend's sports car race.

Regulation changes had also had a big impact on sports cars, which now had a three-litre limit for the Championship. This seemed to favour Aston Martin but at that stage didn't take into account all the work that Enzo Ferrari had done on developing the Testa Rossa, which was one of the reasons Peter Collins had wanted to be in the Ferrari team in sports cars as well as Grand Prix cars.

The entry wasn't very large but the long race round the nearly six-mile circuit was more interesting than had been expected. There were four works 250 Testa Rossas and Jon von Neumann's private car, Trintignant/Picard had a 250 GT LWB and there were a few other private cars, while Fangio had one Maserati 300S and there were two more and some 200S models present as well. Collins and Phil Hill had set fastest time from Fangio/Godia who had eventually come out to South America by another route, having avoided the plane that had crashed killing everyone aboard.

The race got down to a fight between the Collins and Musso Ferraris, or looked to until Trintignant hit Musso on the first lap and put him out. Fangio took up the chase but crashed on lap 24. Magnasco had been killed on lap eight in a 300S, so von Trips/Gendebien/Musso shared the car that chased Collins and Hill. Stirling Moss and Jean Behra got up to second in the amazing Porsche RSK, a car which Moss always enjoyed driving. Phil Hill set a new lap record and then Collins broke it to set fastest lap. The second Ferrari finished on the same lap as the winners with the Porsche third. Peter Collins looked set to take the sports car driver's championship for the second year in a row.

February 2 - Buenos Aires Grand Prix

This race was run as a Formula Libre event with no engine size restrictions. This brought out an interesting array of cars, many with Chevrolet engines, including one for Froilan Gonzales, the ex-Trintignant Monaco 1955 car which Gonzales used for a

229

Froilan Gonzales in a Ferrari 500/625 leads one of the more modern runners.
Photo - Boswell Collection

number of years and which is now in the UK.

Fangio set fastest time but Mike Hawthorn won the first of two heats in pouring rain. Collins had been fifth fastest but his race only lasted for the start, as yet another driveshaft broke, as had happened two weeks before and his weekend was over. Hawthorn retired in the second heat so it was a fine win for Fangio overall, with Musso a good second and Gonzales 6th. Moss had also gone out early after a collision with another car.

Peter and Louise flew back to Italy with the Ferrari team, returning to Modena and then going down to Viareggio to make arrangements for the new boat they were buying, then went back to the apartment at Maranello where they celebrated their first wedding anniversary. Louise wrote home to her parents that she couldn't understand how the year had gone by so quickly. They were then in England for ten days before going back to New York, staying with Louise's parents before journeying on to Sebring.

Having missed the Cuban race, it must have come as a jolt to hear than Juan Fangio had been kidnapped, allegedly by Castro supporters and was held until after the race. Cynics at the time thought it might have been the organisers trying to get some interest in the race! Fangio later said it was the Castro people and they treated him very well. He was probably just as happy to miss it as an early accident killed some spectators, the race was stopped and Moss declared the winner.

March 22 - Sebring 12 Hours

The 1958 12 Hours was a classic Sebring race, with fine weather and a large crowd of 45,000 on hand to watch. Ferrari had built the Testa Rossa very much as a car that would appeal to privateers from the point of view of reliability, ease of maintenance and competitiveness. So three works cars were joined by three private entries.

The works cars were for Collins and Phil Hill again (chassis 0704), Musso and Gendebien, and von Trips/ Hawthorn. The opposition consisted of Aston Martin DBR1s for Moss and Brooks and Salvadori/Shelby. There were some

The drivers' meeting was a rather casual affair!

interesting Corvettes which might do well if they lasted, a pack of Porsches which were now not only good for class wins but had superb reliability. There were three Jaguar D-Types, a Maserati 300S for Bonnier/Dale Duncan and two Lister-Jaguars, one marked for Archie Scott-Brown and Walt Hansgen.

Moss in the Aston set a new record in practice, Scott-Brown was on the pace and the Ferraris were well off Moss' pace. On day two it was Moss, Hawthorn, Collins and Brooks, all within a second of each other. At the start Moss was gone immediately after his usual good Le Mans sprint start. On only the third lap, Scott-Brown spun avoiding another car and was rammed and mounted up the back by the Gendebien/Musso Ferrari. The Lister was out but the Ferrari got back to the pits for repairs. The works-sent Aston Martin DB2/4 MKIII sent over for George Constantine was out early...this car is another still very active in historic racing. The other Lister expired on lap six.

Salvadori steamed up past Hawthorn and Moss as well. Roy then stopped on lap 62 with gearbox failure and all the D-Types had retired well before this. Moss then had his gearbox go on lap 90, the same lap the Bonnier 300S

A DB coupe passes by Gendebien trying to figure out how to remove the Ferrari from the Lister...he did and finished second.

Above: Moss had the Aston in front in the early stages.

Below: Roy Salvadori's DBR1 on the wide open space of Sebring.

Salvadori is boxed in by the Pabst/Jeffords Corvette, the Constantine Aston 2/4MKIII, and the Bueb/Sanderson D-Type. All went out early.

stopped. At one-third distance, Collins and Hill had gone into the lead and, by halfway, the Ferraris had the first four places. As had become their pattern, Collins and Hill had settled down to driving quickly with as little strain on the car as possible. This meant they had a full lap on Musso and Gendebien after Hawthorn/von Trips lost the gearbox after 159 laps. One of the Porsche RSKs, that of Schell and Seidel got up to 3rd from the amazing Lotus 11 of Weiss/Tallakson. While some of the main opposition to Ferrari had been quick, none lasted. Only two Corvettes survived and they were way, way behind.

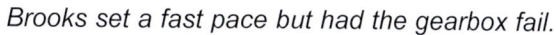

Brooks set a fast pace but had the gearbox fail.

Luigi Musso and Gendebien were second to Collins/Hill.

This Porsche RS was quick but stopped just after halfway, here driven by Jean Behra.

Collins and Hill drove a virtually flawless race to win at Sebring.

As Phil Hill jumped into the victorious Ferrari with Collins to drive onto the victory ramp, Collins was heard to shout "lookout, I haven't got any brakes!" Fortunately, Ferrari pit work had been for the most part very efficient during this race, somewhat in contrast with Aston Martin, where there were long stops. When Moss handed over to Brooks at one point, they were in the pits for nearly four minutes and a lot of strain was put on the car and its

Hill and Collins with big trophies; Kessler and O'Shea, right, won their class in a Ferrari 250GT.

All about the boy!

vulnerable gearbox in the attempt to catch up. There doesn't seem to be a record as to whether Collins derived some satisfaction from having beaten his old team and team mates at Aston Martin.

The Sebring winners trophy today.
Photo - Frank Sheffield

It was after the Sebring race that Mike Hawthorn pulled one of his typical stunts by walking into Peter and Louise's motel room and stepping fully clothed into the bath, then dragging Paul O'Shea's wife in after him. Peter and Louise flew to New York where Louise's father, Andrew Cordier, an important official at the United Nations threw a large party for the couple, attended by some important UN staff, as well as actor Peter Ustinov. They then returned to England for the races at Goodwood and Silverstone and the beginning of the European racing season.

Peter Miller, Collins' former colleague at Astons, saw Peter at Sebring and made this observation:

"Peter looked bronzed and fit, although he had put on weight since his marriage and his whole appearance had been transformed. He wore a neat sports jacket at the pre-race parties, smoked a pipe and seemed very contented with life and I thought he had lost his former lean and hungry look." (Miller, 1962, p.171). Miller remarks a few pages later that, after Sebring, he was not returning to England until late in 1959 and that Sebring was the last time he saw Collins, Hawthorn, Musso and Scott-Brown.

April 17 - Goodwood Sussex Trophy

News in the week up to the Easter races at Goodwood included a report that Ferrari were preparing a 'special' car for the second 'Race of the Two Worlds' at the end of June, one to be driven by Musso and the other by Collins or Hawthorn, though this never happened. It was somewhat reminiscent of the recurring story of cars that Ferrari were building for Indianapolis which never appeared!

A surprise in the Sussex Trophy race turned out to be Peter Collins not driving a 3litre Testa Rossa but an all-new car, the two litre Dino 196/206S. This space-frame chassis had a rigid rear axle and helical springs and it prompted immediate rumours that Ferrari was going to abandon the V12 and go for 6-cylinder engines.

The good looking new Ferrari at Goodwood.
Photo - Ferret Fotographics

236

Collins gets a nice drift going in the new Ferrari. It must have been cold as the radiator is blanked off. Photo - Klemantaski Collection

In the race, Moss started off in the lead but Scott-Brown got the Lister-Jag past and was off, with Collins third chased by Duncan Hamilton in the D-Type. After a few laps Moss got closer to Archie, the Aston DBR2 going very well. Then the Lister steering gave trouble on the tenth lap and it was out, with Collins 20 seconds behind in his first drive at Goodwood in three years, finishing second. Hawthorn took the F1 Glover Trophy race in the Ferrari, a race in which Jean Behra had his crash into the Chicane wall which in those days was brick, not styrofoam! The much-photographed incident was fortunate in that Behra had only minor injuries but the BRM was much worse off.

May 3 - Silverstone International Trophy

Peter Collins was to have driven the Ferrari that Hawthorn used at Goodwood for the BARC 200 at Aintree on April 19 but that had been sent back to the factory for further development. Luigi Musso had taken Dino 246 chassis 0001, Hawthorn's Argentine car, to Siracusa on April 13 and won the race there over a fairly mediocre field but won nevertheless. Chassis 0002 of the new generation Dino 246 was dispatched to Silverstone for the International Trophy, a non-championship race which always attracted a first class entry and was taken as seriously as a Grand Prix.

This was to be Collins' opportunity to see what he could achieve with the new car. While the press had detailed the new Dino, it was still not necessarily clear to the knowledgeable public and perhaps even to some of the competition, that this was no longer a Lancia D-50 or D-50 derivative but Ferrari's all-new hope for the final years of the 2.5litre formula.

The grid was indicative of just how quickly the Formula One scene was changing, as the first three cars were the Coopers of Salvadori, Brabham and Moss followed by Collins in the Dino, then Behra and Flockhart in the BRM P25 and Graham Hill and Cliff Allison in Lotus 12s and all this on the fast Silverstone circuit.

Collins takes Copse Corner with a touch of understeer in the new Ferrari. Photo - Anthony Pritchard/T.C.March Collection

Collins used the power of the Ferrari to take the lead at the start but the charging Behra in the BRM got past on lap five and he stayed there for five laps when a stone broke his goggles and he had to pit for another pair. He came back to 4th but it was left to Salvadori in the 2litre Cooper to try and chase Collins.

Peter was clearly comfortable in the new car and as he got more familiar with it, made full use of the power on the fast Silverstone circuit, drifting beautifully through the corners.

Moss had the gearbox go at lap 18, so Peter eased away to win from Roy Salvadori by some

Collins' win at Silverstone helped to stall thoughts about the threat of the rear-engine cars. Photo - Anthony Pritchard/T.C.March Collection

The racing career - The Ferrari years 1956-1958

24 seconds, sharing fastest lap with Jean Behra. It seemed the new car was very suited to Collin's style of driving, using the power in very fast corners to extend the gap over his rivals without over-stressing the car. He was very smooth during this period, seeming to drive at his best when in the lead. This is not to say that Collins didn't explore the limits of the car. He did just that at Copse Corner and spun onto the grass and though he held his lead, it did allow Salvadori to get a bit closer to him.

May 11 - Targa Florio

It was immediately off to the Targa Florio for some reconnaissance and practice for most of the drivers, especially Phil Hill and Mike Hawthorn, who had never been there before. Hawthorn hated it and said to Hill during a practice run that he was happy it was a circuit he wouldn't have to do again, making it clear that he was planning to retire at the end of the 1958 season.

65 entries were accepted and 53 started this running of the great race, this time over 14 laps of the 44.7 mile circuit. The vast majority of entries were Sicilian and Italian privateers and the real fight would be between four factory Ferrari 250 Testa Rossas, a works Porsche RSK for Behra/Scarlatti and an Aston Martin DBR1 for Moss and Brooks. The Ferraris were for: Munaron/Seidel, Collins/Hill, von Trips/Hawthorn and Musso/Gendebien.

There was no official practice as such and the cars set off with the smallest and presumably slowest first. The fight was between Musso and Collins as reports came in from around the island and Moss in the Aston appeared very late, lost a lot of time repairing a crankshaft weight which had fallen off, and then broke down out in the country. Colin Davis in an OSCA MT4 was an early threat for the lead but it was Musso who seemed in control. When he retired Behra and Scarlatti became a strong challenge as well. Phil Hill took over from Collins but went off the road and had to push himself back onto the circuit, dropping the pair to 4th where they finished. In spite of running

The rural scene before the start. Peter and Louise Collins are on the left walking towards their car while Phil Hill talks to an official. Number 100 is the Moss/Brooks Aston Martin.
Photo - Ferret Fotographics

Collins in the Ferrari before going off the road. Photo - Klemantaski Collection

out of brake fluid, Musso and Gendebien won from the Porsche, Trips/Hawthorn and Collins/Hill while the 4th 250 TR had also retired. It had been a good day for Ferrari and they now led the sports car series by ten points.

May 18 - Monaco Grand Prix

There were 29 entries for Monaco and of these 28 showed up. The non-show was a Maserati entered by Scuderia Sud America for Fangio. There were four Ferraris, three 246 Dinos and a smaller 156 Dino for von Trips but this got the larger engine for the race, three Vanwalls, three BRMs, of which only Flockhart didn't qualify. The two Lotus 12s did well. Brooks, Behra and Brabham had three different marques on row one and the Ferrari drivers felt they were down on power and Hawthorn was down on row three with Moss. Collins was a row back ahead of Musso and von Trips and Trintignant was on the second row going well in the Rob Walker Cooper.

The Vanwalls of Lewis-Evans and Brooks were early retirements, then Behra went out from the lead at 30 laps. Moss and Hawthorn fought it out until Moss' engine broke, followed 17 laps later by Hawthorn with a failed fuel pump. The reliable Cooper of Trintignant carried on steadily into the lead. In the late stages, both Musso and Collins had made ground and were pulling out all the stops but the Frenchman was 21 seconds in front of Musso and Collins finished 18 seconds further back. Cooper had broadcast the message again, loud and clear!

There is some superb colour cine film of this race at Monaco and the cameraman at one point stationed himself inside the old Gasometer Hairpin to get close-up shots of the

*Above: Collins passes Hawthorn's retired car at the entrance to the tunnel.
Photo - LAT*

*Collins at the Station Hairpin.
Photo - Ferret Fotographics*

All about the boy!

The Ferrari strains through the Station Hairpin. Photo - LAT

drivers. Peter Collins is shown lap after lap in car number 36 braking hard into the corner, his arms crossed over as he twirled the steering wheel and applied the power coming out of the corner. His hands fly swiftly back and forth as he corrects and then lets the wheel go as the Ferrari powers away. For most people, it's as close as we will ever get to Peter Collins...a stunning sight.

The racing career - The Ferrari years 1956-1958

The racing world, especially in Britain, was shocked to hear that Archie Scott-Brown had been killed at Spa when his Lister-Jaguar had crashed and burned. The determined Archie had won many friends in his battle to overcome considerable odds and prejudice.

May 26 - Dutch Grand Prix

The Ferraris were not much better at Zandvoort for the Dutch Grand Prix. Hawthorn headed Collins and Musso on the grid but they were all way behind the Vanwalls on a circuit where they could expect to go well. The Dinos understeered through practice and if pushed hard, the understeer turned to sudden and uncontrollable oversteer and there wasn't much power either. Collins and Musso had been having a battle royal in about 9th and 10th places and then Collins had the gearbox seize and he went off and couldn't get restarted. Though Brooks and Lewis-Evans retired their Vanwalls, Moss went on to victory. Hawthorn salvaged 5th and Musso 7th for Ferrari but they had been humiliated. It would get a bit worse before it got better.

June 1 - Nurburgring 1000 Kilometers

After the Dutch race, Hawthorn had strong words with Tavoni about the poor performance of the cars and when he went back to the UK, he wrote a letter to Enzo Ferrari also in strong terms. It is interesting to speculate how Ferrari viewed the Hawthorn-Collins combination and it is interesting that at the next race at the Ring, they were together in the Testa Rossa. This broke up the so-far successful partnership of Collins and Phil Hill. Roy Salvadori felt they were a terrible combination of drivers for Ferrari as *together* they found it very difficult to be serious. Those more sympathetic to Peter Collins would see this as part of the negative influence Hawthorn had on Collins, though Louise Collins never seems to have supported this view.

Collins and Hawthorn were in 0704 and the other three works cars were shared by von Trips/Gendebien, Musso/Hill and Munaron/Seidel. Peter and Mike were fastest of all in practice, obviously able to be serious when

Collins in the Testa Rossa at the Ring. He and Hawthorn finished 2nd to Moss.
Photo - Klemantaski Collection

All about the boy!

needed or wanted, with Moss in the Aston DBR1 next, which Stirling was sharing with Jack Brabham at the Ring for the first time and who was much slower than his partner. Two other Astons were there for Brooks/Lewis-Evans and Salvadori/Shelby.

Moss built up a lead over Hawthorn which was lost when Brabham took over. Then Hawthorn had a damaged tyre and pitted and handed over to Collins. He again caught up the gap to Brabham but Moss again put the car in the lead. When Hawthorn took over towards the end, he managed to put the car in a ditch, losing time but not the position and thus the Ferrari was second to the flying Moss, who was four minutes ahead. The other Testa Rossas finished in the next three places, building Ferrari's title lead.

June 15 - Belgian Grand Prix

Collins on the parade lap in an Austin Healey Sprite, much promoted in 1958. Photo - P3 Motorsport

Peter Collins' chance of a good result at Spa was ruined by the dithering of the starter, who, when Masten Gregory's car wouldn't start, held the already boiling cars for another minute. Collins was on the second row of the grid and the first four had been covered by only six tenths of a second. Vanwall had thought they had the front row tied up and were very relaxed but Hawthorn found his car much better and was on pole with Musso next, then Moss, Collins and Brooks. These last two immediately engaged in a fight for the lead but Collins was quickly out with serious overheating. The paint had been blistering on the engine cover, so hot had the engine become.

Then Moss, Gregory, Seidel, Behra and Musso also went out and the race was only five laps old. Musso crashed and the others all had engine failure. Musso's shunt at Stavelot was huge and he was lucky to come out of it with minor injuries. Hawthorn at first thought it was Collins who had crashed and surely must have been killed. Nixon (1991) says that Hawthorn lost interest in the race, though in fact he did keep up the pace for all the remaining laps.

The race then settled into a dreary procession, with Brooks coming home first but his gearbox tightening as he approached the line. Then Hawthorn had a piston break as he headed for the flag and Lewis-Evans' suspension broke. If the race had been a few hundred meters longer, Cliff Allison would have given Lotus their first Grand Prix victory, three years before Innes Ireland did it in 1961! The race ran well under the 'mandatory' two hours and if it had gone the distance, Allison might well have won.

June 22/23 - Le Mans 24 Hours

The tale of Peter Collins at Le Mans in 1958 is one that has been rather wrapped in myth and exaggeration over the years. It is seen as the trigger that ended

The racing career - The Ferrari years 1956-1958

the 'special relationship' between Peter Collins and Enzo Ferrari. The stories have always been intriguing and in many ways rang true, as Ferrari had a pattern of developing such relationships and then ending them, or seen them end through tragedy.

Ferrari had three Testa Rossas for Gendebien/Phil Hill, von Trips/Seidel and 0704 for Collins and Hawthorn all with new all-enveloping bodies. There were plenty of privateers in support. The works Astons were there for Moss/Brabham, Salvadori/Lewis-Evans and Trintignant/Brooks, as well as several D-Type Jaguars and a pair of Listers. Practice made it clear that the race would be between the Astons and the Ferraris. The weather looked ominous and it was sure to have an influence. No one expected, however, that one of the worst ever rain storms was on the way.

Moss led a train of Astons away from the start though Hawthorn, abusing the clutch at the start, was behind Moss at the end of the first lap. Moss led the early part of the race, with sometimes von Trips and sometimes Hawthorn in second. Just after two hours, however, the news came through that Moss' engine had blown and that was followed almost immediately by torrential rain. Hawthorn, now leading, came in and handed over to Collins and there were cars sliding all over the circuit.

Phil Hill had taken over from Gendebien and was driving brilliantly. There were several accidents and at four hours Lewis-Evans was one of them with the Aston. The Hamilton/Bueb D-Type was catching the two leading Ferraris towards midnight, while Collins and Hawthorn had a number of problems and had made pit stops to sort them. The Jaguar eventually got out in front of the Ferraris as the terrible conditions persisted. That was in the 8th hour but an hour later the Hill/Gendebien car was back in front and that is where it stayed. The Jaguar disappeared in hour 19 to be replaced in 2nd by the Whitehead brothers' surviving Aston Martin.

A two-litre Ferrari, driven by Mexican Pedro Rodriguez and Jose Behra, the brother of Jean, retired at about 3.00 am after a good run. Pedro, 18, was to share with brother Ricardo but the officials would not have a 16 year old in their race. He certainly was more capable than many who were out there!

The Autosport report simply noted that the Collins/Hawthorn car stopped at 2.15 am with clutch failure.

Peter had been forced to abandon the Ferrari out on the circuit and get back to the pits. He couldn't get any gears and there was no indication that the clutch would operate. When he got back, he and Louise and Mike packed and returned to England. Peter was due to do demonstration runs at Oulton Park in a few days for Mercedes with the pre-war W163. Supposedly, what got back to Enzo Ferrari was a story that Hawthorn had said before the race that they didn't want to do this 24 hour event and would get it over. That was in keeping with his usual somewhat joking and sometimes immature behaviour. No one believed that they would do that. Mike was not easy on clutches and made a fierce start. But they did lead the race and were going very quickly while they were running so there was no evidence that they sabotaged the car. Some drivers have done that...Jochen Rindt is an example...but they didn't. When the mechanics retrieved the car, the clutch was working...not surprising after cooling down overnight but it wouldn't have been working after a few laps.

The story gets complicated. Nixon (1991) says that the Le Mans incident started the breakdown in the relationship between Collins

All about the boy!

and Enzo Ferrari. But he also says that moving onto the boat in Monte Carlo was the trigger for the ending of the 'special relationship'. Louise, however, clarified this for the author:

"The Ferraris were always very kind to me and we never "moved" to Monte Carlo. We bought our boat and took it to Monte Carlo but we also kept the villa that Ferrari loaned us in Maranello right up to Peter's death and that's where we stayed when we were in Modena. I know that in '*Mon Ami Mate*' it says that we shut up the house but we didn't because after Peter died I had to pack up our things out of the house so there's a little confusion there."

There appeared to be rumours that Collins was not going to get a Grand Prix drive at Reims. However, these rumours don't seem to have been reported at the time. Certainly Autosport's Gregor Grant didn't report them. He would have had Collins' ear and he did very full Le Mans reports and follow-ups and nothing appears in them. Sheldon and Rabagliati, in their superb statistical summaries of F1 races, didn't report it and they picked up the undercurrents of the period.

There, of course, were Ferrari minions, many of whom spent years presenting selected information to Enzo Ferrari, telling tales, operating on behalf of some drivers rather than others, etc. Musso was desperate to win the upcoming French Grand Prix, so it is feasible to think that someone was working to support that. Or maybe Ferrari did act on wrong information about Le Mans. But if he did, why punish Collins when, if there was any culprit, it was Hawthorn? Yes, it is true that Enzo Ferrari would have been affected by Collins spending time on his boat. Yes, he would have a reaction to Louise having an influence on Peter, as he had seen Peter as something of a substitute for Dino. Yes, it was like him to be impulsive. But, no, the author does not accept that there was a break-up of the 'special' bond as described and that there was a calculated plan to deprive Collins of a race at Reims. The evidence is that Louise says that she and Peter continued to remain on good terms with Enzo and Laura Ferrari.

July 7 - French Grand Prix - Coupe Internationale de Vitesse

In retrospect we have the accounts that Peter Collins arrived at Reims to find that he was driving in the F2 race but not the Grand Prix. There were stories that this was to protect Musso's chances of a win, though why Hawthorn should be driving is not clear or explained. Peter pushed Amarotti to talk to Tavoni and Enzo Ferrari to sort this, especially if he did well and was fit after the F2 race and that agreement was reached...possibly reached too easily for it to have been a firm plan by Ferrari.

The F2 race took place not long after the finish of the 12 hour sports car race. It was a significant F2 event and with such a good grid, helped the cause of F2 in Europe immensely. Collins was in the original F2 Ferrari Dino 156 chassis 0011, suitably updated and with F2 engine, of course. He was in the middle of the front row, with Jean Behra on pole in a Porsche RSK 1.5 which had been neatly converted to single seat format. It was very effective. Moss was on the outside in a Rob Walker Cooper T45. The works Cooper of Brabham broke on the line and Roy Salvadori only lasted two laps.

Behra led for a few laps, then Moss, then Behra again and these two and Collins opened up a gap on the rest. On lap 10 Moss came in with low oil pressure in the Climax and after another lap decided to quit. George Wicken brought his T43 up into 3rd. Ian Burgess got 4th from Henry Taylor and Bruce McLaren. Behra was twenty seconds ahead off Collins at the end and the Porsche performance surprised many.

Peter Collins in the F2 Dino 156 in the Reims F2 race.

Jean Behra surprised everyone with the speed of the converted Porsche RSK.

Stirling Moss catches eventual 3rd place finisher George Wicken after visiting the pits. Moss retired at the end of this lap...and Wicken had some problems at the start!

Collins took the Ferrari through Thillois Corner very quickly.

Another view of the shapely new Dino 156.

Bruce McLaren leads Henry Taylor in their race long duel.

Jean Behra takes the flag 20 seconds ahead of Collins.

In addition to the return of five-time World Champion Juan Fangio, there were several other interesting drivers on hand for the Grand Prix who were not part of the usual Grand Prix scene. One was American Carroll Shelby who was better known for his sports car drives, especially in Aston-Martins in Europe and in Maseratis in the USA. Fellow American Troy Ruttmann was an experienced Indianapolis driver who got talked into trying F1 by Shelby and they were both in the CentroSud Team with now ageing Maserati 250Fs. Gerino Gerini was also in the team, having one of his very few Formula 1 races. Occasional F1 driver Francesco Godia-Sales was in a 250F as was another American, Phil Hill, also in a Maserati but this one owned by Jo Bonnier. Only Fangio was able to make the great old 250F go well against the newer cars and this would be Fangio's last Grand Prix.

The Vanwalls had demonstrated their quality through 1957, though reliability wasn't established until later in 1957 and in the early part of 1958. The Vanwalls were very quick through the first half of the 1958 season but the Ferraris had been getting better and better. Schell in the BRM and Tony Brooks put in quick times at the beginning of practice but Mike Hawthorn showed how much the Ferrari 246 had improved by soon setting pole time. Luigi Musso was desperate to demonstrate that he was the best Italian F1 driver and was pushing his car very hard to qualify 0.7 seconds behind Hawthorn. Schell's early time kept him on the front row but he was almost a second slower than Musso. The Ferrari's top speed was embarrassing the Vanwalls and Peter Collins squeezed in ahead of Brooks on the second row, forcing Stirling Moss back to the third rank. There were reports that Musso was running a slightly lighter, F2 version of the Dino, chassis 0012, though his car has always been reported as chassis 0004. Trintignant posted the same time as Moss in another BRM, ahead of Juan Fangio. The 'master' was quickest of the 250Fs, marginally ahead of Behra in the BRM and Lewis-Evans' Vanwall. Godia-Sales was the next quickest 250F but four seconds behind Fangio, yet still two seconds faster than Phil Hill. Von Trips didn't set a time so started from the back of the grid.

The BRM of Harry Schell and Tony Brooks emerged in front as the flag was dropped, Brooks squeezing between Schell and Musso but Mike Hawthorn quickly got past them both in the first lap and was followed through by Musso and Collins, the torque of the 246 Dino engine being very impressive for the large French crowd. Collins no sooner had joined his team mates when he had trouble with the brakes, a brake air scoop jamming behind the pedal and he went straight on, missing a corner and losing many places. He would have to spend much of the race catching up. He had set a new circuit record on lap three.

Peter Collins lines up again with Behra in the Grand Prix shortly after the finish of the F2 race. Photo - Klemantaski Collection

Schell's BRM and Brooks' Vanwall get the jump on Hawthorn and Musso with Moss, Trintignant and Fangio next.

The whole field rushes up the hill towards the old Dunlop Bridge.

Hawthorn was settling into a dominant pace but Musso, had the Englishman in sight and would not let him go. He hung onto Hawthorn for several laps. On the tenth lap, Hawthorn came past the pits, uphill and down into the right-hander where the road goes to the village of Gueux. Hawthorn managed this corner flat in top gear and Musso tried this as well and it didn't work. He crashed and was killed and that was the end of Italy's best Grand Prix driver. In fact, with Eugenio Castellotti already gone, Italy really didn't have any significant drivers left.

Hawthorn on lap 10 in the lead.

Luigi Musso on lap 10, desperately chasing Hawthorn. He tried to follow Hawthorn flat through the right-hand corner after the Dunlop Bridge and crashed to his death, seconds after this photo was taken.

Given the layout of the Reims circuit, very few spectators knew what happened until after the race. Mike Hawthorn was now leading the Vanwall of Tony Brooks and behind them was a fierce battle between Schell, Moss, Fangio and Behra. Fangio had certainly lost none of his flare and skill and was making the old Maserati go well. Cliff Allison had had his engine fail on lap six and Shelby's Maserati engine went on the same lap that Musso crashed. On lap 16, Brooks brought the Vanwall in, the gearbox having broken. The second place battle was broken up when Behra began to struggle and he would eventually end up unclassified when the fuel pump stopped. Fangio made a brief stop, so Moss then held second on his own, though he couldn't catch Hawthorn. Schell had slowed because the BRM was overheating. Wolfgang von Trips had worked his way up the field and Collins was also recovering very well. Trintignant had an oil pipe break on his BRM on lap 24 so he retired and the Godia-Sales 250F crashed a few laps later. Through all this, Hawthorn pushed on, setting fastest lap at 128.17 mph.

The engine in G Hill's Lotus failed on lap 33 and Lewis-Evans' Vanwall engine also went two laps later. As the race ran out, Hawthorn led Moss, with von Trips 3rd and Collins 4th but Collins' Ferrari ran out of fuel right at the end and this allowed Fangio to slip past. The first five were the only cars to complete the full 50 laps. Mike Hawthorn was right behind Fangio at the end but refused to lap him. This was seen as an act of true sportsmanship from Hawthorn, who was often criticized for his boyish and flamboyant behaviour off the track. His victory would prove crucial to Hawthorn winning the Driver's World Championship in 1958. Though the race was truly tragic for the loss of Luigi Musso, this had been an example of wonderful late 1950s motor racing. Musso had apparently just concluded a business deal to import American cars into Italy and his business partner had said that he must win to pay his debts!

After some braking problems, Collins dropped from 3rd and finished 5th behind Fangio. Photo - LAT

This was Hawthorn's first Grand Prix win in nearly four years and Phil Hill's first Grand Prix finish, though in a Maserati, not a Ferrari.

July 20 - British Grand Prix

The motoring press were full of excitement over what could only be a massive showdown between Stirling Moss and Mike Hawthorn who were tied on 23 points each in the World Championship battle. There was virtually no one else in with a chance if you believed what you read.

Indeed it was Moss in the Vanwall who looked quickest in practice and who put the green car on pole. Next, however, was not a Ferrari nor another Vanwall but good old Harry Schell in the BRM P25. And next to him? It was Roy Salvadori in the Cooper T45...about to have a brilliant weekend in the little Cooper. Then came Hawthorn in the Dino 246 chassis 0003, an amazing Cliff Allison and the Lotus, Peter Collins in chassis 0002 Dino and Lewis-Evans in the second Vanwall. Brooks was a row back and looked unlikely to figure in the fighting at the front.

The Moss-Hawthorn fight more or less disappeared at the drop of the flag as it was Collins who got the Ferrari power down first, shot through the gap and was away...and, essentially, gone. Whatever had been said, or would be said, about Peter's motivation, it was clear that this day all he wanted to do was win. He might have been expected to hang back and help Hawthorn get more points than Moss but the fact was that they couldn't catch him. Nixon has Moss leading to Maggott's Corner when Collins went past him, though *Autosport* clearly has Collins getting by everybody down the straight into Copse. It was academic, however, he was gone.

254

The racing career - The Ferrari years 1956-1958

Above: The Collins Ferrari is wheeled onto the Silverstone grid; (17) is Cliff Allison's Lotus.

Below: Collins fastens his helmet and has words with an official.

The grid was a pretty relaxed place in 1958. Photo - Anthony Pritchard/T.C.March Collection

Collins prepares himself for the start. His preparation worked. Photo - Klemantaski Collection

The racing career - The Ferrari years 1956-1958

At the end of lap one, Collins has pulled out a gap on Moss in the Vanwall.

Peter Collins eases the Dino into Copse Corner.

Moss then lost the Vanwall engine on lap 25, so the highly expected encounter was over. Hawthorn then needed a stop for more oil and this caused anxiety in the Ferrari camp as it was thought Collins might be in trouble with over-consumption as well. Hawthorn didn't lose a place. Salvadori was in a great 3rd spot and Lewis-Evans couldn't catch him. Then came Schell, Brabham and a lapped Tony Brooks. Hawthorn set fastest lap and was 24 seconds behind Collins at the end.

All about the boy!

Hawthorn in the pits for more oil, talking to Tavoni.

*Collins had a flawless run, finishing well ahead of Mike Hawthorn.
Photo - Anthony Pritchard/T.C.March Collection*

The racing career - The Ferrari years 1956-1958

David Brown of Aston Martin recalled that Peter had said to him that he would help Mike at Silverstone and that he would go out and set the pace to draw out the opposition, presumed to be Moss and attempt to get Moss to blow up. Well, that happened but then the 'rabbit' didn't expire so Collins won by a long way.

The Collins entourage returned to Shatterford Grange, the whole family having been at Silverstone. Tony Brooks brought Pina, later his wife, along to the Collins family home. Peter checked them into a hotel and was surprised when Tony asked for separate rooms. Tony had met Pina at Rouen in 1956.

August 3 - German Grand Prix

After their ordeal at the Nurburgring the year before, Vanwall had put a great deal of work into improving their three cars for this year's German Grand Prix. While Moss had said he had thought he had lost his chance of the Championship at Silverstone, he was in fact still a strong contender.

It was a bit of a surprise, then, that Hawthorn was fast enough for pole position, a second quicker than Tony Brooks. Moss was four seconds further back and then Collins, almost three seconds slower than Moss. It was clear, however, that when the race started, the times would be much closer.

Ferrari brought five cars, 0002 for Hawthorn, 0003 for Collins and 0004 for von Trips as well as a spare and 0011, the Dino 156 F2 car for Phil Hill to finally make his Ferrari debut in a Grand Prix. There was an F2 race incorporated into the Grand Prix and Hill and Brabham turned very respectable times in the F2 cars. Brabham hadn't done enough laps in practice so he was forced to start at the back while Hill was on row three.

At the start, Brooks and Moss were at the front,

*The start of the German Grand Prix.
Photo - Fodisch Archive*

259

The first lap and Moss leads Brooks into South Turn, with Schell right behind, then Hawthorn and Collins.

and Harry Schell had come out of the line from the third row, driven down part of the pit lane and was third by the South Turn. He even got by Brooks but he was soon overtaken by several cars. Hawthorn and Collins went by Brooks but Moss soon stretched out a long lead, 20 seconds at the end of the lap.

Hawthorn leads Collins after Moss retired and before Brooks had caught them. Photo - LAT

The racing career - The Ferrari years 1956-1958

Hawthorn and Collins then took nine seconds back from Moss, who got this back a lap later when he had seen a pit signal. Peter Collins had pushed past Hawthorn into second with Brooks a bit further back. On the fourth lap, the two Ferraris came by in front with Brooks 30 seconds in arrears. Moss had his magneto fail and that was that. Collins was leading at the time Tony Brooks decided to make his move, cutting the gap to 11 seconds, then 8 1/2 seconds. As they finished lap nine, Collins had little over a second on Hawthorn and Brooks was now on Hawthorn's tail.

They went past the pits, down around the South Turn, came back past the rear of the pits and on the entry to North Turn Brooks got past Hawthorn. On the next lap both Ferraris were in front of the Vanwall again but Brooks was determined to get past on the tighter sections. He passed Hawthorn in the South Turn, then took Collins in the North Turn. They were on the eleventh lap, flying round the circuit in close company. They approached Pflanzgarten, a climbing right-hander. The report in *Autosport* says that Collins was right on Brooks' tail, other reports that he had dropped back a bit and now was trying to catch him again.

Phil Hill had a theory:

"Brooks won and I got ninth overall and fifth in Formula 2 - but Pete's death upset all of us. He was like a little boy in racing, full of fun and loving every minute of it. We still don't know *exactly* how it happened but my theory is that he didn't or couldn't use his brakes before coming over the brow. By then he was going too fast to get around. Maybe his brakes failed...anyway he never had a chance on that bend." (Nolan, 1996, p.120).

But Hawthorn was there and he saw it and reported it later in his own book, *'Champion Year'*. Hawthorn said that there were only three cars lengths covering them and that going into the dip in 3rd gear Collins seemed to be accelerating too hard, coming through too fast. Hawthorn's view was that Peter did not turn in early enough, was trying so hard to catch Brooks, that he went wide on the exit, his rear wheel caught the bank.

Collins' Ferrari struck the bank and flipped over, throwing Peter out. Hawthorn saw the 'blur of blue' as Peter was flung out. Hawthorn drove on, not quite knowing what to do. He passed the pits, and then his engine stopped some miles further on.

A first hand account by journalist Peter Lewis said the cars went through with a few car lengths' gap between each of them, Collins not being right on Brooks' backside. Lewis saw Collins run wide on the exit, almost not turning in at all and then rolling.

Peter had been thrown out and struck a rather small tree and had received very serious head injuries. He was being flown to a hospital in Bonn. As Tony Brooks won, Louise was completing her lap charts, when Tavoni came and told her about the accident and that it was serious. Tavoni drove Louise to the hospital. There had been the usual confused and contradictory reports, some that Collins was not badly injured, some that he was badly hurt and everything in between. Louise didn't make it to the hospital on time. Peter Collins had died in the helicopter.

There were the usual discussions about what had happened and there was an argument that the brakes might have been fading...that had happened to Hill and von Trips. The accident looked like one in which the car hadn't been slowed enough into the corner. But the stronger argument seems to be that Peter made a mistake. He was not about to lose this race like

261

All about the boy!

he and Hawthorn had the previous year. It seemed much more likely that he said to himself 'he's not getting away from me' and pushed just that bit too hard.

The great and joyous story was over in a flash.

*****

As Louise arrived at the University of Bonn clinic where Peter had been taken, she received a telephone call from her father who had already heard the news from one of his many world-wide contacts. He had decided it was best coming from him. He also arranged for the news to be delivered to the Collins family by a friend and associate who had his boat moored near the Genie Maris, where the Collins family was celebrating the engagement of Tricia to Michael Whittall.

Louise was brought back to England by Mike Hawthorn and they went directly to the Black Boy in Bewdley, as Mike couldn't remember how to get to Shatterford Grange.

Peter was cremated and his ashes buried near his paternal grandparents at St. Mary's Church at Stone. While the British press covered the funeral and memorial services, behind the scenes there was serious tension. The owner of Honeybrook House returned to Louise the £500 deposit Peter had paid on the house but more or less at the same time, Pat Collins asked Louise to sign away her claim to Peter's share in Kidderminster Motors. (Nixon, 1991, p.337).

It was after this that Louise went back to wind up arrangements for the Mipooka in Monte Carlo and to then return to Maranello. She discussed a number of the events in her letters home. When she was invited by several people to come to the Italian Grand Prix, including an invitation from Enzo Ferrari, she saw Mike Hawthorn again and she realised that the friendship the trio had shared was over. Louise returned to the United States and picked up her career as a stage actress, returning to the use of her stage name, Louise King.

The 'mon ami mate' phrase had been picked up by Hawthorn and Collins shortly after the Four D. Jones comic had first appeared in the *Daily Express* in May, 1957. It was Hawthorn's initiative and he used it to be referred to the two of them rather more than Peter did. They were 'mates' in a sense that meant something more than just friends and at the time it symbolized their position as the 'Brits in Ferrari'. They saw that as a good thing but not everybody else did. It was as much a declaration as a friendly motto. In retrospect, it may have obscured some things about them as individuals. Their relationship was only a short part of their lives. They were different in many ways. Peter was a person in his own right, a bright and charming young man and in many ways an eternal 'boy'. There remains something enigmatic about him...was there a deeper, less accessible side...or was it very much a case of what you saw was what you got? The tragedy is that not many people ever knew the answer to that question.

The racing career - The Ferrari years 1956-1958

There were countless tributes to Peter Collins. Mick Marriott found this one from the *BARC Gazette* dated July-August 1958 with the commentary by H.J. Morgan, the BARC's General Secretary:

"TRAGEDY AT NURBURGRING

What more can one say about Peter Collins? Except that his tragic passing is a grim reminder, if ever a reminder were necessary, of the risks which these young men who engage in top-flight motor racing regularly undertake.

They lead a glittering life, moving around in a sort of international circus from track to track throughout Europe and America and to the observer they appear to carry very lightly indeed the severe risks of their calling. They are men of immense courage and their life is one they would exchange for no other.

We remember Peter Collins from earliest days - the days when, with his father, he used to come down to Goodwood with a '500' Cooper in tow and stay with us all at the Richmond Arms. His pleasant and cheerful personality, combined with so much skill at the wheel, inevitably established him as a favourite when, in a relatively short space of time, he developed into a driver of world rank.

We also recall one particular example of his boyish enthusiasm immediately before the first post-war meeting at Crystal Palace (in 1952). It was a Sunday and Peter and some friends, including the late Bobbie Baird, turned up to see how we were getting on. Preparations were lagging somewhat in the hot sunshine but without further ado Peter doffed his jacket and shirt and spent the afternoon driving in fencing stakes and doing other odd jobs so that the place will be ready in time for racing tomorrow."

All about the boy!

The younger, dashing, car-oriented and dog loving Neville Hay in the days when he was an associate of Peter Collins. Photos - Neville and Dorothy Hay

264

WHAT THEY SAID ABOUT HIM...

Neville Hay

Neville Hay is one of Britain's best-known motor racing commentators, and filmmakers. He has been a lifelong participant in motor sport on many levels, and, as we will see, had a close and long-term relationship with the Collins family. He knew Peter very well, shared some adventures with him, and followed his career from beginning to end.

"The Collins family was a Kidderminster family and a well-known Kidderminster family. Pat Collins, Peter's father, or Percy as we used to call him, had had a very successful time during the war. He had built up a very large truck depot, and had a quite successful business. Peter was a young man just after the war and because when he started racing he was associated with the business, the local people knew quite a bit about him. There had been a few problems associated with the truck business and the British Road Services take-over just after the war but Peter was clear of that. I suppose the beginning of the Collins dynasty was through owning a piece of land in Kidderminster and they built the local Ford distributorship there. This was when Peter was growing up. He had a Ford 'special' and that is pretty much what he learned to drive in and learned about cars by working on it.

"Peter's mother, in comparison with the size of her husband and Peter, was quite a big woman. She had taught at King Charles I Grammar School for some time, and I remember her, not very well, but as a very nice lady. I suppose my real link with the Collins family started in two ways. My father and Mr. Collins knew each other quite well, they had the same kind of social life at the time, so the families knew each other, not well, but they knew each other. Secondly, Peter had a sister called Patricia and she went to the same school I went to, Knoll School. I went there from age eight to eleven. She was a year younger than I was. In those days, not everybody had a car and the Collins family used to bring her to school because by that time they were living at Shatterford Grange. They brought her to school in the morning, and when they collected her, if they were going back to the town, where I would be walking because my grandparents lived there, I would sometimes get a lift down with them...so I was younger than Peter but I knew the family and I knew him from a pretty early age. I knew Tricia and she was sort of a 'mouthy' sort of girl...she had an answer for everything. Most of her answers were sardonic rather than sarcastic, and she never changed!

"She never changed in all the time I knew her, and I recall much later in life I was talking to the sales director of the garage I was working for at the time. They were BMC agents and they wanted to buy a Ford for a client, so he summoned me to his office and asked me about this and I advised him to talk to Mr. Collins. He rang up the Collins garage and he was on the speakerphone and the voice that answered on the other end said 'Yes?' and my associate, Mr. Morris, said 'Don't you say 'yes' to me young woman, who are you?' 'We're Kidderminster Motors, who are you?' 'I am the sales and marketing director of the BMC depot in Birmingham and I want to speak to the dealer principal, I want to speak to Mr. Collins, and the first thing I am going to tell him is that I have had an extremely rude reception

All about the boy!

The young and erudite Neville Hay, friend and escort and driver to Peter Collins. Photo - Neville Hay Collection

from a telephonist.' And she said: 'I'm his daughter!'

"I was in school with Tricia from 1947 to 1950, so by this time I knew Peter. Sometimes it was Peter picking us up from school or possibly his mother, but I was definitely being driven by Peter Collins when I was in my youth! That was quite exciting because he was already racing in Formula 3 by that time. I had been going to Shelsley Walsh since 1946 and of course one of the first events Peter ever did was Shelsley Walsh. In those days, immediately post-war, there were no circuits, so Shelsley was a pretty special place. It was pretty much the same pre-war as well, so hill climbs were important right up until the mid-Fifties. They were much more important then than they are now in relation to motor racing as a whole. At that time he was racing quite a lot at weekends, but he and his father did not always hit it off all that well. That was understandable. They were about the same height, and they were actually very similar in temperament. I wasn't very good at sport but one thing I could be competitive at was swimming, and I used to swim every day. I got to know Peter better because I used to see Peter because if he was having a bit of the up and downs with his father, he would retire to the swimming baths where he would loaf around for a day or two.

"He was also a very strong swimmer, but we used to talk motor racing because even then I was into anything about motor sport and would read Autocar or The Motor or Motorsport. That's how I came to know Peter from that point of view. As I got older, he was away more, and then he lived in France for a while. There was the fuss at that time about National Service. The problem with Peter was very simple. He understood how to take a car apart and put it back together again...well, he was good at taking it apart, and I'm not sure how good he was at putting it all back together. I suppose from that point of view you might say that he had served a motor trade apprenticeship. Well, he never really did a real apprenticeship, but hands on he was okay.

"However, it was quite difficult in those days to get deferred unless you had, for want of a better word, a *proper* deferment arrangement centred around an apprenticeship, which could be a three or five year apprenticeship. Normally, therefore, at the age of 18 you got called up for your National Service. If you got a three-year deferment, that was ok until you were 21. Some people managed to stretch it to five and that took them to 23 but the trick of the game, if you could possibly do it, was to get some sort of deferment arrangement so you got to 26 and they lost interest in you. In Peter's case it was very clear that at the time that the Mike Hawthorn thing came about, which was about '53 or '54, there could be trouble. I think this has all been told pretty well by other

What they said about him...

people, but suffice it to say there was no way that Moss was ever going to pass a medical. As far as Peter was concerned, this was a far more deliberate attempt to avoid his career being interrupted by military service than ever it was in Mike Hawthorn's case. Mike Hawthorn became the victim, and he was the one who had all the publicity. He also had a lot of misery: the sad death of his father in a road accident, and he had the burns he had sustained at Syracuse which put him out of racing for a while. I'm not saying that he didn't indulge in a little hard work to dodge the situation by that stage because it was going to interrupt his career.

"But to understand Mike's situation, you have to go back a bit. At the beginning of 1952 there was the Cooper-Bristol and that was put together by Mike's father Leslie Hawthorn and he made a damned good job of it like everything else he did because he was a very fine mechanic. Like Freddie Dixon with the Riley, these guys knew how to put a car together properly. So throughout 1952 this car went exceptionally well. By the end of the year, two things had happened. Hawthorn had got a lot of really great publicity. Hawthorn went to drive for Ferrari. He knew a lot of people, and somehow, he could go to a race, finish second, and he would get more publicity than whoever finished first. If you mentioned Mike Hawthorn in 1952/53 most people who were even vaguely interested in motor racing would know who Hawthorn was. Perhaps a few would know Peter Collins, but they would all know Mike Hawthorn. As far as the others ...Peter Collins, Tony Rolt and Lance Macklin, who were often finishing ahead of Hawthorn in those years, nobody knew them at all. So the second thing was that Hawthorn was a star, Moss with British cars winning places, particularly in sports cars getting places. It wasn't winning but it was getting places. And Mike would always have a go. In those days he was fit, I mean really fit...wild, but fit.

"Towards the end of the year, he had got the Ferrari deal sewn up. He was actually going to drive a Ferrari at Modena. They had taken the Cooper-Bristol out to do Monza and Roy Salvadori was out there. They wanted somebody in the car and Roy could be very quick and he was there. Before Roy went out in the car, Mike decided to take it round. He had been driving the Ferrari in testing, and he decided to compare the two, and the result was catastrophic. He had a very big accident and the accident caused him a lot of damage. He had a lot of internal damage and he was in hospital for a long time and that was the beginning of his kidney problems. Then, move on the clock to his win in the 1954 Spanish Grand Prix in Barcelona with the Squalo Ferrari. He went into hospital then and had an operation and had a kidney removed and it was very clear by that time, because of Mike's personal habits, that is, his very hard drinking, the other kidney was not all that healthy, and that was in the days before dialysis.

"Peter said to me, and this is out of the context of the time we are talking about, he said in 1958 that 'this is Mike's last season and he's never going to get a license to race again. He will not be fit enough to get a license.' Those are more or less his exact words. They were mates...mon ami mate...well, I don't think Mike's influence on Peter was particularly a good one. When you are at school and you are a little bit in the shadow of a guy who is captain at rugby or cricket, and he's bigger and stronger than you and you want to be his friend. Well, I think that is sort of what their relationship was like. Peter fell into that category where Peter was either very nice, or very nasty. He wasn't very often nasty...he could cover it. Not many people noticed it, or would notice it. But that was what Peter was like. You wouldn't know that you

All about the boy!

had upset him until maybe a year or two years later...and he had a very long memory. He could be your best mate but he'd not forgotten that you'd upset him. I think other people might say he bore a grudge. If he lost an argument, if he felt in some way he had been belittled, he didn't forget it.

"So, Peter had managed to get himself a five-year apprenticeship, which took him up to the age of 23, which he would have been in 1954. His father would have drawn up the apprenticeship papers and Newnham, the company secretary, would have signed them. His deferment would have run out after that. There would have been a statement that said 'this young man has an apprenticeship from.....etc'. By the time deferment would have become an issue again, he would have been driving for Aston Martin in 1952 and had the Paris job. By 1952 he was driving for H.W.M., so he would have made the move from 500 c.c. cars, and this was a successful year in professional terms. He was having a good professional season, so he wasn't going to throw it all away, so he went and had a word with David Brown at Aston Martin, and it was arranged that he would go and live in France. This was before the Hawthorn hoo-hah, it was before it came up in Parliament, those discussions about putting helmets on racing drivers and putting them in the army. It was quite clever and Peter's father had helped sort it out before it became a story in the newspapers, before it became an issue. But Peter was thinking 'it would be a good thing if I'm not living in Kidderminster without an apprenticeship otherwise I'm going to get called up'. He certainly wasn't the only one stretching out their deferments and he was trying to protect his embryonic career.

"So he decided to live in Paris, and lived there throughout 1952 and 1953 and he seemed to manage to stay 'out of trouble' as far as being called up was concerned, because he would have been possibly called up until he was 26 in 1957, not that long before he was killed. He was spending some time in the UK in these years, but also spending a lot of time out.

"He did that rally with his father in 1947 and I suspect he didn't get into racing until 1949 simply because he wasn't old enough. I think he would have but he wasn't 18 until 1949 so that was when the racing started. There were some problems in the business at that time and that might have contributed to the delay in so far as his father helping to support a racing car was concerned. Something had gone wrong in some deals with some motor traders. I think Peter's mother protected her husband...and her son...and her son from her husband because Percy had quite a temper and she was a right-thinking lady. The father had very strong views. One was how he didn't approve of Peter's marriage to Louise and given the way they were and could hide feelings and attitudes, you might not be aware just how strong his view on this was. People wouldn't have known about that at the time when we all went out somewhere together. But Louise was basically left without any visible means of support after Peter's death. She remained on very friendly terms with her sister-in-law until Trisha died and she was also on good terms with her brother-in-law, Mike Whittall, but not with the rest of the Collins family.

"But Peter and his father were close in some ways, particularly motor racing. In fact, when Peter started, he wanted to do it with him. If it hadn't been for the business, I think his father might have been racing as well. As far as Peter was concerned, his father was all for it. I'm not so sure how his mother felt. I didn't discuss it directly with her. I don't think she objected but I think she knew the dangers involved. In those days, women perhaps didn't voice their views so strongly, but they would have listened

What they said about him...

to her, as they...Peter...had a very high opinion of her.

"Percy and Peter bought the Cooper together, though I expect Percy put up the money. Percy wanted to race it but he didn't want to be in competition with Peter and Peter didn't want to be in competition with him. It's difficult to say whether he was intending to be a racing driver at that time, and I would guess if you had asked him, he would have said 'mind your own business'. I don't think he would have told you, but I think his intention was to go motor racing and certainly by 1950 and 1951, he would have had sight of Stirling Moss who was by then a full time professional racing driver. He was the first full time professional British racing driver. Richard Seaman had had a large bag of gold to go racing with, though he was supported by the racing by the time he was with Mercedes Benz. Peter could see that Moss was doing it and then quite a lot of people built a living out of it in those days. By 1952 several drivers were capable of it, Roy Salvadori being one of them. It became clear in those days that if you had an Aston DB3S or a Jaguar, a Connaught or a Cooper and you wanted to race it with a 'hotshoe' driver, it became that you might say 'let's see Collins and see what he wants' and a driver might have wanted one hundred pounds and split the starting money. Peter had a reputation by 1951 so he got into the position where he could do that. In Peter's case, I think once he had got his legs down into a cockpit of an H.W.M. and he had gotten into an Aston Martin, there was no doubt that he was intending to go motor racing full time for a living, still managed to a degree by himself and his father. He didn't get involved with anybody managing him until 1955.

"With the Cooper, they did some of the work themselves and it was largely run out of the Collins' garage business. There was a chap called Walter Moule who is now dead, but worked for Collins, and there was also a fellow called Ron Lowe...he was associated with a car called the Dellow. Ron Lowe and Ken Delingpole were the partners in Dellow and their sleeping partner was Lionel Evans who had a body shop called Radpanels. They were all near Birmingham, and Ron Lowe was in at the very start of the 500 c.c. Formula 3 and was the president or chairman of the Hagley and District Light Car Club. That club was more a racing club than an ordinary motor club as it had a lot of younger members who were into racing. Radpanels would look after the bodywork on the Collins' Cooper if Peter dented it. Peter and his father would do what I would describe as the basic looking after it. These were quite simple cars and people like Francis Beart would build the engines, but there was little in the way of adjustment that you could do, only a bit to the suspension. Percy Collins was primarily paying the bill. By 1952, every serious driver would have some kind of deal with an oil company, and the oil companies and fuel companies were very good. They would pay a good retainer, pay a bonus and sometimes buy a car. That was more serious for Peter when he was at Astons, but he would have had some money even in the Cooper days which would go into the car and the racing.

"In the days they were running the Cooper, they would sometimes be running in as many as three classes in a single day. They only had one Cooper chassis but they would swap engines during the day. That work was being done by Peter, and by Walter Moule who worked for the team. There were other people around, and I can remember when I went to watch Peter there was a chap called Alf Williams who used to spend a good amount of time on Peter's cars. One way or another, there was always someone there to give him a hand. I think the 'old man' gave him some money for this but I don't think he had a regular, paid

All about the boy!

Hawthorn ever was. John Surtees is another good example of this kind of driver. Peter was amongst the drivers who would look for cars that would provide them with an advantage, because others hadn't found them. Hawthorn's approach was much more about just getting in the car and driving it. More recent examples are probably Lauda and Senna.

"Hawthorn, perhaps in 1958, would say about the Ferrari 'this is crap and I can't do anything with it', but he didn't or couldn't say what should be done about it. Moss or Peter or later Brabham would say 'it's too soft at the front and maybe we can change the toe-in, etc'. Peter was knowledgeable enough about cars to be able to do that, even though his so-called apprenticeship was problematic. Hawthorn would try and was capable of driving round the problem and Peter would try and solve the problem. Peter had honed his skills in driving those three seasons in 500 c.c. F3 and he had learned to race against the best. I disagree with some people who have written about this, but I believe Peter was a totally professional driver. His attitude towards his driving and his attitude towards the business of driving a racing car for a living was 100% professional. It was as true of him as it was of Moss from the word go. It is very easy if you have immense personal ability, bordering on genius, to play a very good game of rugby. But if you are not very fit....you are going to have trouble. If you look at Mike Hawthorn, he was one of these people who had brilliant aptitude, but in comparison to Peter, or to Stirling or to Tony Brooks...well it's difficult to make a comparison. If he felt like going off to have a beer and the car wasn't going well in practice, well he would go off and have a beer. That would be the last thing Moss would do and certainly Peter, especially in the years up to the end of 1956, would never wander off and go have a few drinks. He would drink after the race, or even during the week, but the difference was that Peter's attitude towards racing was thoroughly professional and Hawthorn's wasn't.

"There was another parallel about Peter and Mike in that their fathers both owned garages. But the similarity pretty much ended there. Peter helped at the garage but he wasn't going to take over the business. Hawthorn had inherited the garage when his father was killed in a road accident. He had a good manager in there, his mother, but he was paying more attention to it and that was one of the reasons why he drove for Vanwall and for BRM, because he actually wanted to be in the UK. He also didn't really like the Continental life style. Mike was a steak and kidney pie and beer man. Peter was someone who liked the 'better things' in life. But going back to this comparison of drivers...if you thought somebody played a good game of rugby you would try to emulate him. Well, that is how it was with Mike and Peter. If Mike smoked a pipe, Peter would have a pipe. I don't think Peter ever smoked a pipe before he was spending more time with Mike, but then you would see pictures of him with a pipe. There were other examples like that, indications that Peter had a tendency to be influenced by Mike.

"You could say 1952 was the start of Peter's professional career from the point of view that he was now going to drive for a team in Grand Prix races and that he would no longer be running his own car, or not very often anyway. He started that season doing the Monte Carlo rally with David Murray in a Ford Anglia. I think that car was almost certainly a Kidderminster Motors demonstrator. Although he was about to start driving for H.W.M. one of the things you have to understand about Peter Collins was that he loved driving. He didn't actually care what it was, from the county snowplough which was parked at Kidderminster Motors to the garage's wrecker

What they said about him...

to a rally car to a sprint car. He would drive anything and he really loved it. I think that was part of him for most of his life, up until the time he found things that might replace driving. That was not long before he was killed, when he had met Louise and he was thinking about what he would be doing after racing. There was the house that they bought, or were going to buy. He told me about this house, but if they had actually bought or were about to sign the papers, I am not certain. The house mattered to him and Louise mattered to him. He wanted to do something else and he had a plan. The plan was to have a motor agency and to stay in motor racing at some level. I know there were conversations going on at the time about Peter going back to drive for Aston Martin in sports cars. The actual words John Wyer had used were 'my door is always open, Peter.' Actually what John Wyer wanted was for Peter to drive the Aston Martin Grand Prix car but what he didn't tell Peter was that he already had two drivers, although he considered one of them a bit 'iffy' as a potential Grand Prix driver.

"The H.W.M. drive came about, as much as anything, by word of mouth. John Heath and George Abecassis were what you might call 'chancers'. They had picked up that Stirling Moss was very good and they were watching F3 very closely. They also saw that Peter was very good. They had been talking to Moss and wanted to do something with him, and he did some races for them in 1951. In 1952 he was also 'dazzled' by what Leslie Johnson was planning with an E.R.A. and had agreed to do some races for him when the car was ready. I think he was pretty disappointed when that never turned out to be what it promised. Peter ended up driving in the H.W.M. team in 1952 and it is fair to say that he took a while to settle down. If you look at his results, the car wasn't bad but I think Peter was particularly good in it initially, and there were times when the car was on the pace but he wasn't. It is difficult to say but there were races where he did not achieve what was expected of him. The expectations of him in the H.W.M. were pretty high. I think his under-achievement didn't do him a lot of good internationally at the time.

" It was almost as if, in 1952, his career, other than winning the Goodwood 9 Hour race, stalled. I don't think, at that time, that things were going terribly well at home. He was spending a fair amount of time at home then, and I think there were a number of conflicts and he wasn't a very happy man. I met him to go swimming a number of times because that was one of the places he would hang out or hide out. During 1951 Peter had gotten to know John Wyer and had spent a lot of time trying to get a drive in the Aston team. He would pop up at places and he got to know Tottie Wyer and Tottie pushed John to give him a drive. I believe she said something like 'oh give the boy a try and see if he is any good'. Peter was very persistent and worked hard to get what he wanted. So when they agreed he would drive in the race at Monaco which was to be a sports car race that year, he got something out of that by being the one driver who was really able to preserve the engines. I think he was then very anxious to do more that year but didn't get another chance until the Goodwood race.

"He was already well established with Aston Martin by the time the Goodwood race took place, because he was a known driver and he was doing some testing. He clearly established himself in a lot of other people's eyes by winning the Goodwood race. By the end of the 1952 season, Lance Macklin had left the Aston team. Reg Parnell and his nephew Roy Parnell did a lot of the development work on the Aston. But by 1953 they decided they would do their development work at Monza, which they did. They didn't quite have the level of preparation that Mercedes had but they did quite a good job. They did some preparation at Monza for

All about the boy!

the Mille Miglia which was a race which in the future Peter would excel at and he nearly won it on one occasion. As far as H.W.M. was concerned, they were going through their final metamorphosis by this time and Alf Francis had left, tired of the efforts to squeeze more power out of old kit. There were a lot of internal wrangles within the team and it was their last full year as a team. Meanwhile, Peter knew that Astons had something new on the stocks and that the DB3 would be replaced by the DB3S, which was a well kept secret to most of the rest of the world, but Peter knew about it.

"Aston started off 1953, after the testing, using the DB3 at Sebring. Peter came in and handed over to Geoff Duke, but Geoff Duke tripped over a back-marker and they had to retire. The other car of Parnell had an incident as well but finished second. The Collins/Duke car had been leading at the time of their incident. Well, Peter threw all his toys out of the pram when that happened. He made a venomous attack on Geoff Duke whose feelings were seriously hurt by the personal attack on him. He went to John Wyer and said he wasn't prepared to drive with someone who would be so personal as Peter had been. Geoff Duke was something of a gentleman of the old school and he took it very badly.

"What this brought out, which not many people knew, was that Peter had a vicious temper. Over all the years that I knew Peter, I only saw his temper twice, but I saw his father's temper a few more times. They were so similar...they would really 'throw all the toys out of the pram'. This was part of his character. He didn't wear his heart on his sleeve. He was fun loving, he could be great as a member of a team, but it was being a driver where it was very difficult to know the real Peter. The real Peter was much more serious about life than most people believed. Most of the people who met Peter Collins said what a nice chap he was, always smiling, always laughing. But I don't think you got to where Peter got, and you don't drive the way Peter drove unless you are a very determined character. It was in his genes, and his father was the same. I think very few people knew him really well. There was a bloke he was very 'pally' with named 'Vick' who ran the Washington Hotel in London. He spent time with him and I think they were close friends and there were a few others. He was a little bit secretive, he didn't want people knowing about or prying into his private life. He had a life outside Shatterford Grange, Ferrari and motor racing where he wanted to be a normal bloke and enjoy himself. He could go out and enjoy himself at Alistair Wilson's pub but he was always the 'gaffer's son' and there was a sense that he was always under his father's 'thumb'. Some of the times he went out with me was to get away from that.

"It was interesting what happened to him after 1953, where he had done some good sports car races and now had a reputation as a very competent driver. He went into 1954 and there was no H.W.M. At the beginning of 1954 the Vanwall made its first appearance at the International Trophy driven by Alan Brown. About the same time, Hawthorn had been invited to drive for Vandervell on occasions with the Thin Wall Special. That had happened a couple of times in 1953 with other drivers and Vandervell was obviously looking for a driver for his embryo Grand Prix effort. Among the people who would be an obvious choice would be Peter Collins. This was very good for Peter. He drove the Thin Wall Special first at Aintree in the wet. This led to him driving the Vanwall at the British Grand Prix. He did a few more races in it but I don't think he finished in it in any of the international races. He also drove it at the end of the year at the Spanish Grand Prix, and I am sure it was Vandervell's intention to have Peter driving the Vanwall in 1955. But something went awry with the deal.

What they said about him...

I believe Peter thought, that having done all the hard work, if Mike Hawthorn was going to drive as well, he had no intention of being number two to Mike Hawthorn. Then there was a big row at the 1954 Spanish Grand Prix which started when Prince Bira fell out with the BRM team. Bira wanted to 'borrow some fuel' from BRM and they said no! An accident to Bira's 250F Maserati had occurred in the British Grand Prix. Ron Flockhart, BRM's reserve driver for their Maserati 250F, took over Bira's car by prior arrangement as during the race Prince Bira was suffering from malaria and had arranged for the takeover if he felt too ill to continue. Flockhart rolled the Bira Maserati 250F at Copse on his first lap out of the pits and Bira was upset to say the least. He had another race with good starting money the following week. Bira had had a good season so far and he hoped to be able to make good money at Silverstone if he was well placed. Peace reigned when Sir Alfred Owen agreed to exchange their undamaged Owen/BRM Maserati chassis for Bira's damaged one. Unbeknown to Owen/BRM, Bira's car had a slightly shorter chassis than the Owen 250F. This caused Tony Rudd and the 'boys at Bourne' great heart-ache as certain bits, such as their new and superb prop-shaft did not fit! It took a long time and was very expensive to rebuild the car. Ken Wharton, who drove the BRM car was 'not as quick as he perhaps once was' and had not achieved much except a fourth at Berne and was now 'wound up' by a bloody-minded Bira because he was refused BRM's fuel. Hard words were exchanged and Ken Wharton left the Owen Organisation team in a huff.

"So Raymond Mays invited Peter Collins to drive in the team for 1955. He had impressed Mays because he had been doing Grand Prix races, so Peter went to drive for BRM instead of Vanwall. Mays had known Peter also from the events they were both doing at Shelsley Walsh. It may be that after Peter crashed the Vanwall in Spain at the end of 1954, Vandervell then decided not to pursue the efforts with Collins for 1955.

"From what I knew of Peter, I can see him getting in a state over this and blaming someone else for any problems at Vanwall, blaming the car and just saying 'I'll go to BRM' and that's what he did. I doubt that there was a written contract with BRM, just an agreement he would drive for them. Of course he fell out with BRM at the end of 1955. He had a storming row with Raymond Mays. He had asked permission to drive the works Maserati in the Italian Grand Prix and Mays had said 'No' and so had John Wyer who didn't want him to do it. But Peter did it anyway and when he got to Monza and went into his hotel, John Wyer and David Brown were sitting there. Peter was a bit sheepish and asked what they were doing there and they said 'we've come to watch you race' and laughed it off. The car that he drove is the one that is still in the Donington Museum.

"Then there was more trouble. After Monza, he had two more races to do with BRM. Because he had driven in the Targa Florio with Moss for Mercedes, he now had Ken Gregory looking after him as a manager. It was Ken Gregory who got in the middle of the discussions about whether Peter would drive for Maserati in 1956 or whether he would drive for Ferrari. Somewhere in the middle of all this was Moss. I think the intention was for Ken to have them both driving for Maserati. So Peter left BRM somewhat under a cloud, and in the end he went to drive for Ferrari in 1956. His Ford Zephyr with the three carburettors went back to Ford. The Aston Martin went to Duncan Hamilton...I know, I took it there. When Peter did the Targa with Mercedes, he thought that might well be one of his drives for 1956 and he didn't know at that stage that Mercedes were

All about the boy!

going to announce that they were leaving. I think most people thought they would stay in racing for another year. The thought was that at least they would stay in sports car racing. The deal to drive with Stirling in the Targa Florio was brokered by Ken Gregory. The other driver who had a one-off drive with Mercedes was Desmond Titterington who retired in 1956 after finishing third at the Oulton Park Gold Cup in the Vanwall. Mercedes had Moss, Karl Kling was still around, so Peter was in the picture for a drive. Then they made the decision after the Targa to stop and that left Peter somewhat in the cold. What isn't clear to me was why Ferrari offered Collins a drive because he had so many other people to choose from who he knew...Fangio, Castellotti, and Musso. The only reason I can think of was that Ferrari had adopted the policy of signing up everybody in sight and that would stop them from signing for anybody else. It is still a mystery because he allowed Collins to keep his contract with Aston Martin so he would be driving against Ferrari in sports car races. The only person who was doing the hiring and firing at Ferrari was Ferrari himself. I think Enzo Ferrari thought Collins was going to Maserati and there were three things he didn't want. He didn't want Fangio in a Maserati, he didn't want Moss in a Maserati and if Collins had won the Targa with Moss, he must be good and he didn't want him at Maserati. He couldn't get Moss, he had Fangio, so he thought if he had Collins, he had a very good hand that no one could beat.

"At that point in 1956 Peter effectively went to go and live in Italy. I was working at Kidderminster Motors in 1956 and I saw him occasionally. Then I saw him towards the end of 1956, and we went out together and that was before he went out to Argentina and before he married Louise.

Neville Hay today, as erudite as ever. Photo - Pete Austin

What they said about him...

"Before that, he had that very good 1956 season with Ferrari. I suppose a lot of people believed that the 'mon ami mate' notion with Mike Hawthorn had come about before then, but Collins and Hawthorn hadn't originally come into contact with each other until the back end of 1954 when Hawthorn was invited to drive the Vanwall on a couple of occasions and Collins was also driving the Thin Wall Special. They were both at that time going through a rather strange period. They knew each other, they were at some of the same races, but they weren't 'best mates'. Collins, partly because he was spending some time in London, was certainly closer to Moss than he was to Hawthorn.

"I think it fair to say that it was at this time Hawthorn was anxious to 'drive British', following the death of his father earlier in the year and his impending serious operation which was partly as a result of his accident in late 1952 and his physical condition. Mike joined Vanwall for 1955 and Peter felt that his own position as a Vanwall driver had been/would be diminuated by having the well established Hawthorn in the team. Hawthorn was already a Grand Prix winner twice by the end of 1954. Hawthorn left Vanwall after an argument at Spa in June 1955 and nearly went to Maserati; He ended however up back at Ferrari for whom he drove one of the Lancias (which were 'gifted to Ferrari') at the Gold Cup at Oulton Park in late 1955, its first race under Ferrari's banner.

"Peter accepted the offer from BRM to drive the Mk2 V16, their 250F and the new P25 when ready. He had success with the latter two and drove the P25 in practice at Aintree in 1955 when it spewed oil over itself and had a minor but damaging accident. At Oulton Park the car made its debut from the back of the grid and Peter climbed to 3rd until it is claimed a faulty oil gauge indicated no oil pressure and he retired. Peter had driven a works Maserati at Monza in 1955 and Ken Gregory, who arranged the Mercedes drive, started to manage Collins' affairs instead of Peter and his father. There was a famous mix-up over telexes about whether Peter should join Moss or as happened go to Ferrari for 1956.

"Hawthorn still wanted to live in the U.K. and went to BRM in Peter's place to be joined by Brooks. After two accidents and five retirements in all, Mike went back in the Italian team at the end of the year too.

"The relationship between drivers, Collins and Moss, who were both driving for Astons, saw them share a DB3S when they were second at Le Mans that year after which Peter left Aston Martin. There had been a bit of 'argy-bargy' at the sports car race at Rouen where Collins reckoned that the Aston Martin with drum brakes was quicker than the car with disc brakes. There was disagreement in the team and amongst the personalities about this which developed into a first class row at Aston Martin between the 24th of June and the 28th of July. First Hawthorn and Collins shared a car for the first time and won the Supercortemaggiore race for Ferrari on June 24th, Collins then blew up with the Aston at Rouen. Collins had won the French Grand Prix, was second at the British Grand Prix and then finished second with Moss at Le Mans on July 28th. Did Hawthorn play a part in this? First there had been a problem at the Nurburgring in the 1000 Kilometers, where Collins had been slow in comparison with Tony Brooks. Why? Well I think no one knows. But at Aston Martin between the Ring and Le Mans there was a feeling that Peter Collins wasn't trying. They felt he wasn't the driver he had been and that his interest was at Ferrari and that to some

277

All about the boy!

extent Tony Brooks was his 'protege' and the protege had made him look stupid. I can't believe that anyone of the experience of Peter Collins couldn't adapt himself from driving a Ferrari to driving a DB3S. I also can't believe that anyone who was capable of lapping Dundrod as Collins was at the end of 1955 could be so slow in 1956. I also believe that Collins wanted to be sacked by Aston Martin.

"There was nothing about John Wyer that was ever going to lead him to avoid what he saw as the truth. Only in 1955 had they made a big fuss over Collins breaking his contract with him. I think John knew he wasn't committed to the team and he was no longer able, for whatever reason, to command the same respect as he earlier had when he was a member of the team. The strange thing is that whenever I saw Peter from the autumn of 1955 until late in 1956, when he gave me some cigarettes and we went out to the Winter Gardens in Droitwich he was comparatively unchanged. He had been driving full-time for Ferrari for a season by then.

"The thing that had changed was that Hawthorn had moved to drive for Ferrari in 1957.

"Now Hawthorn had lived in Italy but he didn't like it too much. When he was with Ferrari in 1953 and 1954, he was living out of Britain a lot of the time, partly avoiding 'the hoo-hah' about National Service and he was getting very homesick. As far as Peter was concerned, he was comfortable in France and comfortable in Italy with Ferrari. He hadn't met Louise yet and there were no serious relationships at the time, with no indication that he would do anything except go on the way he was.

"I didn't see him until July 1957 at the British Grand Prix. While looking through some car bits and pieces recently I realized that it was when we met later in 1957 that he seemed very 'down'. The Lancia-derived car was going very badly and they weren't very happy about it and it was about this time the larger-engined 'Dino' appeared. Although Peter had had this wonderful season initially, the 1957 season was pretty miserable for him because after the early non-championship races he didn't do very much and neither did Mike. They had both been totally out-driven by Fangio at the Ring and in general terms it hadn't been a very good year for them.

"It seems to me the Hawthorn/Collins relationship was strongest towards the end of Peter's life. It had started in 1957 and grown through 1957 and 1958. Musso was still in the team but basically you had Peter and Mike who were driving probably better than Musso and they were playing about with each other and in 1957 they had got caught out at the Nurburgring by Fangio playing 'after you Claude, no after you Harry'...it was a silly game. Ferrari had become very much an 'Anglicised' team, they had become very much anglophiles in the whole of their attitude and it seemed to me their attitude was childish.

"When I went to Goodwood and Silverstone for the Easter races and International Trophy in 1958, that was the first time I really saw them, for lack of a better word, as a 'foursome'...the two of them and the Grand Prix car and the sports car. Peter drove the sports car at Goodwood and it didn't seem to handle very well and Mike drove the Grand Prix car. Then they reversed the positions when they went to Silverstone where Peter won it.

"I remember I had gone up on practice day for

What they said about him...

the International Trophy and because Peter won the F1 race in the car Hawthorn had won Goodwood in, that helped cement the view in the public's eyes that these two were very close. By the time Peter was killed these two had battled on with the Lancia-Ferraris, and been made, quite frankly, to look a bit stupid at the Nurburgring, and had got to the end of a bad season in 1957 where they were often beaten by Fangio, Moss, Behra and Lewis-Evans. But the new car came along and things started to look pretty good for 1958. Still the new cars weren't very good in Argentina, they weren't very good in Holland and Monaco. Peter only finished one of those races. They had been very 'pally' when they had come across to the UK for Goodwood and Silverstone because it was just the two of them. This was a 'splitting of the camp'.

"After the Dutch Grand Prix, there was a very foul letter exchanged between Ferrari and Hawthorn, and they (Collins and Hawthorn) were both very fed up with what was going on. It was then a little better at Spa and Peter's drive was ruined by being held at the start. Hawthorn was second behind Brooks and then Mike won the French Grand Prix and of course Musso had been killed there.

"Then they went to Silverstone for the British Grand Prix where von Trips was going to drive the third Ferrari. There was some doubt during practice as to whether Mike was going to be allowed to race as he was not well. In fact it was clear to those who knew him that his physical condition had deteriorated and many people were sure he would not be able to go on driving, and his life style was not particularly helpful to his health. At Silverstone, Peter went off and was quicker than anybody else including Moss' Vanwall while it lasted. Peter was so much quicker in the race, quicker than he had been in practice, and quicker than all the rest.

"I think by this time Peter had several things happen that were important to him. First, he had not been provided, at first, with a Grand Prix car for the French Grand Prix. Several people had acted on his behalf to get him a proper car for the race, then he had a problem in the race with something jamming the brake pedal and on the last lap he ran out of petrol and lost what would have been third place. The second thing was that he had realised that, as there was no more Mille Miglia, the days of the road races were over, even though there had been a Targa Florio that year. That eliminated those events where Peter could really excel, as he was so good on those kinds of roads. He was beginning to think his way around the circuits and he had realised that he could drive very wisely if he thought his way around rather than just getting in the car and driving. The third thing was that he was negotiating to buy a house and was going to supervise the work on it and was thinking about family. He had spoken to John Wyer and John told me this some ten years afterwards. Peter had spoken to John and had asked John how he felt about coming back (to Astons) next year and John said that he had told Peter that his door was always open to him. Peter had said to John Wyer that he wanted to come back and drive and that he was tired of being at Ferrari. Wyer had asked him if he wanted to drive a Formula One car but Peter had said 'I've already got a deal there'.

"Now I believe, but have nothing to prove it, that he had a deal with Cooper. He had had that drive at Monaco in practice when Jack Brabham arrived a little late, so he drove the car and saw how good it was. Because Peter was Peter, he could find and bring a 'bag of gold' to Cooper, or Cooper could use Collins to find this money. Collins hoped he would win the Championship in 1958 and then would go to Astons for sports cars and drive for Cooper. By then, anyone could see that a 2.5litre

279

All about the boy!

engine in the rear of a Cooper was going to be a winning proposition in 1959.

"But of course, then there was the German Grand Prix. He showed Cliff Allison round the circuit. He was impressed with Cliff's driving at Spa and Cliff told me that he, Peter, had mentioned his name to the Ferrari team.

I think the Ferrari problems in the race were that, although the Vanwall was quicker on the twisty bits, the Ferrari was faster in a straight line. Once Peter and Hawthorn were with Brooks, I'm sure Peter was thinking that as long as I can stay 'up his chuff' I will get by him and put distance between me and him by the end of the straight. I think it might have been different had it been anybody other than Brooks. Peter felt he had been made to look foolish at the Ring in the sports car race and though there may have been other contributory factors, like a return to Astons I think, still eating away at him was being slower than Brooks and he just said to himself 'I'm not having this'. Peter was never noted for having accidents or for making mistakes and a mistake of that magnitude is hard to understand. He knew that he still had a chance for the Championship, and the races that favoured Ferrari were still ahead, so he would have wanted to win at the Ring or at least get some good points.

Sue Palethorpe

Sue Palethorpe was one of Peter's school friends, who, along with her brother Peter Vale, remained a friend all through Peter's motor racing years.

"I knew Peter from the time I was about 14. The family was known from the garage they had at Kidderminster. He had a sister called Tricia, and we all knew each other quite well. We had lots of pictures when we were around that age. He was then just what I would call one of our gang and as a boy was lots of fun, a great chap. When I left school I went to work for Bob Gerard who of course was also very involved in motor racing and that meant I was able to keep up some contact with Peter through motor racing. I was a 'gopher' at Bob Gerard's...go for this and go for that...when he needed parts for the car. When things broke on the car I would have to dash off to places and pick things up. I also went to the races and did some of his lap charts and I did that from time to time. I left working for Bob Gerard when I was 21, so I had been with him for four years from the time I was 17. Then I went off to London where I was working as a model and then I got married.

"But we still saw the Collins, Peter and Tricia, they always came to us at Christmas. There were lots of stories, lots of things that happened at parties that Peter was involved in. I remember we had a roof space in our house and some of us got locked in there for sometime when the door shut and we had to bang on the door until someone came and let us out. There was a group of us who were friends together during that period. We managed to stay in touch with each other and I stayed in contact with Peter, as we would all go back and forth to home. I remember he came to my twenty-first birthday and really we stayed in touch right up until he was killed, which was of course terribly sad for all of us. I also knew his sister Tricia well and we stayed friends.

"I usually saw Peter at the races, particularly when I was working for Bob Gerard. I remember, as far as I was concerned, that Peter was always kind. We all got on very well and he was a great friend. Later Peter introduced me to Mike Hawthorn who I also got on with quite well and we all used to go around together."

What they said about him...

Peter Vale

Peter Vale is Sue Palethorpe's younger brother, who managed to tag onto Peter Collins through his sister's connection with him.

"My parents were friends of the Collins. I was younger than Sue...a few years younger but when Peter started racing and doing hillclimbs, there was a kind of open invitation to Sue to go around and look at the cars and as a 14 year old I took advantage of that and made arrangements to go around to the garage as well. That was in about 1951 and I remember it being very relaxed and it just seemed normal to go and see Peter and be taken around the garage. That was when I started following his career. When he started racing with Astons, he would sometimes just come around to our house with whatever car he had at the time. He would come around to see Sue and one day he said 'did I want to go to Droitwich with him?' So we went to Droitwich and I remember that was the first time I ever went over 70 miles an hour! At that age, that was quite an experience. He was a charming fellow, he really was. Although he was famous, he would come back and he was always a normal person. I think it was important to him to just be a 'normal person'. I later went to a lot of the races when Sue was working for Bob Gerard but I think I was still too young to really understand what it was all about. I went to Shelsley a number of times and especially remember Peter running the Cooper with the bigger engine, which was an exciting thing to watch. When he became more famous, I know I was quite proud to know him but at the same time he was still just the same person I had known for years. Of course I can recall how much fun motor racing seemed to be in those days for the people who were in it and for us they were all so much more approachable then they are now.

"Peter certainly had an influence on me and my interest in motor racing. I wanted to do some racing, so when I left school and was working and earning some money, I bought myself a car and did a few years in the clubmans' series. I found I wasn't quick enough and of course if you were working, there was the time needed if the car broke down but I really enjoyed my time doing it and Peter was at least partly responsible for it. Through him I met a lot of people and I recall going to the Goodwood Nine Hours when he was there.

"It was a shocking experience when Peter died. I remember hearing it on the news. I just walked out into the garden and was thinking about how I would not see him again and that was strange when I had not experienced many people dying. I wished then that I had had more contact with him."

John Francis

John Francis is amongst the many people who were part of Peter Collins' social life in and around Kidderminster.

"I was working behind the bar at the Black Boy at Bewdley in the 1950s when Alistair Wilson was running it and of course I knew Alistair and his wife quite well. We worked together but we were also friends and we considered ourselves as friends with many of the people who came to the Black Boy Hotel in those days. I was working there at the time when Pat Collins had been coming in and then he brought Peter there when he was old enough. Peter Collins treated it very much as his 'local' as a young man and would often be there either on his own or with friends. He of course knew most of the other people who came there regularly and as he became more well known, there was a larger group of people who knew him.

All about the boy!

"Peter was always an affable fellow, you know, he bought his rounds, he was generous and he was always friendly. I would say he was just a 'normal' sort of person and that was one of the places where he would be just an ordinary person, even though he had become very well known. I, like many people, followed his career. I do remember that day, when Peter had been killed. Then Mike Hawthorn came back from Germany and brought Louise to the Black Boy...it was a terrible time. 'Mac' Wilson and Mike took Louise up to Shatterford Grange, the Collins' home and we sent along a bottle of whiskey with Mike. It was a very sad occasion of course and I remember it well."

Mick Marriott

Mick Marriott is the Assistant Editor of the Ferrari News for the UK Ferrari Owners' Club and an area organiser for the Club. He is not only very knowledgeable about Ferrari and motor racing history, but has a particular interest in the 1950s and Peter Collins specifically and has an impressive Collins memorabilia collection. He spoke to the author about his interest and fascination in Peter Collins.

"I have always been interested in the 1950s and early 1960s era of sports car and Formula 1 racing. As the years have gone by I have maintained that interest in sports cars but not so much in F1. To me, many of the men from that era were like frustrated Spitfire pilots. They were a bit too young to have been in the war, so they took to motor racing which was a very high-risk sport at the time. So I have a lot of admiration for the guys like Brooks, Moss, Peter Collins, Hawthorn and Salvadori. They had no seat belts, inadequate helmets, no flame-retardant overalls, no deformable structures and the cars were potentially death traps. For those men to drive at the speeds they did, in those cars, on the dangerous tracks where they raced with no Armco barrier, and often no run-off areas, well, to me they were heroes. They were the dashing young men that you could look up to.

"As you get older, you look not only at them driving the cars, but you also want to look at the personalities and to read and know more about them. Stirling Moss, for example, always comes across as a real professional, utterly dedicated; Hawthorn as fairly loud and rather arrogant, presenting a strong image because he was very tall and had that blond hair but maybe was not the nicest of people. I came across Peter Collins fairly late I guess. I knew about him but I never read very much about him, and when I did he seemed to me to be not one of the ultra-professional drivers, but he had a very strong image. He was very good looking, and he died young so he never ages in the memory. He just seemed to have a bit more rounded character than, say, the Hawthorns of this world. He seemed a very decent person, with some flaws no doubt, but no obvious major ones, and he just seemed to be a very nice guy. And of course he died before his time, and so that is just the kind of thing that captures your imagination.

"For some reason, he has an appeal as the kind of person who as a friend wouldn't let you down, and you could get to know him. I was just starting secondary school around the time he died, and I don't really remember that having a lot of impact, as there seemed to be a lot of drivers getting killed in that period. It was a long time later, when I started collecting motor racing books written by people like John Wyer and Peter Miller; and then later Chris Nixon wrote his book which

What they said about him...

seemed mainly about Hawthorn, and I was surprised that no one had written anything specifically on Collins. But now a lot of early film is on video and DVD and the old footage is readily available. In the last ten or fifteen years I have become much more aware and interested in Collins and others of that period. I like sports cars and my imagination was really captured by those photos of Collins driving in the Mille Miglia with Louis Klemantaski sitting alongside him. To me however, Collins always stands out as an interesting and underrated character. He was a very successful sports car driver, he won some notable Grand Prix races and he managed to finish quite high up in the World Driver's Championship. Then there was the time when he gave the Championship to Fangio by handing over his car and that brought him acclaim as a sportsman. I found

The view Louis Klemantaski had from the passenger seat. Photo - Klemantaski Collection

All about the boy!

the handing over of the Championship to Fangio at Monza in 1958 rather strange. It was all very 'nice' and it was fantastic public relations but if he was the consummate professional whom I think he was (there was the Rob Walker story about Collins pushing Horace Gould off and that made Rob Walker understand what a professional driver was) well if he was that professional, why would he hand the car over? That was always a bit of a strange event to me. It is still enigmatic, that choice.

"When it comes to saying what I thought his greatest races were, he certainly had some good races in the Mille Miglia. Obviously his Grand Prix wins were all quite notable ones...the '56 French and Belgian races and the '58 British Grand Prix. I think his win in 1955 in the Targa Florio in the Mercedes with Moss has to rate very highly as an amazing performance. The Mille Miglia and Targa must have been nightmare races to drive, with so many problems to face. Obviously there were some difficulties on some of the closed tracks but on the open road circuits, on public roads with huge crowds on some parts of them, a wall of spectators, that must have been a nightmare for drivers and Collins did very well in those. If a driver could do the distances they did, in those conditions, then you're pretty much a superman in my book.

"Peter Collins just seemed a well-rounded character and I admire the fact that he was a very good driver, in the top handful of the time but he was this strange mixture. He had a kind of playboy image with all the women attracted to him but there was the serious side to him as well, where he was involved with his local school, acted as a governor and put some time and effort into that. Then, despite a non-academic background, he learned enough Italian to endear himself to Enzo and the workers at Ferrari. It seems that he was very approachable, without an edge to him, not a nasty side, a very pleasant human being."

Tony May

Tony May was another person to have contact with Collins through his father Austen May, a distinguished author and another of the pioneer 500 c.c. racing drivers. Tony and his brother Tim saw Peter Collins race on many occasions as boys.

"I think the story I remember best about Peter Collins was when Peter's father rang my father and said 'Oh, Peter wants to buy one of these funny little Cooper five hundreds. I'm a bit worried about whether he can drive it or not and I wonder if you think you can teach him and show him what to do?' Of course, my father had not yet met Peter at that time, so when he did meet him he was, like so many people, completely enchanted by...as he called him...'the boy'...and later 'the boy wonder'. Well, this spurred my father into also going out and buying a Cooper 500 himself. Peter went and bought a car from the Cooper Car company and my father bought the car that had been Stirling Moss' first Cooper 500 and the real difference was that Stirling's was now much more expensive than a brand new one!

"They did go to a local airfield and Peter was there with his father and both the Coopers were there and my father was asked to show Peter the correct lines to take. We then recognised what a phenomenal talent he was to become and my father was always pleased to have been there right at the beginning, and to have been in the position of trying to tell 'the boy' the right lines in the corner!

What they said about him...

"Before the war my father had done many, many trials and then did a number of events in the ex-works MG 'Cream Cracker', a lovely car which is still around today and it does trials with Ian Williamson. Then the war came and that put a stop to all forms of fun and motor sport and everything else. After the war my father had a V-8 trials car and then he got interested in the new 500 c.c. formula, so he bought Stirling's car and went circuit racing straight away. The first meeting he went to was at Goodwood and he did very well and was on the second row of the grid. He was absolutely amazed at this and shot off at the start, was second or third and at one point had got into the lead. Then there was a huge bang and he didn't understand what he had done. After the meeting they got in touch with Stirling's father, Alfred Moss, and he said 'Ah, yes, forgot to tell you, that was the sprint engine!' They had been running two engines, one for sprints and one for races.

"My father knew the Collins family. I think a lot of those people knew each other because pre-war there hadn't been a lot of them competing. I can remember through my childhood how all these people knew each other, whether it was Stirling or Ken Wharton or Ken Tyrrell. The old man seemed to know all these people quite well...and there was an interesting chap called Bernie Ecclestone! Bernie started racing 500s the same time as the old man, and they all knew each other.

"I can remember being at the British Grand Prix at Silverstone, walking across the paddock with my father, who typical of him, had just showed up, no passes or tickets and had talked his way in and we bumped into Ken Tyrrell. The next thing I know we were swept into the pits and suddenly there I am among all my heroes. It was the most incredible experience. Of course, everything then was so easy, so free and then I was sitting in one of the Tyrrell cars.

"I didn't have much direct experience with Peter, though I was at races when he was there. He and my father shared a car transporter, which they used to take the cars to the various circuits. I think I'm right in thinking that this was because they both wanted to do European races and my father raced at Monte Carlo and he went to Clermont Ferrand and all sorts of places. It was probably just for one season but he and Peter Collins shared the transporter. I think it was Peter's father's idea to use the transporter, something he came up with from his own Ford agency, Kidderminster Motors. My father was very close to Peter and his family. His father had done trials pre-war, just as Alfred Moss and even Mrs. Moss had done, so that was how they all knew each other."

Tony May. Photo - Pete Austin

It was Tony May's father, C.A.N. May who had written a number of books about motor sport including *Formula 3 - A Record of 500 c.c. Racing* and *Speed Hill-Climb*. The first of these is a very detailed account of the men and machines responsible for what May termed 'racing for the impecunious enthusiast'. May wanted to withdraw that description of the class when the 1948 Cooper 500 was selling for a whopping £575!

All about the boy!

May described his entry into F3 himself:

"Several factors, unrelated in themselves, then contributed to my taking a firm decision to enter 500 c.c. racing. Firstly, I was visited by a youthful Peter Collins, from Kidderminster, whose father I remembered as being contemporary with me in the trials and rallies of 1938 and 1939. Collins junior now owned a Cooper and although as yet he had not raced it, but had only practiced with it on local airstrips, his enthusiasm for 500 c.c. racing was infectious and in no time I found myself catching a little of it. An invitation was issued for me to try out his car but, unfortunately, when I came to avail myself of this opportunity mechanical misfortune had overtaken the Cooper and I did not get a ride." (May, 1951, p.78).

May then spoke to John Cooper and Eric Brandon who both had their 1948 cars for sale. He then heard that Stirling Moss' very successful Cooper was also up for sale, and knowing the Moss family, went up to Bray to examine the car, which he duly bought. Over the Christmas period, he describes early attempts to get to grips with starting and driving the Cooper, finding that he managed to get the engine to slide about in the chassis:

"It was that same afternoon that Peter Collins threw a chain on his Cooper and had it tangle round the gearbox and clutch assembly, and Dennis Kiteley's green Cooper flatly refused to start." (May, op. cit, p.78).

The local airstrip must have indeed been a very busy place.

Ed McDonough and Tony May discuss Peter Collins at Race Retro in 2008.
Photo - Pete Austin

What they said about him...

Tony May's father C.A.N. 'Austen' May in his Cooper 500 at Goodwood in 1949.
Photo - May Collection

Mike MacDowel

The former British Hillclimb Champion, Mike MacDowel...he pronounces it MacDool!....had a varied and active career. He made his Formula 1 debut at the wheel of a Cooper at the French Grand Prix at Rouen in 1957.

" I first encountered Peter when he was with Mike Hawthorn at Aintree in 1956. They were staying at the Adelphi Hotel, which had a big revolving door. I appeared on the scene just as they were having a competition to see how fast they could get this door to revolve. There was a bit of a fuss amongst the staff but that seemed to be very much the way they were.

"I remember my race at the French Grand Prix very well. I had driven at Rouen in 1956 in a Cooper sports car; I raced with Colin Chapman; he seemed to just disappear in the race', he was a very skilled driver. The Lotus, however, was faster through the corners than the Cooper and another problem was that the Cooper had a far lower gear ratio. The Cooper spent a lot of time going sideways and sliding and drifting around the corners which isn't the quickest way of driving but at least it prepared me for being

All about the boy!

there in the Grand Prix.

"My F1 debut was pretty brief. My team mate at Coopers was Jack Brabham. It wasn't until some months ago that Jack told me he was in a 1900 c.c. car, not a 1500 c.c. car. He spoke to me recently in his broad Australian accent, simply saying, 'That's why you couldn't keep up mate.' However, he stuffed his car into Horace Gould's 250F Maserati. I remember, as I was coming down the short straight near the pits, very clearly seeing a BRM in the ditch. The driver, Ron Flockhart, was sitting beside it on the grass. Another wonderful experience!

Mike MacDowel . Photo - Mike Jiggle

"As for people like Fangio, Collins and Hawthorn, I didn't really see much of them. I was standing beside Fangio in the 'Gents' however! On the track he was in a 250F Maserati, and if you look at the photographs of the race you will see the distinctly damaged nose. I remember, too, in practice, driving down the hill, it was quite a long straight. In my mirrors I saw Fangio coming behind me, and I couldn't keep up. I had this wonderful thrill of seeing him just chuck the 'Maser' from lock to lock, the car controlled but sliding, his strong arms above the cockpit. Again, a terrific mental picture of seeing the great man in action, unbelievable car control. To me, being in such company was almost surreal. There I was in the company of these drivers....Fangio and Collins."

Sir Stirling Moss

Stirling Moss is, of course, the most distinguished driver from that late Forties and early Fifties period, one of Britain's very great drivers and of course he still competes today. He was arguably the person closest to Collins in racing, having known and raced against him longer than anyone else.

"If I think back about Peter Collins now, I first think of him as a person with a 'fun personality'. He was a good driver, yes, I would have always considered him a good driver but I tend to remember him more for being a fun person rather than for his driving. He was always a joy to be with, even when we were in different teams and competing against each other. It never mattered whether we were opposing each other, or fighting on a circuit, we were always good friends and that's what I look back on.

"I suppose one of the things that many people may not know is that we were friends for a very long time. He started very early like I had done and I remember meeting him as 'a boy from Kidderminster' as I think someone introduced him to me. In those days, we seemed to have more time to meet people and of course we were driving in a different environment. We

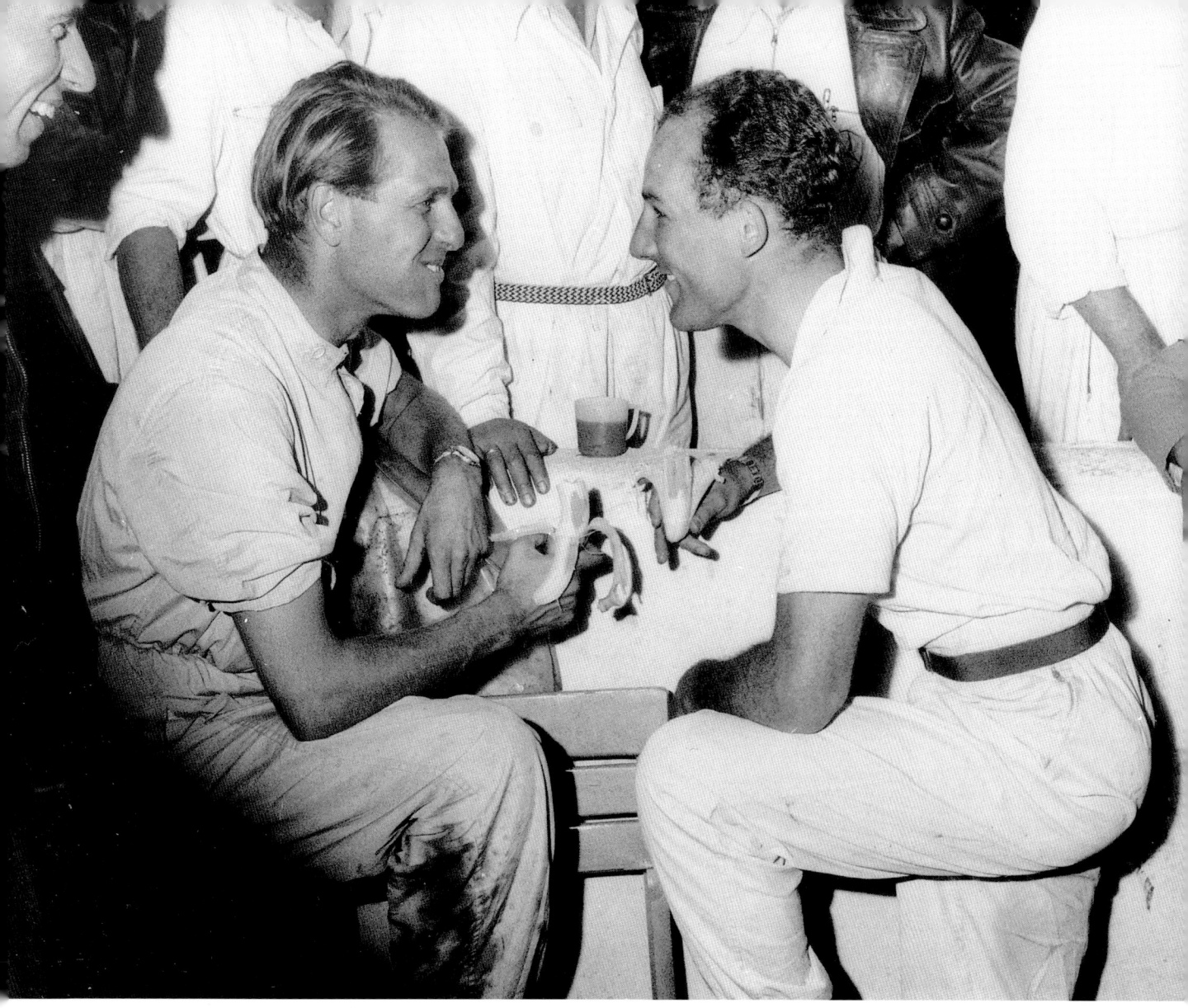

Peter Collins and Stirling Moss in jubilant mood after winning the 1955 Targa Florio for Mercedes Benz. Photo - Daimler-Benz

were doing a lot of hillclimbs in those early days and that's when I got to know him very well. Back in that early period, I was racing against a certain group of people all the time and from 1949 when Peter started he was one of those who came along who I got to know. It was clear to me that he was one of the good drivers at the time. This was in 500s which was what we were both driving and he was someone who seemed to know what he was doing. He had his 'act together' as you would say, was easy to race with and was very competent. If you look at him now, in modern terms, I guess you might say that he was a 'good Red Bull driver, a sort of Mark Webber type'. You could recognise the skills he had even if they weren't necessarily producing the results in the early days.

"Looking back, again over fifty years ago, the way Peter was seen then is different from how he was later portrayed. I know much is made of his 'friendship' with Mike Hawthorn but I suppose I was on close terms with him for quite a longer period of time, even back in the days before we were getting known and getting publicity. Now that I think about it, I suppose I was as close to Peter as anybody was, actually. We also had a later sort of business connection when we were

289

All about the boy!

both involved with Ken Gregory. Ken was the assistant competition manager at the Royal Automobile Club, which was how we got to know each other. I remember the deal with Peter driving with Mercedes, where I helped get him in for the Targa Florio, one, because I knew how good he was and two, because of the kind of person he was. I couldn't at that time think of anyone who was any better for what we were trying to do. I had seen him on road circuits and knew that he had the skill and the determination and that he was the kind of person I could do well with. As it turned out, it was a very good decision all around. In 1955 the Targa Florio was a very demanding circuit but you could learn it, so we had set out to go round it enough to learn it, which you really couldn't do with the Mille Miglia. Driving the Mercedes was not easy, as the 300 SLR was not an easy car to drive. We both had 'slight offs!' and we were well matched because we both seemed to be able to get a lot out of the car on those tight and narrow roads. Yes, I think you could say it was one of his best races because he was in a new car he had never driven and he could get the very most from it. I knew the car better and had some experience of it, yet he was able to adapt to it and drove it very well.

"Later, along came Louise who became Louise Collins. I had met her in 1956 through Donald Healey, who was a friend of hers, and through that I got to know her fairly well. It was later that I introduced her to Peter. I think you could say about Peter that not many people knew him very well and I wouldn't have discussed a lot of things with him, like politics! We raced together and we socialised together and we would have considered each other as good friends. But he, like many drivers, would have kept a great deal to himself and you could say that there were many things about him not shared with others."

Tim Parnell

Tim Parnell was for some time the competition manager for BRM, having been an F1 driver himself. His father was among the best known and respected racing drivers of the immediate pre and post-war periods, and Tim has spent a great part of his life involved in motor racing.

"My father Reg was close to Peter. They were in the same team of course when they drove for Aston Martin, they were co-drivers in some races and were in many races together even when they weren't in the same car and then Reg went on to manage Aston Martin in racing. I knew Peter very well myself, partly through the association with my father and through his later racing days. Of course the first time I remember Peter was when he was driving a 500 and I think he and Curly Dryden were driving the J.B.S. and I think they had a team together. I certainly recall they did a lot of races together and that's when Peter was beginning to get some attention. That was in the early days of 500 racing, out of which so many drivers came and went on to better things.

"That was a long time before I started competing myself and I started just going along to races with my father and I did that from quite a young age. I knew a lot of drivers before they became famous. My first recollection is going to races with my father before the war, going to Brooklands and that would have been back in 1938 and 1939.

"I thought Peter Collins was a very good driver from the beginning of his career. It wasn't even a career in those days when he first started. I think he was probably serious about it but as far as I was concerned he was just another young man going racing but he stood out as one of the best. I have always thought he was

What they said about him...

'top of the tree'! It wasn't that long before it was clear that he and Stirling Moss and Mike Hawthorn were the leading lights among the British in world championship racing in the 1950s...without a doubt. I think if you look back, you might not say that Peter stood out amongst all the 500 racing people. Stirling stood out in that type of racing and you heard a lot more about him. Then there was a period when Jim Russell was seen as outstanding, but it was clear that Peter was very good at it. He was a leading runner in those days. He did a lot of racing and the people who knew racing well knew how good he was.

"It was when he made the move to H.W.M. and when Stirling was also driving for H.W.M. and doing the same races, that Peter really started making his name and his mark and that was well before he went on to drive for Ferrari. Of course, he drove for Aston Martin long before that, at Monaco in 1952 for the first time. I remember that well, not surprisingly because my father had the engine blow up in his car, going down to Mirabeau I think and that caused absolute chaos. Several of the cars were damaged and out of the race. I was there for that race and I remember my father just said that he had been going very well and the engine blew. I remember him saying that the man who really saved the day was the waiter at the Tip Top Club or one of those places who waved his tablecloth to give everyone a good warning as they came over the crest from Casino Square!

"I think Peter got into the Aston team because they had watched him and wanted him in the team. He had worked his way up through the ranks. John Wyer would have known about him and would have seen what great potential he had, particularly as he had been a team mate of Stirling Moss in the H.W.M. John Wyer was a top man in motor sport and he would know who was good and coming up. He was a tough guy to work with, was very strict. With Moss and Collins and those boys he tried to be very strict with them but they knew how to get round him. He was very good with them and they all respected him.

"My father thought that Peter was a great team member and of course they got up to all sorts of tricks with each other in those days. It was quite amazing some of the escapades they got up to in some of the hotels. I remember on one occasion they moved a wardrobe across in front of a door to one of the rooms so one of them couldn't find his room and they would do that so one of the drivers couldn't get out of his room, or fixed it so that he could open his door and walk into the wardrobe! There was wonderful camaraderie and loads of escapades, all gone today. There were interesting characters in the Aston team in those days, like George Abecassis who was very different to the others, a real 'dry bread' compared to the others but he responded to all the fun and games. Of course, Peter was quite a lad for the girls...he had a hell of a following of girls all over the world. I think he and Mike Hawthorn might have promised to marry several girls. I think their 'mon ami mate' sort of label came about after they had both joined up with Ferrari and became team mates and they were living out in Italy together, so they were seen as the English twosome to some extent. Of course there was a lot of controversy about why 'those two' didn't do National Service. There was quite a hullabaloo about that. I think that was a situation where there might have been some explanations but the daily press wasn't interested in that, they just wanted to give them, especially Hawthorn, a hard time.

"Much of my own view of Peter was influenced by the way my father saw him. They knew each other very well, their careers went back a way together and I think my father got along with Peter very well. I think it was different with

All about the boy!

someone like Roy Salvadori who was a strong character. But these were all big, strong characters...Moss, Hawthorn, Salvadori and Collins, all at the absolute peak of their abilities. It was quite amazing in that Collins could drive anything, like Salvadori could get in and drive anything. They could drive sports cars, open cars, they could jump into saloon cars, go to a race meeting and drive four or five races. Peter was in the group of people who had the chance and the ability to do that. He was a little different from those in that Peter was very easy going, a 'hail and well met' sort of a lad. He had had to put up with a lot of things. I don't think I ever saw Peter lose his rag over anything, or lose his temper. He may have but I didn't see it and it wasn't like him to do so. He had a way of taking everything on, a wonderful guy."

Tim Parnell. Photo - Mike Jiggle

A drawing of Reg Parnell in the Aston Martin DB3 in 1951. Drawing by Dave Alford

What they said about him...

John Pearson

John Pearson is a well known figure in British motor racing, a member of the BRDC, and has been coming to events at Silverstone since the late 1940s when he was a young teenager. His father, Douglas Pearson, knew Pat Collins through pre-war association with motor sport and John himself admits to having 'disappeared' from school on a number of occasions to see what was going on at Silverstone. He soon found himself an active part of the circuit as he did jobs for officials, timers and for the scrutineers. He thus had access to some very well known people over a very long period. He later became an integral part of historic racing, as a restorer of important cars and a driver himself.

"I first saw Peter Collins in 1949, recognising him as a serious talent in 500 c.c. F3 racing and I was at Silverstone on May 5, 1951 on the occasion when Collins came flying into Woodcote very rapidly and went ass-over-tip at the corner. I was pleased to see him walk away from this as I had been introduced to Peter in the paddock and it was not long before I saw him in fairly heroic terms. I recall several of the Silverstone 500 races where Collins not only took part but where it had been clear that Collins had more than his fair share of talent.

"As I had met Raymond Mays at races, I got to know Mays well over a long number of years and later in life visited Mays at home. Raymond Mays confided in me that he had been 'disappointed in Peter Collins' with whom he had had a hand-shake arrangement that Collins would drive the BRM in 1956 and then he walked out on that agreement. Raymond Mays was thought to have seen Collins in a negative light after that event though I viewed 'Ray' as very much a 'gentleman' and not inclined to speak

John Pearson. Photo - Mike Jiggle

negatively about people.

" I believe that Collins also raced a Ford Consul at Silverstone. My memory and this is going back a long time indeed, was that Collins appeared in a green Consul and it was the very first example of that Ford model which I had ever seen. I was at Oulton Park in 1955 when Collins competed in a race with the BRM P25 for the very first time, having crashed in practice earlier at Aintree. I remember vividly the sight of Collins rushing from his starting position in mid-field through a whole pack of red cars until he was nearly at the front. He just seemed to fly past the other cars and I remember, because it was the first time I had seen that car, which was very low, just how fast it was and how well Peter drove it. I've never forgotten that. I also recall Collins' stunning drives in Libre races in the BRM MkII

All about the boy!

V-16 where he could out-drive just about anyone else.

"I also saw him in other races, in the Allard in 1951 and also when he drove the Owen Organisation Maserati 250F, which he seemed to be able to drive very well. He seemed able to adapt himself to new and very different cars without much problem."

Don Truman

Don Truman, as we see, was another 500 c.c. racer from the period of Moss and Collins. He was a successful driver himself and in later years became well known as an official of the BRSCC where he continues to remain active. He was characteristically ensconced behind the crossword page in the Sunday paper when the author talked to him at Silverstone.

"I was already in 500 c.c. racing when Peter Collins came on the scene, as I started in 1947. It was a marvellous period. The issue of money was very different then and everybody was very friendly...well, maybe there were a couple of drivers who weren't but 99% were. Almost everyone was friendly and drove in a sportsman-like manner. I remember Peter for always having a grin from ear to ear. I argued with him...no, it wasn't an argument...I called him a rotten bastard actually because he had gotten the latest works Norton engine and the engine I had according to Norton was a 'good un'! He had a good five more horsepower than I did and I couldn't live with him when we were together on the circuit. Peter and his father took their motor racing very seriously right from the beginning. I remember one incident with Peter when I was arriving at Goodwood when I was cut up very badly on the approach to the circuit by a low, red sports car. I pulled up behind it in the Goodwood paddock and went over and said 'Peter, you cut me up!' 'No' he says, 'it wasn't me, it was this mad bastard here!' That 'mad bastard' was Juan Manuel Fangio who had been driving Peter to the circuit! That was when Peter was driving for Ferrari. I guess Peter was the only person ever to refer to Fangio in those terms!

"I can't quite remember when I was first aware of Peter being there in racing. There were a number of good drivers around at that time and he came out of that group in 500s. When he got the Norton engine for his Cooper, then I was certainly aware of how fast he was going and that I couldn't get near him. We used to do about 20 to 25 events in a season in those days, so you tended to be very busy all the time and we were doing a lot of hillclimbs then, that was because there were very few circuits. As soon as the circuits developed, the hillclimbs started

Don Truman on duty at Silverstone, with his crossword. Photo - Pete Austin

What they said about him...

to lose their appeal. You learned a lot from doing hillclimbing. My first event was at Shelsley and I remember being frightened bloody stiff on the line....and making slowest time of the day! You had to do an awful lot of work for 40 or 50 seconds racing. Then, when you came to a circuit, where you could do 50 miles, it made a big difference. But you had learned a lot about narrow roads and not hitting trees when you were doing the hills.

"I did the 100 mile race at Silverstone, and that was a big thing when we started doing races of that length. Peter won one of those big 100 mile races I remember. We had to start learning to fit special tanks in the car. I remember being told that after so many laps I had to turn the tap up otherwise there would be an air lock. As I came by the pits up went the board 'tap' and I thought 'what the bleeding hell are they talking about?' and the next lap he was waving the board frantically. All of a sudden the engine cut out and I thought 'Ah, tap!' The only thing that comes anywhere near the sensation of being in a big group of 500 c.c. cars in a race like that is Hyde Park Corner in the rush hour! It wasn't unusual to have tyre marks on both sides of your cars. I can remember certain things clearly...like taking the old Woodcote Corner flat for the first time in my life. That was in 1952 and that memory stays with me and always has done. I remember racing at Aintree in the Cooper Mk V or VI with a fixed calliper and the floating disc. Unfortunately it used to wear the brakes out in about twenty miles! I arrived at Tatt's Corner with no anchors...that was off-putting! I recall coming into the pits with my helmet hanging off and the mechanic said 'you obviously weren't going fast enough or you'd have hit the wall'. He said it more colourfully, however. That was Moss' fault of course. I was talking to Moss before the race about Melling Crossing and he had said: 'Well, you know Don, you grit your bloody teeth and keep your foot in, you can take it flat'. I'd had about six tries and on the seventh I got my wind up and said 'I'm going through here flat' and I did and that's when I ended up with no brakes!

"Part of racing then was that there were a lot of great characters around...Eric Brandon, Moss of course, who I always saw as a gentleman amongst drivers, and he would never do anything that would put people in any trouble, and would always give signals if he was going to change direction; he was very good and you realised just how fast he was when you chased him around a corner. There was Frank Aitken, and Don Parker...perhaps not as sporting as some other drivers...he was tough. There was Curly Dryden...I used to stay with Curly at that boozer he ran, and we went down to Brighton together. I hung my jacket up there because we had to do an engine change and somebody nicked my bleeding wallet!

"It was an interesting time, there wasn't a lot of money around. I bought a Marwyn to start with, and that has the distinction of possibly being the worst racing car ever made in history! God knows where there's one now! I had an RAC vehicle report on it and the final paragraph, which I sent to Marwyn, said 'this vehicle is not only not safe for racing, it is not fit to be used on the road'. There was Clive Loens who was around from the beginning. I wasn't one of the 'first 25', I was possibly in the 'second 25' of pioneers in 500s. I went to the original 500 Club meeting which was supposed to have been held at Silverstone but the farmer chased us off and we went to the Easton Neston estate to play, at the invitation of Lord Hesketh's father. I think Alan Brown was at that one, and there was also Austen May who was a friend of mine. One of my early pictures appears in the book, maybe the first photo in the book!

"I think 1953 was the most successful season for me, and I was placed in every race but one.

295

All about the boy!

That one was at Oulton Park when I rushed through Cascades and was supposed to have pushed Jim Russell off into the lake. The guy who wrote as *Grand Vitesse* in the *Motor* said 'Truman pushed Russell off into the lake'. I hadn't and I bloody told him so. I saw Jim the next week and said 'what's this about me pushing you in the lake' and he said 'you effing well did!' So I had to apologise to *Grand Vitesse*.

"I had been serious about racing, but when people like Collins and Moss moved on to bigger things, I was working for 'the old man' in his business and was going to take that over. I wasn't able to give racing that kind of commitment. These blokes were then professionals and they were at it 24 hours a day, and I could manage two nights a week and the weekend. Peter was able to go on because his father was very well fixed so it easier for him. I was invited to a couple of the parties at the Collins house and everybody in the motoring world was there. It was huge house at Shatterford Grange and there were so many racing people there. I didn't have much to do with Peter's father, but Peter was a very nice bloke. I thought he was genuine...not like Hawthorn, who I saw as a nasty piece of work. They were completely different kinds of people. Peter was a likeable bloke and Hawthorn wasn't. My opinion was that Hawthorn wasn't a good influence on Peter. Peter wouldn't do a dirty trick but I wouldn't have put it past Hawthorn to do any dirty trick. There were other people like that, some who had to work their way up the hard way and that left a scar on the character.

"I used to read Autosport in those days, and followed Peter's career, so I sort of kept up with what he was doing. The magazine used to be all forms of motor sport and was a good source of information about people. Even I used to get good coverage...of course I had been boozing many, many times with Gregor Grant...and that helped! Those were different times when you could seem to do a lot more with the money you had, and that is why 500 racing was so good.

"In those days even the people like Peter who had backing would get a good race from drivers with much less in the way of resources. It all came down to being close to the action and being able to deal with that. Some of the early races at Silverstone had 40 starters and if you could come through that and do well, you were good."

Louise Collins King

One of the highlights of working on this book has been the opportunity to develop a correspondence with Peter's widow, Louise. In the course of conversation, when asked whether she preferred to be called Louise King or Louise Collins, her irrepressible character emerged with the reply that "I have a friend who likes to call me Louise Lanette Cordier King Collins King Burwash King! I always go back to King because it's a simple four letter word that never confuses

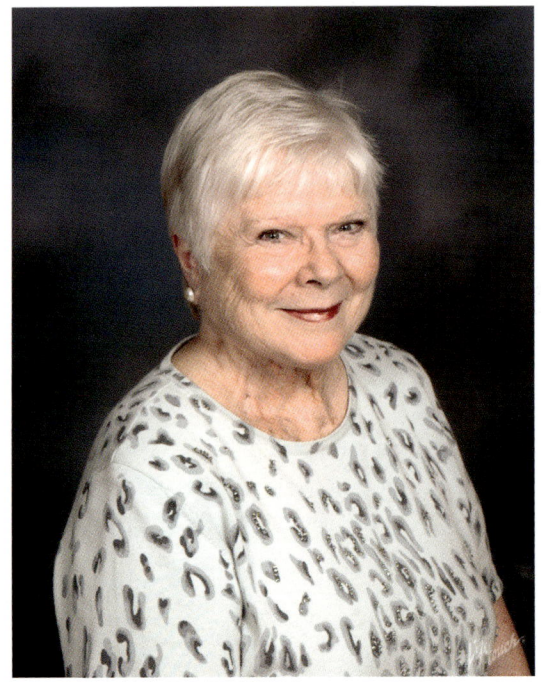

Louise today. Photo - Louise King Collection

*A portrait of Peter and Louise at their wedding in February, 1957.
Photo - Louise King Collection*

All about the boy!

anyone but I do answer to just about anything!" She has been very helpful and open in answering the author's questions and gone out of her way to find photos and useful material, getting Denise McCluggage to agree to the reproduction of some of her writing about Peter and Louise.

"In 1953, I bought one of the first Austin Healeys to come into the United States and I became involved with the Sports Car Club of America. Through the SCCA I got to know a lot of the drivers who were racing then. I was an actress and was working at the time doing "The Seven Year Itch" in Chicago. I was going on rallies then whenever I had the chance. I met Stirling Moss back then and that may have been at Sebring or in Nassau as I had gone to both of those places whenever I could. I had gone to Europe and to England for the first time in 1955 where I got to know more of the racing crowd. I had even won the Michigan Mille in 1954. That was a 1000 mile rally around the lakes so obviously the whole scene had fascinated me as did the drivers!

"What was going on in Peter's head at the time is hard to know but I do know that when we met in 1957 that we both 'fell' for each other within the first few minutes of getting together, which was about 11.00 pm after the show at the Coconut Grove Playhouse just south of Miami. He asked me to marry him on the Wednesday afternoon and I said 'Yes!' without hesitating. Another factor is that I was about to go on to another acting job within two weeks and Peter was off to Cuba and then back to Europe so this was the only way we could be together. In those days I wouldn't have dreamed of going off with him without being

Peter and Louise enjoying a 'regular' night out with Fon Portago at the El Morocco nightclub in New York.
Photo - Autopresse

What they said about him...

married. Things were quite different then! I think that we both felt that we had sown all the 'wild oats' that we needed to so we were quite ready to settle down which made us open to the marriage commitment. Denise Mc Cluggage wrote a lovely story about the two of us.

"We had a very busy life in that short time we were together and managed to fit in a lot of travel. If we were in New York, El Morocco was a standard visiting place to go when we were there, as was Rene Dreyfus' restaurant Le Chanteclair and Sardi's. In those days we went out almost every night to pretty nice, popular places. We dressed up a lot then as well so it may seem like that an evening at El Morocco was a special occasion but I considered it a pretty normal evening.

"I don't ever think of Peter as a very private person. He was very open and friendly with

Louise was keen to accompany Peter wherever he went, and they did a great deal of travelling in their 18 months together. Photo - Louise King Collection

Peter and Louise staying at Mannerbio before the 1957 Mille Miglia...studying the route map!
Photo - Louise King Collection

What they said about him...

just about everybody and the Grand Prix drivers were a pretty tightly knit circle. We travelled together and ate together and drank together and a lot of us stayed in the same hotels so we considered a lot of the drivers our friends. Certainly Mike Hawthorn, von Trips, Phil Hill, Olivier Gendebien, Louis Klemantaski, Tommy Wisdom, Duncan Hamilton, Donald Healey, Jo Bonnier, Joan and Bernard Cahier, Masten Gregory were and more but all of these people I would say were our friends. We did have many great times together full of laughter and lovely experiences.

"Much seems to have been written about Enzo Ferrari and the way he viewed my relationship with Peter. The truth is that the Ferraris were always very kind to me and we never actually 'moved' out to Monte Carlo. We bought the boat and took it to Monte Carlo but we also kept the villa that Ferrari loaned us in Maranello right up to Peter's death and that's where we stayed when we were in Modena. I know that in 'Mon Ami Mate' it says that we shut up the house but we didn't because after Peter died I had to pack up our things out of the house so there was a little confusion there. Who knows, maybe I am wrong. I'm sure Ferrari would have been happier if we were there all the time but we loved being on the boat and it was very convenient during the racing season of 1958. Ferrari was very kind to me after Peter died and I have nothing but good thoughts about him so there never was a need for a change of view.

"In answer to the question I sometimes get about how I remember Peter, it's easy. Peter simply loved life, his family and me. He was a very happy person and very serious about his racing and the cars but he was full of fun and joy which gave me the happiest year and a half of my life. We had a great marriage and were very, very close through every minute of it so I think of that period of my life with much happiness and gratitude.

"I could have stayed in touch more with people I knew but I don't enjoy writing which is a drawback in keeping up relationships but for a while I always looked forward to seeing Bette Hill when I visited England but now I've lost track of her and I've only seen a few people occasionally. Chris Nixon took me to see Pina and Tony Brooks' house but I think they moved since then. About six years ago I became closer to Phil Hill's wife Alma for a while and I saw them in Naples, Florida briefly. The phone calls get fewer and far between...we all need more time!"

Louise King was kind enough to allow her personal letters to be reproduced in this book. They had been published previously but she told the author she "was pleased to be published twice!"

This letter was from Peter and Louise to Peter's parents, dated Monday, Feb. 18, 1957:

"Dear Mum and Dad:

Well, hello! I hope you received the photographs etc. OK and not too bent up. Louise and I have spent quite a lot of time sorting out pictures and things to bring home to show you after Sebring. The church was beautiful and an unexpected crowd of friends turned up for the wedding. The reception was held afterwards in the Cadillac Hotel and there were about 100 people there. It all went very well and they even had a singer over from Cuba to literally sing us on our way. It was a wonderful day for both of us and we both wish you could have been here.

"For the first time in my life I am able to realize what it means to have someone for whom I have so much love, respect and tenderness that I'm afraid of things that may in any way spoil

All about the boy!

about the same place. It was Stirling's fault because his brakes failed and caused a wooden fence to fly around a bit and stop Peter and Mike. Anyway, Peter walked back to the pits, we hopped into the speedboat and did the same as the previous day.

"To top it all off, on Monday we were cruising around in the boat and a large yacht was trying to leave the harbour but had several anchor chains caught on its anchor, so Peter came to the rescue and was in the process of removing the chains when he slipped and at last fell into the water. It seems the harbour had its eye on him and it was inevitable that he should go for a swim."

Peter and Louise with Lufthansa's PR Director Peter Easton at a Lufthansa/Mercedes Benz cocktail party. Photo - Lufthansa Airlines.

What they said about him...

Anthony Carter

Anthony Carter is a well-known author and historian, and he wrote the nostalgic 'Reflections of a Lost Era'. Anthony was a first-hand witness to a number of Peter Collins' exploits.

"Peter Collins was the quintessential 'Boys Own' hero of the late 1950s. Fifteen years earlier and he would have been flying Spitfires.

"I remember him well, receiving the cup for winning the International Trophy race at Silverstone in May 1958 driving a Ferrari Dino 246. There he was, changed from his overalls and now wearing a tie, navy blue blazer, cavalry twill trousers and suede 'brothel creepers' - smart wear for a young man about town. At the time this country was blessed in having a quartet of drivers at the top of their game and winning Grand Prix - the supreme professional Stirling Moss and the deceptively quick Tony Brooks in Vanwalls and the fun-loving duo Mike Hawthorn and 'mon ami mate' Peter Collins in Ferraris. Today the media, television in particular, builds up new heroes overnight and then indulges in the peculiarly British habit of shooting them down. Fifty years ago reputations were built the hard way on success or failure and we savoured every snippet of news on the racing and the private lives of our heroes. They were public property!

"When Peter married beautiful American actress Louise King in Miami, February 1957, it made headlines across the world. It was the sort of story newspapers thrive on, a human story for everyone to enjoy. Sadly it was short lived. Eighteen months later Peter went off the road at the Nurburgring in his Ferrari and was

Peter Collins receives the Daily Express International Trophy from Sir Max Aitken, Chairman of Beaverbrook Newspapers, at Silverstone 1958. Photo - Anthony Carter

All about the boy!

killed in full view of the pursuing Mike Hawthorn. To this day I vividly recall the pictures on the front pages of every newspaper showing a dark side of motor racing as Mike Hawthorn gently accompanied Louise Collins down the steps of the aircraft on arrival at Heathrow, their faces etched with grief. It summed up the feelings of an entire nation.

"Mike Hawthorn was famed for his inconsistency, driving with supreme aplomb one day, mediocre the next. Now he was tested to the ultimate, demonstrating remarkable courage and commitment by finishing second in each of the three remaining championship Grand Prix of that fateful season, 1958. He had become the first Englishman to win the Drivers World Championship, outwardly jubilant but inwardly a broken man. The long months had exacted a high price, the loss of his great friend following hard upon that of his Ferrari team mate Luigi Musso at Reims in July. Mike Hawthorn retired from the sport but within three months he was dead, killed in an accident on the Guildford bypass in January 1959. It was the stuff of fiction, ending a momentous era that had already witnessed the withdrawal of the Vanwalls which, at the conclusion of the season, had won the inaugural Constructors Championship and taken Stirling Moss to within one point of the Drivers Championship. Vanwall's third driver, Stuart Lewis-Evans, died when his car caught fire in the last race which decided the championship - the Moroccan Grand Prix at Casablanca. It was too much for Tony Vandervell. Enzo Ferrari mourned the loss of two young men who had become almost like sons to him.

"Peter Collins and his deceased colleagues, Rest in Peace."

Peter Collins with his Ford Zephyr on Monday before the German Grand Prix, shown here at Adenau. Note the Ferrari transfer on the back of the Zephyr.
Photo - Anthony Carter

What they said about him...

Michael Whittall

"My home was Shatterford from 1946, the big house at the other end of the village!

We knew the Collins family well from middle 1950s when they moved to Shatterford Grange. I first met Tricia when she was still at school (Malvern Girls College) so that would have been 1954/55. As our friendship grew so did my closeness to the family. I met Peter from time to time, but by then his visits home were infrequent. However I do have several vivid recollections!! I am sure that I would not be breaking new ground if I mention what a lovely person Elaine was, but Pat Collins was in a somewhat different mould. He and Peter did not always see eye to eye!

"I met Louise on her first visit to Shatterford following their wedding. Peter was the hero of the area and the speed of events caused a few ripples - not the least with Pat! However it would be imprudent for others to take up too many details based on hearsay though I did know some of the ladies who were part of the contemporary local social scene!

"I was privileged to meet up with Peter and Louise at Kidderminster and Dartmouth on their rare trips through my closeness with Tricia and the family. I was of course at the famous party in Dartmouth following the wedding and reports that I have read are understated!! If I recall rightly the piano was taken apart piece by piece by Mike Hawthorn, who was there with Cherry Huggins. The chest of drawers levitating from the balcony was true, but a human also did a similar exit (I *can't* remember the name!) mercifully with no permanent injury. I can not recall many of the racing fraternity as I was not particularly involved in those circles. However I remember a long conversation I had with Tommy Sopwith. The party could not have been too large as the Queens Hotel was not large. There were many friends of Pat and Elaine there.

"The last time that I saw Peter was after his win at the British Grand Prix. He came back in the evening to my parents' house when the well-quoted and true tale of trying to persuade Tricia and I to announce our engagement took place. Two weeks later he was dead. I shall never erase the desolation of that moment when Pat, Elaine Tricia and myself, who were aboard the *Genie Maris* at Dartmouth, heard the news of the accident on the radio with Basil Payne arriving at the boat shortly after to break the terrible news.

"I still remember the day of Peter's funeral. A lonely grave and a window memorial mark the spot. The day passed in somewhat of a blur but I have a clear vision of Louise supported by Mike Hawthorn.

"It was an all too brief a time spent with Peter, and with Peter and Louise together. We did see quite a lot of Louise between 1958 and her return to America a few years later. Whilst in Britain she did return to her acting career and I remember her on the *What's My Line* TV show with Gilbert Harding and Isobel Barnett. We also saw her in a play whilst on tour.

"Tricia and I were married in November 1959 at Stone Church. Louise was Matron of Honour. I have a later photo with Sarah (daughter no 2) at her christening. Louise is godmother, and she attended with a well known motoring figure - I think Bernard Cahier - who took the pictures. Sarah remained in Jersey when Tricia moved there in 1966, where she still lives with husband Peter and son Luke. Eldest daughter Deborah returned to the UK to live with me in 1972 at age 11 shortly after my remarriage to Judy. Deborah has two daughters, Laura and Julia. Deborah lives in the Midlands still with partner Ian. She was

All about the boy!

married to John Mould and has two daughters. John's late father was a notable amateur racing driver - Peter Mould. Tricia had another son, Chris Brookes, following her remarriage. Judy and I have three children - Kate, Fred and Jemima.

"Pat Collins sold Kidderminster Motors in about 1964 (he was not tolerant of the Ford Motor Company putting pressure on him as to how he should run his business!). They retired to Jersey in 1964 where Tricia and I visited them frequently. Tricia decided to move to Jersey mid 1966, so there was a separation and we divorced a few years later.

"Another memory that has just flashed through my mind was one evening when Peter came home for a flying visit. Pat, Elaine, Tricia and I had arranged to meet at the Dog at Harvington for supper with Peter arriving later. For some reason he arrived in Pat's Bentley which he had driven at speed from Shatterford. This apparently included an "interesting" moment at the famous Honeybottom Bend. Peter referred to scratches on cars as "beer stains". Pat was not amused! On an earlier occasion he had rolled a car there."

WHAT THEY WROTE ABOUT HIM...

Robert Edwards

Author Robert Edwards described the early relationship of Moss, Collins and Ken Gregory, who would become their 'manager':

Ken Gregory and Stirling Moss had a nodding acquaintance via the RAC which was cemented in the autumn of 1949, after Gregory had been appointed to assistant to the secretary of the 500 Club at the salary of £1 a week. It was something of a boost, this moonlighting, as it upped his income by exactly 20 per cent. One of Gregory's first tasks was to organise the Club's first end-of-season dinner dance at the Rubens Hotel, Victoria, where he found himself no doubt deliberately sharing a table with Moss and Peter John Collins, an affable young sprig from Kidderminster. All three were firm friends from that day on, particularly Moss and Gregory. A small deceit had allowed Moss to stay, ostensibly, at Gregory's tiny flat - more of a garret, really - instead of going home with his parents. The reason was, unsurprisingly, a girl. Plenty of them had been brought to the dinner by both Collins and his apparently shy friend. (Edwards, 1997, p.29).

Edwards goes on to describe how Collins joined Moss for the Targa Florio in 1955:

There was one more race left on the sports car calendar and the Mercedes team had drawn dead level with Jaguar. Ferrari were three points in the lead and Neubauer, taking the view that one should always leave things as one would want to find them, performed a fairly brutal reshuffle in the Mercedes team. Gone were von Trips and Andre Simon, so Ken Gregory was asked to find and deliver two top line drivers, one to partner Moss, the other Fitch. This was heady stuff; Neubauer was in effect allowing Gregory to select two drivers for the race which would decide the World Championship - not a task to take lightly. Gregory and Moss put their thoughts together and came up with, unsurprisingly, two Brits, Peter Collins and Desmond Titterington.

Peter Collins, chum of both Ken and Stirling from the 500 days, was a works Aston Martin driver and something of a veteran. Like many British drivers, he was frustrated at the lack of a home-grown product. Like Moss, he had spent two years with H.W.M. and had driven a Maserati (for Alfred Owen). His Formula 1 mount for 1955 had been the Vanwall but he had had little success with it. Moss would drive its successor.

But that is where the resemblance between the two men ended. Whereas Stirling Moss was (and is) a focused, introspective man, given to intense self-criticism and fanatical about such social imperatives as punctuality, Peter Collins was, ahem, not. He got away with it though. Even the vinegary John Wyer, team manager at Aston Martin and disciple of Neubauer, couldn't find it in him to stay angry very long with this charming, affable fellow, even when he was hours late for an appointment. Collins pursued his social life with the single-minded resolution which characterises the true Hedonist. The completely carefree sybarite is a rara avis in Britain but commoner south of the Alps, so a trip to Italy was perfect for him. Gregory was, of course, concerned that he would miss the plane, or meet a girl, or forget, so virtually frogmarched him to the airport,

All about the boy!

rather as you would see off a nine-year-old to school. (Edwards, op.cit. p.160-161)

Edwards made further comments about Collins after his race with Moss in the 1955 Targa Florio:

Collins was occasionally unreliable, if utterly charming. Once Collins was in a racing car, however, he changed totally. Gone was the irresponsible (and irrepressible) public schoolboy; in his place a fierce if insecure buccaneer. He was to prove this several times, but the Targa Florio had lifted his reputation out of the also-rans and into the first league, where it would stay. (Edwards, R. 2001, p.161).

Denise McCluggage

*L*ouise Collins King told the author that Denise McCluggage had written a lovely story about Peter and Louise, and Denise has kindly given permission for these extracts to be reproduced from By Brooks Too Broad for Leaping, her poignant account of a number of racing people. They had originally appeared in Denise's column in 'Autoweek' in the 1980s, Song For a Sad year as I Remember Distinctly, and Enzo and Louise as A Ferrari Footnote: Enzo Ferrari and the Widow Collins.

Song For A Sad year

Volare was the song that year, "de blu del pinto de blu," something like that.

A group of strolling musicians played along the quay at Monaco. "*Volare*!" we called out from the deck of *Mipooka* and they played it and we threw coins and they moved on to the next yacht tied up there in Monte Carlo. *Volare* floated back often on the soft evening air.

When the Grand Prix is run the boats on this side have to be moved out into the center of the harbor. Ascari plunged into the drink one year just about where *Mipooka* was docked.

Ascari. Ancient history, as anything that wasn't happening right now seemed to us in the arrogance of our youth. Stage center was ours. What went before was an opening act - entertaining as it might have been. But all leading to this. Now.

And Now moved with us like a bubble. We didn't move *through* time, we moved *with time*. Our time. (Another song, much later: *"Those were the days my friend, We thought they'd never end."* Well, they end.)

The year 1958 was clearly Peter Collins' time. Peter, from the Midlands of England, at 27 was handsome, talented and personable. A lover of laughter. He was one of the promising young Britons ready to take over international motor sport after Fangio's domination. Stirling Moss. Tony Brooks. And Peter and his good friend, Mike Hawthorn - "Mon ami, mate" they called each other -were the fair-haired lads of the Ferrari team.

Peter's road car was a Ferrari. *Mipooka* was Peter's boat. Between races he lived aboard *Mipooka* with his American actress wife, Louise King - much to Enzo Ferrari's irritation. (Ferrari preferred his drivers single and living in the *albergo* across the street from the factory in Maranello.)

Louise had those bright, sunny good looks people like to think of as typically American. Not unexpectedly, every man in the paddock went all buttery around her but even the often jealous wives and girlfriends adored Louise.

What they wrote about him...

Denise McCluggage was a serious, successful and highly respected racing driver. Here she practices for the Le Mans start at Sebring in 1960.

She was a special person. There was depth behind the twinkle.

I was spending a few days with Louise and Peter on *Mipooka*. It was between races - probably midsummer, between Reims and Silverstone but I wasn't on my way to England, just back to Italy where I was staying. That was the year of the blue Alfa and I was going to race it at the Nurburgring before the Grand Prix.

Peter, Louise and I laughed a lot those few days and listened to *Volare* coming across the water and were invited to lunch aboard the *Christina*, the Onassis yacht.

Peter won convincingly at Silverstone, so it was a happy reunion two weeks later at the 'Ring. His victory had pulled him out of the Ferrari doghouse and back into contention as a successor to Fangio.

Aug.3, race day. I drove my little curtain-raiser event. Then it was time for the Grand Prix.

What a race it was for the British - both cars and drivers. Englishers were four abreast across the starting line - Collins, Moss, Hawthorn, Brooks (Ferrari, Vanwall, Ferrari, Vanwall.) Stirling took off like a scalded cat and shattered the "untouchable" lap record Fangio had set in his dramatic race here just two years previously (*one year, in 1957- author*) (He'd run down Hawthorn and Collins to win despite a midrace pit stop.)

Moss led by as much as 20 seconds but by the fourth lap (more than nine minute laps, remember) he was out. Magneto. Then the *mon*

Denise at Sebring in 1960, with the OSCA she drove.

All about the boy!

ami mates were 1-2 - Peter leading, Mike second.

But Brooks was catching up. Shades of 1957.

Louise was in the pits keeping careful lap charts, as she always did, timing the cars with a stopwatch with a split second hand and recording it all. I popped in and out, amazed at her calm. Two red Ferraris flashed by, a green car in their wake. Whoosh...Whoosh...Whoosh. I went outside so I could hear the PA system better.

Was that something about Peter crashing? Back to the Ferrari pits as Brooks came by. Hawthorn. Whoosh...whoosh...then the loud silence. The jerking progress on the unstopped second hand on Louise's watch. No Peter. Deliberately she wrote down Mike's time.

I dashed back outside. Reports on the PA were sketchy, conflicting. Peter had crashed at *Pflanzgarten* - that seemed clear. But what then? One report had Peter walking to a car and getting a ride back to the pits. Louise was still intent on her watch. Mike, now, was gone, too. Stopped somewhere on the circuit. (He had been trying to get back to the site of the crash and his clutch - damaged at the start - had given out.)

The race ended. Brooks won. Louise completed her charts and set them aside. Then I could see the calm erode a little behind her eyes. "I don't know whether to go back to the hotel or wait here," she said, adding with a little laugh: "Peter and I have a way of just missing each other."

A man, an official, with a stricken look, pushed through. "Mrs. Collins. Mrs. Collins. Come with me!" He whisked her out. She turned and smiled a little. A tiny wave. Believe with me, it seemed to say.

We didn't hear anything. There had been a helicopter we had been told. They had taken Peter to Bonn. And time stretched on.

I don't remember whose room we were in at the Sporthotel under the stands, or exactly who was there. Eight or ten others. We were waiting - an understood but unacknowledged waiting. Anyone close to racing is familiar with it. And in the meantime we talked and laughed. I was cutting Jo Bonnier's hair.

Jo and I were the only ones facing the open door and we saw Mike first and froze in place and then everyone else turned and froze too. Mike Hawthorn was big and square-jawed and fair-haired. So fair, one of those English schoolboy faces that said "Goodbye Mr. Chips" to Robert Donat. He was still in his driving clothes - dirty white pants, his trademark green battle jacket. His face was streaked. And tired.

He didn't have to say anything. Slowly in his hands he turned a shattered brown crash hat that we all recognized as Peter's.

Pflanzgarten was not a fast turn - less than 100 mph - but Peter had been intent on retaking the lead and he was too fast for the turn. His car had peeled off, airborne and his head had hit high on a skinny lone tree. He was dead by the time Louise reached the hospital. What had she said? Peter and I have a way of just missing each other...?

I don't remember if I finished Jo Bonnier's hair cut or not. I do remember sitting on my bed that night, holding in my hand the one shoe I had just removed and then finding myself exactly like that 45 minutes later, stiff and bone chilled. I had been thinking of Louise, of Mike - the last of the *mon ami mates*. Thinking.

Mike was himself dead before the year was out (*early 1959 - author*), killed on the

What they wrote about him...

Guildford Bypass in a highway accident in his Jaguar in the wet shortly after winning the 1958 driving championship and then retiring.

Volare.

For a lilting song one exceeding sad, I think.

Enzo and Louise

The place was Miami, the year was 1957. Louise King was starring in a winter stock version of the *Seven-Year Itch*. Peter Collins was passing through after racing in Argentina. Instead of going home to the English Midlands before races in Cuba he was going home to America's Midlands - Kansas - with Masten Gregory. Peter had never seen Kansas. He never did.

Peter Collins had never met Louise King, either. Or at least he didn't think he had. Friends had suggested he look her up. The two arranged to meet at a bar near the theater after the show. "It was rather strange," Louise recalled recently. "Bob Said and his wife were there talking to Peter when I arrived. We had a drink at the bar. Then we felt we ought to go to dinner, but Peter said, 'No, I have to meet someone here.' I said, 'Who else are you meeting?' And he said 'Louise King.'"

They weathered that identity crisis rather well. 'That was on Monday, he proposed to me on Wednesday and we called our parents. Friday, my Dad flew down.'

Dad was Andrew Cordier, assistant to Dag Hammarskjold at the United Nations. "He looked at Peter and said, 'Why Louise, you two met last year in Monte Carlo. There's a photograph at home of the two of you.' He was right. Jim Kimberly had taken a picture at the beach when he introduced them and sent a print to Louise.

Somehow Eros had wrapped a blindfold around Louise and Peter's eyes instead of his own. 'Turned out we had even met at a party at Joan and Bernard Cahier's,' Louise said, 'but neither of us remembered the other at *all.*' So much for love at first sight. On February 11, Peter and Louise were married. For the next 18 months, until Peter was killed at the Nurburgring August 3, 1958, they were apart only one night. 'That was when Peter went to practice for the Mille Miglia.'

I was at Louise's house in Connecticut to gather any recollections she might have of Enzo Ferrari for some articles I was doing. 'Ferrari never went to races so I never saw that much of him,' she said. 'We shared no language so there was never any great communication.'

The bachelor Peter Collins had lived during the racing season near the Ferrari factory, ready at a moment's notice to test the race cars. He loved wandering around the factory, too. That, and Dino's death, was a tie to the Old Man. Dino, Ferrari's 24-year-old son, just a year younger than Peter, had died June 30, 1956.

Now barely seven months later, Ferrari faced another loss: Peter's sudden marriage. Louise said: 'I know people said that Ferrari would have preferred Peter did nothing but race but he never showed me that side. He was always very gracious to me.'

Ferrari refers to Peter in his autobiography as 'un bel regazzo' (a handsome lad). He remarked on his pleasant, open face and on his enthusiasm for racing matched by his expertise in mechanics. 'He was a driver who assimilated his machine.' But when he wrote of Peter's marriage, his tone changed subtly. He described

All about the boy!

the American girl Peter 'fell for as a divorcee, a slim, pretty blonde who made a career for herself on stage and TV.' Peter Collins after his marriage, Ferrari wrote, still preserved his old skill and enthusiasm but 'his happy character" changed. "He became irritable."

Ferrari is keenly perceptive, but sometimes his perceptions suffer from misinterpretation. Peter was, indeed, irritable but the source of his irritation was Ferrari himself, not his own marital status. 'Peter felt that he (Ferrari) was still mourning too much for his own son and not paying enough attention to the racing,' Louise said. 'He had a meeting with Ferrari and told him as much. Peter may even have threatened to quit, I don't know. Anyway, it was right after that Ferrari called us both into his office and gave us his villa in Maranello - to stay in, not to keep - and gave me a ring with three big diamonds. I don't think many people talked to Ferrari the way Peter did.'

And there was the Lancia. 'Ferrari was upset that we bought a Flaminia instead of a Ferrari. Peter told him there was a rather important difference in price. I don't know what financial arrangements were involved, but Ferrari took the Flaminia and gave us a Ferrari - a Pinin Farina prototype of the Superamerica. Dark blue and incredibly beautiful.'

For living arrangements during the 1958 season Peter and Louise chose (over Maranello) a boat which they called Mipooka, docked at Monte Carlo and outfitted with two Siamese kittens. Life was good. In England in July Peter won the Grand Prix and they put a down payment on a house. He was going to retire at season's end to a Ferrari dealership.

There was an off-week between the English and the German Grand Prix. Louise can't remember whether or not they went to Maranello between the races. Ferrari, with his aptitude for drama, places them there. In his book he wrote of Peter: 'My last memory of him was when I shook his hand before he left for the Nurburgring. Looking at him I was suddenly seized by a strange feeling of infinite sadness. As I went back into my office I could not help wondering if it was some sort of presentiment.'

After Peter's death Louise went to see Ferrari (he was used to a near-parade of the widows and bereft girl friends of his drivers.) 'Through an interpreter he said that he had not gone to races for years but that if I would go to Monza he would break his habit and meet me at Monza for the Grand Prix,' Louise said.

Louise went to Monza. 'But he never showed up,' she said. How did she feel about that? Fine. 'I thought he had told me he would meet me there so that I would go to a race again; that it would help me deal better with Peter's death,' she said. 'I was not alone. I was with Taruffi and a group of friends and they all said, 'Well, he got you here and that was what was meant to happen.'

Enzo Ferrari as a youngster, had dreamed of being an opera tenor. Certainly he played the death scenes as well as any of them.

****

Denise wrote, in her Now and Then column, a piece about an earlier adventure with the then Louise King. Stirling Moss had introduced Louise to Denise and Louise was her co-driver on the Great American Mountain Rally. Denise was driving a Volvo which lapsed onto three cylinders and Louise got out into the snow and pushed the Volvo, gaining her the title as the 'fourth cylinder'. The rally, especially through the snowy hills of upper New York State and Vermont was a series of adventures and the pair got to know each other well. Louise had served her apprenticeship early in the motor sport game. They are still friends.

What they wrote about him...

Denise shared Abarth (65) with American Ruth Levy at Sebring in 1958. They retired but this is the race won by Peter Collins and Mike Hawthorn.

Enzo Ferrari

I've mentioned Peter Collins' name several times. I had great respect for him as a racer and as a man. To illustrate his moral strength, let me go back to the year 1956, which I discussed before in relation to Manuel Fangio. The world championship was evolving in such a way that people were predicting him to be the winner. Then, one day I called him up and said, 'Collins, I'd like your opinion on this matter. I'm not asking you to yield to Fangio. I've never asked that of anyone because I was a racer myself, so I know what it means. But I want to know what you're thinking, now that we're down to the bottom line.' He replied without hesitation, 'I never thought that a 25 year old guy like me could take on such a big responsibility. I have lots of time ahead of me: Fangio should stay world champion for another year because he deserves it, and I'm willing to give him my car if it makes it any easier for him.' Unfortunately he didn't have a 'lot of time' ahead of him because he died two years later on a tragic day at the Nurburgring'. He was exhibiting his tremendous. and perhaps still growing, style in a duel with Brooks on that insidious, arduous course.

315

All about the boy!

Peter was a handsome fellow, not terribly tall but well built, with an open face. His passion for racing was equal to his passion and talent for mechanics. In fact, his family had a large machinery and transportation business. Peter was a man who would get into a car and know exactly, within one lap, the engine's maximum speed, the best performance, and so on. He was a racer, in other words, who could virtually assimilate the car, interpret its potential and indicate all this to the technicians, not only approximately but often with utter precision. This was a precious contribution to the fine-tuning and development of the vehicle. As a racer, he was consistently fast, and above all he was indomitable. That is, he was a racer who never gave up. Moss admired him so much that he wanted him for a co-pilot in a Targa Florio, which because of their exploits was unforgettable.

After he started racing with us, Peter decided to marry. The beautiful slender blonde divorcee he had met in Florida was an actress who had worked with Orson Welles in the movies. They had first met the previous year in Monte Carlo, but she hadn't made much of an impression on Peter. This woman, Luisa, was one of those typical feminine creatures who hang around the pits whom I've only mentioned in passing. But that tournament in Florida was decisive for Peter. The American woman fascinated him and won him over; he phoned her father and married her. Collins maintained his enthusiasm, his bravura. And although he continued to be dazzling, his happy personality began to crack: he became nervous, and word got out that America was keeping him awake at night. And the last memory I have of him is shaking his hand before he left for Nurburgring; when I looked at him, I was overcome by sadness. And as I went back into my office, I wondered if it was a presentiment.

APPENDIX A - LIST OF RACES

Year	Date	Event	Car	Number	Result	Information
1947	June	Blackpool Rally	Aston Martin		1st Cl.	Concours
1949	10/4	Brough	Cooper 500		8th	Unconfirmed
	18/4	Goodwood	Cooper 500		DNS	
	22/5	Prescott	Cooper 500		9th	
	12/6	Prescott	Cooper 500		7th	
	9/7	Silverstone 100	Cooper 500	11	1st	
	17/7	Prescott	Cooper 500	56	DNF	Crash
	30/7	Zandvoort	Cooper 500	38	DNF	Unplaced
	20/8	Silverstone	Cooper 500	8	8th	
	3/9	Silverstone	Cooper 500	51	DNF	
	11/9	Prescott Int.	Cooper 500	47	7th	
	17/9	Goodwood	Cooper 500	8	1st	
	24/9	Shelsley Walsh	Cooper 500	7	3rd	
	8/10	Weston Speed Trial	Cooper 500		8th	
1950	10/4	Goodwood Easter	Cooper 500	15	DNF	
	13/5	Silverstone GP	Cooper 500	14	3rd	
	27/5	Goodwood	Cooper 500	5	2nd	
	29/5	Blandford	Cooper 500	30	2nd	
	10/6	Shelsley Walsh	Cooper 500		2nd	
	11/6	Prescott	Cooper 750		1st	
	24/6	Bo'Ness	Cooper 750		1st	
	2/7	Rest and Be Thankful	Cooper 750		2nd	
	3/8	Bouley Bay	Cooper 750		1st	
	26/8	Silverstone Int.	Cooper 500	21	7th	
	2/9	Brighton Speed Trial	Cooper 500		3rd	
	2/9	Brighton Speed Trial	Cooper 750		1st	
	10/9	Prescott	Cooper 500		3rd	
	10/9	Prescott	Cooper 1200		1st	
	23/9	Shelsley Walsh	Cooper 1200	3	3rd	
	23/9	Shelsley Walsh	Cooper 500		1st	
	30/9	Goodwood	Cooper 500	11	4th	
	7/10	Castle Combe	Cooper 500	24	1st	
	7/10	Castle Combe	Cooper 1200		3rd	
	16/10	Altcar Sprint	Cooper 1200		1st	
1951	3-4/3	Burnham Rally	Ford Consul			
	26/3	Goodwood	Cooper 500	12	DNF	
	26/3	Goodwood	Cooper 1200	10	1st	
	31/3	Castle Combe	Cooper 500	40	DNF	2nd in heat
	5/5	Silverstone Int.	Cooper 500	10	DNF	Crash

317

All about the boy!

	Date	Event	Car	No.	Result	Notes
	5/5	Silverstone Int.	Dyna-Panhard		3rd Cl.	21st OA.
	12/5	Altcar Sprint	Cooper 750		1st	
	12/5	Altcar Sprint	Cooper 1200		1st	
	12/5	Altcar Sprint	Allard		2nd	
	19/5	Prescott	Cooper 1200		1st	
	26/5	Boreham	J.B.S. 500	133	2nd	1st in heat
	2/6	Ulster Trophy	J.B.S. 500	6	1st	
	2/6	Ulster Trophy	Cooper 1200		DNF	
	14/6	Isle of Man	Allard		DNF	Crash
	23/6	Shelsley Walsh	J.B.S. 500		Unplaced	
	23/6	Shelsley Walsh	Cooper 1200		1st	
	24/6	Prescott	Cooper 750		2nd	
	24/6	Prescott	Cooper 1200		1st	
	1/7	Boreham	J.B.S. 500	9	Unplaced	
	9/7	Rest and Be Thankful	Cooper 1200		1st	
	14/7	Silverstone GP	J.B.S. 500	40	Unplaced	
	15/7	Bouley Bay	J.B.S. 500		DNS	
	21/7	Windfield	J.B.S. 500	40	1st	
	28/7	Croft	J.B.S. 500	40	1st	
	4/8	Ibsley	J.B.S. 500	83	1st	
	6/8	Gamston	J.B.S. 500	46	1st	
	6/8	Gamston	Allard		1st	
	11/8	Boreham	J.B.S. 500	24	Unplaced	
	18/8	Silverstone 100	J.B.S. 500	22	DNF	
	1/9	Silverstone	J.B.S. 500	76	1st	
	9/9	Croft	J.B.S. 500	42	DNF	
	9/9	Croft	Allard	17	1st	
	9/9	Croft	Allard	17	1st	2 Races
	15/9	Tourist Trophy	Allard		DNF	
	22/9	Shelsley Walsh	J.B.S. 500		3rd	
	22/9	Shelsley Walsh	Allard		2nd	
	22/9	Shelsley Walsh	Cooper 1200		1st	
	23/9	Westwood Park	J.B.S. 500		1st	
	23/9	Westwood Park	Allard		1st	
	6/10	Gamston	J.B.S. 500	57	1st	
	6/10	Gamston	Allard		3rd	
	7/10	Brough	J.B.S. 500	17	Unplaced	
1952	22-29/1	Monte Carlo Rally	Ford Anglia		3rd Cl.	
	14/4	Pau GP	HWM-Alta	22	DNF	Chassis 2-52
	27/4	Marseilles GP	HWM-Alta	22	7th	Ch. 2-52
	10/5	Silvertsone Int.Tr.	HWM-Alta	29	9th	Ch. 2-52
	18/5	Swiss GP	HWM-Alta	18	DNF	Ch. 2-52
	22/5	Luxembourg GP	J.B.S. 500	2	3rd	
	25/5	Montlhery GP	HWM-Alta	22	4th w.Macklin	Ch. 2-52
	1/6	Monaco GP	Aston Martin DB3	74	7th	Ch. DB3/4
	15/6	Le Mans 24 Hrs.	Aston Martin DB3	25	DNF	Ch. DB3/5
	22/6	Belgian GP	HWM-Alta	26	DNF	Ch. 2-52
	29/6	Reims GP	HWM-Alta	18	DNF	Ch. 2-52
	6/7	French GP	HWM-Alta	22	6th	Ch. 2-52

Appendix A - List of races

	Date	Race	Car	No.	Result	Ref
	13/7	Sables d'Olonne GP	HWM-Alta	22	2nd	Ch. 2-52
	19/7	British GP	HWM-Alta	29	DNF	Ch. 2-52
	3/8	German GP	HWM-Alta	111	DNS	Ch. 2-52
	10/8	Comminges GP	HWM-Alta	22	DNF	Ch. 2-52
	16/8	Goodwood 9 Hrs.	Aston Martin DB3	17	1st w.Griffith	Ch. DB3/5
	24/8	La Baule GP	HWM-Alta	24	4th	Ch. 2-52
	7/9	Italian GP	HWM-Alta	54	DNQ	Ch. 2-52
	14/9	Cadours	HWM-Alta	20	DNQ	Ch. 2-52
1953	8/3	Sebring 12 Hrs.	Aston Martin DB3	31	DNF w.Duke	Ch. DB3/4
	26/4	Mille Miglia	Aston Martin DB3	551	DNF w.Keen	Ch. DB3/4
	3/5	Bordeaux GP	HWM-Alta		DNS	Alternate
	9/5	Silverstone Int.Tr.	HWM-Alta	24	12th	Ch. 2-53
	9/5	Silverstone Int.	Aston Martin DB3		4th	Ch. DB3/4
	16/5	Ulster Trophy	HWM-Alta	26	DNF	Ch. 1-53
	25/5	Crystal Palace	HWM-Alta	4	7th	Ch. 1-53
	31/5	Eifel GP	HWM-Alta	11	3rd	Ch. 2-53
	7/6	Dutch GP	HWM-Alta	36	8th	Ch. 1-53
	13-14/6	Le Mans 24 Hrs.	Aston Martin DB3S	25	DNF w.Parnell	Ch. DB3S/2
	21/6	Belgian GP	HWM-Alta	26	DNF	Ch. 2-53
	5/7	French GP	HWM-Alta	28	13th	Ch. 2-53
	12-16/7	Alpine Rally	Sunbeam Alpine	509	DNF	
	18/7	British GP	HWM-Alta	2	DNF	Ch. 2-53
	18/7	British GP	Aston Martin DB3S	18	3rd	Ch. DB3S/2
	26/7	Aix le Bains GP	HWM-Alta	16	DNF	Ch. 2-53
	9/8	Sables d'Olonne GP	HWM-Alta	12	5th	Ch. 1-53
	22/8	Goodwood 9 Hrs.	Aston Martin DB3S	6	2nd w.Griffith	Ch. DB3S/4
	5/9	Toursit Trophy	Aston Martin DB3S	20	1st w.Griffith	Ch. DB3S/4
1954	24/1	Argentine 1000 Kms	Aston Martin DB3S	40	3rd w.Griffith	Ch. DB3S/4
	7/3	Sebring 12 Hrs.	Aston Martin DB3S	24	DNF w.Griffith	Ch. DB3S/4
	2/5	Mille Miglia	Aston Martin DB3S	609	DNF w.Griffith	Ch. DB3S/4
	15/5	Silverstone Int.Tr.	Aston Martin DB3S		8th	Ch. DB3S/1
	29/5	Aintree	Thin Wall Ferrari	39	DNF	Ch. 375-10
	7/6	Goodwood	Thin Wall Ferrari	3	1st	Ch. 375-10
	12-13/6	Le Mans 24 Hrs.	Aston Martin DB3S	20	DNF w.Bira	Ch. DB3S/6
	19/6	Crystal Palace	Connaught	4	2nd	

319

All about the boy!

	Date	Event	Car	No.	Result	Chassis
	4/7	GP d l'ACF	Vanwall	50	DNA	Vanwall Spl.
	12-15/7	Alpine Rally	Sunbeam Alpine	504	DNF	
	17/7	British GP	Vanwall	20	DNF	Vanwall Spl.
	17/7	British GP	Aston Martin DB3S	20	1st	Ch. DB3S/1
	24/7	Fairwood	Aston Martin DB2		4th	
	14/8	Snetterton	Thin Wall Ferrari	3	1st	Ch. 375-10
	5/9	Italian GP	Vanwall	10	7th	Vanwall Spl.
	11/9	Tourist Trophy	Aston Martin DB3S		DNF w.Griffith	Ch. DB3S/2
	25/9	Goodwood	Thin Wall Ferrari	9	1st	Ch. 375-10
	25/9	Goodwood	Vanwall	8	2nd	Vanwall Spl.
	2/10	Aintree	Thin Wall Ferrari	9	DNF	Ch. 375-10
	2/10	Aintree	Aston Martin DB3S		2nd	Ch. DB3S/2
	26/10	Spanish GP	Vanwall	42	DNS	Vanwall Spl. Crash
1955	17/1	Monte Carlo Rally	Aston Martin DB2/4		95th w.G.Whitehead	
	4/2	Olton Park	Aston Martin DB3S	42	8th	Ch. DB3S/2 (PC's Car)
	11/4	Goodwood	BRM V-16 MkII	25	1st	Ch. MkII 01 or 02
	11/4	Goodwood	Aston Martin DB3S	84	5th	Ch. DB3S/2
	1/5	Mille Miglia	Aston Martin DB3S	702	DNF	Ch. DB3S/5
	7/5	Silverstone Int.Tr.	Maserati 250F	3	1st	Ch. 2509
	7/5	Silverstone Int.Tr.	Aston Martin DB3S	12	7th	Ch. DB3S/2
	28/5	Snetterton	BRM V-16 MkII	27	DNF	Ch. MkII 01 or 02
	28/5	Snetterton	Aston Martin DB3S		2nd	Ch. DB3S/2
	30/5	Crystal Palace	Maserati 250F		1st	Ch. 2509
	11-12/6	Le Mans 24 Hrs.	Aston Martin DB3S	23	2nd w.P.Frere	Ch. DB3S/6
	16/6	British GP	Maserati 250F	42	DNF	Ch. 2509
	16/6	British GP	Aston Martin DB3S	1	2nd	Ch. DB3S/6
	7/8	Swedish GP	Aston Martin DB3S		DNS	Ch. DB3S/2
	13/8	Snetterton	BRM V-16 MkII		DNF	Ch. MkII 01 or 02
	13/8	Snetterton	Ford Zephyr		1st Cl.	
	20/8	Goodwood 9 Hrs.	Aston Martin DB3S	2	3rd w.T.Brooks	Ch. DB3S/6
	27/8	Olton Park	Aston Martin DB3S		3rd	Ch. DB3S/2

Appendix A - List of races

	Date	Race	Car	No.	Result	Chassis
	3/9	Aintree	BRM P25	9	DNS	Ch. 252
	3/9	Aintree	BRM V-16 MkII		1st	Ch. MkII 01 or 02
	11/9	Italian GP	Maserati 250F	32	DNF	Ch. 2515
	17/9	Tourist Trophy	Aston Martin DB3S	16	DNF w.T.Brooks	Ch. DB3S/6
	24/9	Olton Gold Cup	BRM P25	10	DNF	Ch. 252
	1/10	Caslte Combe	BRM V-16 MkII		DNF	Ch. MkII 01 or 02
	1/10	Castle Combe	Maserati 250F	14	DNF	Ch. 2509
	16/10	Targa Florio	Mercedes 300SLR	104	1st w.S.Moss	Ch. 0004/551
1956	22/1	Argentine GP	Ferrari 555 Squalo	36	DNF	Ch. 555-3
	29/1	Buenos Aires 1000	Ferrari 410S	44	DNF w.L.Musso	Ch. 0596 CM
	5/2	Mendoza GP	Ferrari 555 Squalo	36	5th	Ch. 555-3
	24/3	Sebring 12 Hrs.	Aston Martin DB3S	26	DNF w.S.Moss	Ch. DB3S/6
	8/4	Giro d'Sicily	Ferrari 857S	337	1st w.Klemantaski	Ch. 0584M
	15/4	Syracuse GP	Lancia D-50	28	3rd	Ch. 0008
	29/4	Mille Miglia	Ferrari 290/860	551	2nd w.Klemantaski	Ch. 0628M
	5/5	Silverstone Int.Tr.	Lancia D-50	2	DNF w.J.Fangio	Ch. 0004
	5/5	Silverstone Int.Tr.	Aston Martin DB3S		DNF	Ch. DB3S/7 Crash
	13/5	Monaco GP	Lancia D-50	26	2nd w.J.Fangio	Ch. 0007
	27/5	Nurburgring 1000	Aston Martin DB3S	6	5th w.T.Brooks	Ch. DB3S/5
	3/6	Belgian GP	Lancia D-50	8	1st	Ch. 0008
	10/6	Targa Florio	Ferrari 860 Monza	112	DNF w.Castelloti	Ch. 0602M
	24/6	Supercorte-maggiore	Ferrari 625LM	62	1st w. Hawthorn	Ch. 0642M
	1/7	French GP	Lancia D-50	14	1st	Ch. 0008
	8/7	Rouen GP	Aston Martin DB3S	18	DNF	Ch. DB3S/9
	15/7	British GP	Lancia D-50	2	2nd w.Portago	Ch. 0008
	28-29/7	Le Mans 24 Hrs.	Aston Martin DB3S	8	2nd w.S.Moss	Ch. DB3S/9
	5/8	German GP	Lancia D-50	2	DNF	Ch. 0008
	12/8	Swedish GP	Ferrari 290MM	1	2nd w.Trips	Ch. 0626M
	2/9	Italian GP	Lancia D-50	26	2nd w.J.Fangio	Ch. 0008
1957	13/1	Argentine GP	Lancia D-50	10	DNF	Ch. 0009
	20/1	Buenos Aires 1000	Ferrari 290S	6	DNF w.Hawthorn	Ch. 0656 Shared 0628-3rd
	27/1	Buenos Aires GP	Lancia D-50	12	3rd w.M.Gregory	Ch. 0009
	24/2	Cuban GP	Ferrari 500TR	38	4th	Ch. 0654
	24/3	Sebring 12Hrs.	Ferrari 315S	11	6th w.Trintignant	Ch. 0674
	7/4	Syracuse GP	Lancia D-50	32	1st	Ch. 0009
	28/4	Naples GP	Lancia D-50	11	1st	Ch. 0008
	12/5	Mille Miglia	Ferrari 335S	534	DNF w.Klemantaski	Ch. 0700

All about the boy!

	Date	Event	Car	No.	Result	Chassis
	19/5	Monaco GP	Lancia D-50	26	DNF	Ch. 0008
	26/5	Nurburgring 1000	Ferrari 335S	5	2nd w.Gendebien	Ch. 0700
	2/6	Belgian GP	CANCELLED			
	16/6	Dutch GP	CANCELLED			
	23-24/6	Le Mans 24 Hrs.	Ferrari 335S	6	DNF w.P.Hill	Ch. 0700
	7/7	French GP	Lancia D-50	12	3rd	Ch. 0008
	14/7	Reims GP	Lancia D-50	4	DNF	Ch. 0007
	30/7	British GP	Lancia D-50	12	DNF	Ch. 0008
	4/8	German GP	Lancia D-50	7	3rd	Ch. 0008
	11/8	Swedish GP	Ferrari 335S	4	2nd w.P.Hill	Ch. 0700
	18/8	Pescara GP	Lancia D-50	DNA		
	8/9	Italian GP	Lancia D-50	30	DNF	Ch. 0008
	20/10	Spanish GP	CANCELLED			
	22/10	Modena GP	Ferrari 156	28	4th	Ch. 0011
	27/10	Morocco GP	Ferrari 156	2	DNF	Ch. 0012
	3/11	Venezuela GP	Ferrari 335S	14	1st w.P.Hill	Ch. 0700
	8/12	Nassau Trophy	Ferrari-Healey	18	11th 1st Cl.	
1958	18/1	Argentine GP	Ferrari 156	18	DNF	Ch. 0012
	26/1	Buenos Aires 1000	Ferrari 250TR	2	1st w.P.Hill	Ch. 0704
	2/2	Buenos Aires GP	Ferrari 156	18	DNF	Ch. 0012
	22/3	Sebring 12 Hrs.	Ferrari 250TR	14	1st w.P.Hill	Ch. 0704
	17/4	Goodwood	Ferrari 206S	2	2nd	Ch. 0740
	3/5	Silverstone Itn.Tr.	Ferrari 246	9	1st	Ch. 0002
	11/5	Targa Florio	Ferrari 250TR	98	4th w.P.Hill	Ch. 0704
	18/5	Monaco GP	Ferrari 246	36	3rd	Ch. 0002
	26/5	Dutch GP	Ferrari 246	4	DNF	Ch. 0002
	1/6	Nurburgring 1000	Ferrari 250TR	4	2nd w.Hawthorn	Ch. 0704
	15/6	Belgian GP	Ferrari 246	14	DNF	Ch. 0002
	22-23/6	Le Mans 24 Hrs.	Ferrari 250TR	12	DNF w.Hawthorn	Ch. 0704
	7/7	French GP F2	Ferrari 156	2	2nd	Ch. 0011
	7/7	French GP	Ferrari 246	42	5th	Ch. 0001
	20/7	British GP	Ferrari 246	1	1st	Ch. 0002
	3/8	German GP	Ferrari 246	2	DNF Crash	Ch. 0002

APPENDIX B - LOUISE'S LETTERS

Reproduced by kind permission of Louise Collins King.

March, 1957 - letter to her parents:

"Saturday evening, we arrived in Dartmouth and I got my first look at the yacht (Genie Maris). We have to leave Wednesday morning for Italy and as far as I'm concerned I'd much rather stay right here. I love the boat and it is extremely comfortable to live on and all of a sudden I just couldn't care less about going anywhere. We've been on board for three nights now and I love it. The skipper is a very intelligent person who thinks I shouldn't work too hard, which is the opposite of how Peter feels about the situation. The three of us get along beautifully, though. Yesterday we were busy sanding, re-varnishing and painting a launch - you should see my nails!

"I've been cooking believe it or not and I think the salt air gives the boys such a good appetite anything will taste good. The skipper is a good cook, so he kind of supervises me. Anyway, we're far from starving.

"I wish so much you could see Dartmouth. It is a tiny little village surrounded by pretty, pretty hills and its awfully un-commercial. Must have been like this for years.

"The Royal Navy College is here so most of the boats are Navy ones. I'm sure this must be about the quietest place in the whole world so we sleep like logs, eat like fiends and keep busy, busy all day. A couple of weeks of this and I'll be the healthiest person I know."

April, 1957 - a letter home:

"Mr. and Mrs. Ferrari have been wonderful to us. She has taken a liking to me and insists on going everywhere with me, which is quite funny because I can't understand one word she says, but somehow we get along. They have offered to let us have their villa at Rimini after the race in Naples, so I hope we can go bake in the sun for a while on their beach. What a life!"

July 13, 1957 - a letter to her parents:

"Dear Family:

There doesn't seem to be much to report in this letter. After our small stay in England we went to Rouen and had quite a nice time. Mike Hawthorn had his plane there and every day after practice the three of us flew to Deauville for some fun in the sun. The race was rather dull as about midway the cars were in their finishing position and my lap chart showed the same old thing lap after lap. Monday Peter and I drove back to Deauville for two nights and had a lovely time, as usual, with some friends who happened to be there. Now at Reims we are enjoying ourselves with silly mystery books. Everyone has been kidding us because Mike, Peter and I (we're quite a threesome) have our books with us during breakfast, lunch and dinner. Actually the reason for all this is we came across a store with English books for change and we just about bought the store out...

"Sorry I can't dream up more news for you but everything with us is quite happily normal.

All about the boy!

We miss you muchly and hope you're all well and happy.

love, Louise and Peter"

August, 1957 - a letter home:

"Ferrari has decided that he would keep us in Modena more if we had a nice place to live, so he has given us his villa near the factory at Maranello to use for as long as we want. They haven't lived in it since the war, so the day before yesterday we opened it up and started to clean the place. Its quite modern and we're thrilled to death with it. All we had to do was open the windows and peasant-type people came streaming in to help. Peter has been getting some exercise getting weeds out of the driveway and I'm working miracles with soap and water inside. On the first floor we have two big rooms and a huge hall - both with marble floors - a small john and kitchen, and on the second floor three bedrooms, very big modern bathroom, a small room which will be a bar and a balcony that runs the full length of the house."

October, 1957 - a letter home:

"Peter is now going through a change of life, or something, because he is talking more and more about stopping racing and building houses and raising little Peters and Louises. We've been searching the American housing magazines like mad and cutting out things, etc. I think we want to build a modern American-type house near Peter's home (and that's unheard of here). We have a piece of land about three minutes walking distance from Shatterford Grange that's on top of a hill, with a view both ways that goes for miles and miles."

October, 1957 - another letter home that month:

"The big news is that Peter and Donald (Healey) might become partners in a business in Nassau. Donald has a factory there which is not in use as yet, but when it gets operating it will assemble Healey cars and speedboats for shipping to the States. They would save a great deal of money by assembling them in Nassau and shipping them the short distance between Nassau and Miami. Donald wants someone to manage the factory and the shipping, etc., and would like that someone to be Peter. Also, if Peter wanted to make it a partnership, Donald would be quite agreeable to that. This would mean that we would live in Nassau almost continuously for about a year starting next September. In December, when Peter races for Donald in Nassau they will be able to get much further along in their discussions."

Peter and Louise have a joint birthday party at Dartmouth in November 1957. Photo - LAT

Appendix B - Louise's letters

December, 1957 - a letter from Peter to his parents from Long Island:

"The trip to Nassau was very interesting and except for the weather was most enjoyable, the race week being one long laugh from beginning to end, all attempts at organisation failing miserably. The car (Healey) arrived two days after we did and it soon became apparent that if any work was to be done on it I was the one to do it, so I spent a lot of time wiring loose nuts and bolts and generally doing things that should have been done at Warwick.

"The first day's practice was very interesting for me because I found that when the fuel tank was full the ground clearance was zero and the exhaust pipe took the place of the rear suspension! So we had to re-adjust the rear suspension to suit as best we could and run on less fuel.

"I only did one day's practising as I thought any more would really wreck the car completely, but on race day I must say that it ran quite well and in the whole race of 250 miles I only had to stop once for oil. Much to my surprise we won Class D (up to 3litres), beating all the remaining cars in this category. I should add though, that these were mostly junk.

"Stirling drove a very fine race in a 3.5litre Ferrari to win the main event after the girl he had lent his 3.7litre Aston to up-ended it three times the day before. This annoyed J.Wyer, Esq., but pleased Stirling as it had not been going worth a damn anyway."

February, 1958 - a letter home from Louise:

"We had a wonderful day of staying at home (in Maranello). Peter is building a complicated model boat out of wood on our dining room table, so that kept him and is keeping him pretty busy. Where this year went, I'll never know. I realize we've covered a lot of territory, but maybe that helped time to fly so fast. It's been a marvellous year and we just seem to get happier and happier. Who could ask for anything more"

May, 1958, a letter to her parents from Monte Carlo:

"I can't tell you how many friends came to see us. Every day from early in the morning until late evening we had visitors. Phil Hill stayed with us over the race weekend and all in all we had a grand time, even though it was rather hectic. On Sunday, before the race, I served lunch for 16 people, which is not really the easiest thing to do on a boat our size. Finally, on Tuesday, one couple felt rather sorry for me and arranged a picnic lunch for 12 people (done by the Hotel de Paris, which is fantastic) and we went to a quiet bay for a wonderful meal, sunning and swimming. It was better than a birthday ever could be."

July, 1958 - a letter to her parents from Monte Carlo:

"We've been here on the boat ever since Reims, except for last weekend, when we went to Silverstone. That was really a good and happy race. Peter was first from start to finish and of course his family was there and we were all quite thrilled by the whole thing. But here is the *real* news about that weekend - we arrived at Shatterford Thursday evening and Peter's parents told us about a house for sale about five minutes away from theirs. Friday morning we had a look around the grounds - Sunday we had a look around the house - Monday a plumber and a roof man checked through it and Tuesday we *bought it,* or at least said we would.

325

All about the boy!

"I never really believed this would happen as Peter loves boats so much. It's an old Georgian house called Honeybrook House, sitting on or in 4.5 acres of land. For the past ten years a Bishop Fyffe (aged 90) and his wife have been living in it and haven't had the money or energy to do a thing to it, so its quite run down... We aren't intending to live in it until next year, so we shall have plenty of time to do a lot of necessary work...I suppose you think we are out of our minds getting such a large place, but all of this costs £4,500 or about $13,000, so we feel we have a pretty good deal. At least we have plenty of space for cats, dogs and any small children that might come along.

"By the way, we are keeping our boat at least through next year, so we shall have a home while we're away from England. We shall probably sell the Ferrari though, as we never use it around Monte Carlo (its too crowded) and we're much happier flying to races than driving.

"We're off to Germany Wednesday and I will be back here Monday for nearly a month if Portugal is cancelled (I hope). Sorry I didn't write sooner but I hope this will make up for it.

Love - Peter and Louise"

August 28, 1958 - letter from Milan:

" I have never seen Ferrari as upset as he is now over Peter's death. He said that since his own son died he regarded Peter as his son and wanted to give us the villa and to give Peter part of the Ferrari factory. He was so much like Peter's father with so many plans for his future and now all that is just finished. Well, its wonderful that Peter did have such a marvellous relationship with Ferrari.

"Ferrari has asked me to come with him to the races at Monza on Sept. 7. He *never* goes to the races, but he told me it would be his last Grand Prix and he would like me to be there. He's made no announcement of this decision publicly, so please don't say anything to anyone about it. I don't know how my friends would react to my being there and I haven't made up my mind yet as to whether I'll go, but I sort of feel I should if Ferrari wants me to. He is sending only one car for Mike and after that there just will be no more. Of course, there is always the possibility that someone will talk him into continuing, but I really doubt it. Peter's accident was just too much for Ferrari to take.

"Mike is racing in Portugal today and I am really a nervous wreck. I had an awful time going to sleep last night, probably through just being silly. Its impossible for another accident to happen so soon but I did get a bit worked up. I'll be so happy when today's race is over. This must be why I always insisted on going to every race with Peter. While I was there I never worried, but just not knowing what's happening is terrible."

BIBLIOGRAPHY

Collings, T. *The Piranha Club - Power and Influence in Formula One* Virgin Books, London, 2001.

Cooper, J. with J.Bentley *John Cooper: Grand Prix Carpet-Bagger* Haynes, Somerset, UK, 1977.

Coram, D. *Aston Martin - The Story of a Sports Car* Motor Racing Publications, London, 1957.

Edwards, R. *Managing A Legend: Stirling Moss, Ken Gregory and the British Racing Partnership* Haynes, Somerset, UK, 1997.

Edwards, R. *Stirling Moss - The Authorised Biography* Cassell & Co., London, 2001.

Ferrari, E. *Piloti, Tre Gente* Conti Editore, Bologna, Italy, 1989.

Frostick, M. *Works Team - The Rootes Competition Department* Mercian Manuals, Balsall Common, Coventry, UK, 1964.

IOTA - Official Organ of the 500 Club 1947-1953 Transport Bookman Publications, Middlesex, UK, 1980.

May, C.A.N. *Formula 3 - A Record of 500 c.c. Racing* G.T.Foulis, London, 1951.

May, C.A.N. *Speed Hill-Climb* G.T.Foulis, London, 1962.

McCluggage, D. *By Brooks Too Broad For Leaping* Fulcorte Press, Santa Fe, New Mexico, 1994.

McDonough, E. *Marquis de Portago: The Legend* Mercian Manuals, Balsall Common, Coventry, UK 2006.

McDonough, E.*Vanwall: Green For Glory* Crowood Press, Ramsbury, Wiltshire 2003.

Miller, P. *The Fast Ones* Stanley Paul, London, 1962.

Moss, S. with D. Nye *Stirling Moss: My Cars, My Career* Guild Publishing, London, 1987.

Nixon, C. *Mon Ami Mate* Transport Bookman Publications, Isleworth, Middlesex, UK, 1991.

Nolan, W.F. *Phil Hill: Yankee Champion* Brown Fox Books, California, 1996.

Nye, D. *Cooper Cars* Osprey Publishing, Oxford, 1983.

O'Neil, T. *The Bahamas Speed Weeks* Veloce Publishing, Dorchester, UK, 2006.

Pritchard, A. *Aston Martin - The Post-War Competition Cars* Aston Publications, Buckinghamshire, UK, 1991.

Salvadori, R. and A. Pritchard *Roy Salvadori - Racing Driver* Patrick Stephens, Wellingborough, UK, 1985.

Sheldon, P. and D. Rabagliati *A Record of Grand Prix and Voiturette Racing Vol. 5* St. Leonard's Press, West Yorkshire, UK, 1988.

Sheldon, P. and D. Rabgliati *A Record of Grand Prix and Voiturette Racing Vol.6* St.Leonard's Press, West Yorkshire, UK, 1987.

Sheldon, P. & D. Rabagliati, R. Page *Formula 3 1947 - 1954* Paul Sheldon West Yorkshire, UK, 2007.

Wimpffen, J. *Time and Two Seats - Five Decades of Long Distance Racing* Motorsport Research Group, Washington, USA, 1999.

Wyer, J. *The Certain Sound - Thirty Years of Motor Racing* Automobile Year Edita, Switzerland, 1981.

Yates, B. *Enzo Ferrari: The Man and the Machine* Bantam Books, London, 1992.

Journals

Autocar
Autosport
IOTA
Motor Racing

All about the boy!